Border Crossings

BORDER CROSSINGS

The West and Russian Identity in Soviet Literature

1917–1934

Carol Avins

UNIVERSITY OF CALIFORNIA PRESS

Berkeley • Los Angeles • London

University of California Press
Berkeley and Los Angeles, California
University of California Press, Ltd.
London, England

Library of Congress Cataloging in Publication Data

Avins, Carol.
Border crossings.

Includes bibliographical references and index.
1. Russian literature — 20th century — History and
criticism.   2. Europe in literature.   3. United States
in literature.   I. Title.
PG3026.E95A94   891.7'09'324   81-19729
ISBN 0-520-04233-6   AACR2

Printed in the United States of America

1 2 3 4 5 6 7 8 9

To my parents,
Ellen Sharfstein Avins and Jack Avins

CONTENTS

vii

CONTENTS

CONTENTS

ACKNOWLEDGMENTS

Many people have helped this book cross the border between conception and completion. Michael Holquist, who directed the Yale doctoral dissertation in which some of these ideas are rooted, offered valuable advice on this project as well. As teacher and scholar, he has stimulated my thinking in many ways. I am grateful to Katerina Clark for generously taking the time to make detailed and discerning comments on much of the manuscript. Simon Karlinsky provided important encouragement and support in the final stages of writing. To my former teachers Elliott Mossman and Victor Erlich, my thanks for their insight into twentieth-century Russian literature. I am indebted also to Alfred J. Rieber, whose teaching deepened my interest in Russian culture, and whose wide-ranging comments on the manuscript taught me much.

I have profited from the suggestions of a number of scholars who were kind enough to read parts of the manuscript. Robert C. Williams, Deming Brown, Sidney Monas, Clarence Brown, and Victor Terras are among them, as are Edward J. Brown, Robert A. Maguire, Elizabeth Beaujour, Richard Sheldon, Barbara Monter, George Gibian, and Jane Gary Harris. I greatly appreciate their assistance and interest. At every stage, Irwin Weil and my other colleagues in Northwestern University's Department of Slavic Languages and Literatures have provided a supportive environment in which to work.

ACKNOWLEDGMENTS

Aspects of my research and part of the publication cost were funded by Northwestern's University Grants Committee. I am also grateful to Northwestern for a leave of absence that enabled me to write. Some of the research was done at the Lenin Library in Moscow. At home, my access to source material was considerably broadened through the efforts of June Pachuta of the Slavic Reference Service at the University of Illinois at Urbana-Champaign. Two students, Rebecca Ranich and Robin Ropar, helped with details of the research; Natalie Hector was the expert typist of the final draft. I appreciate the roles of William J. McClung, Marilyn Schwartz, and Peter Dreyer of the University of California Press in bringing this book to the reader.

Thanks of another dimension are due my husband, Rayman Solomon, for his editorial help, his sustaining presence, and the sacrifice of his own time so that I might have more. For their understanding and encouragement, I am grateful to my parents, to whom this book is dedicated.

NOTE ON TRANSLITERATION

Russian names and words are transliterated according to the Library of Congress system, with diacritical marks omitted (System II in J. Thomas Shaw's *The Transliteration of Modern Russian for English Language Publications* [Madison: University of Wisconsin Press, 1967]). The following modifications are made in the text for the convenience of non-specialists, but not in bibliographic citations: soft signs are omitted; *y* is used for endings of Russian surnames; names with an accepted English spelling are given in their common forms.

INTRODUCTION

The sense of a place beyond one's homeland is felt by every people, however vast or isolated its domain. To live in "the land of the rising sun" is to relegate other lands to darkness; to claim earth's "middle kingdom" is to place other kingdoms on its fringes. Self-definition, a central feature of any nation's history, entails defining what one is not. In Russia this process has been in the foreground of national life, shaped by successions of rulers, thinkers, and artists. History and geography — Russia's Mongol and Byzantine legacies and its borders with Asia and Europe — have compounded the complexity of resolving what is Russian.

Literature has long been a principal arena of this debate. In fiction, as in other spheres, Russia could not be mapped through internal exploration alone: its terrain had to be distinguished from what lay beyond. The borderland most mapped by literary surveyors has been that realm referred to as the West. Russian writers of the last century, celebrated for their insight into the landscape of the mind, were engaged in probing the national mind as well. Their works, ventures into human nature and Russia's nature, often involve an interrelation of Russian and Western. Gogol's eye in *Dead Souls* roves both Russia and Europe; Tolstoy needs Kutuzov and Napoleon to dramatize his view of history; ideas of European origin possess the characters of Dostoevsky. "Does there exist a Russian," he asked mockingly in 1862, ". . . who does not know Europe twice as well as

Russia?"[1] Dostoevsky's jibe suggests that his compatriots' knowledge of Europe is largely pretense; his writing makes clear that coming to terms with Europe is essential to understanding themselves. Aleksandr Herzen, who spent much of his life in voluntary but painful exile, wrote that Russians "need Europe as an ideal, a reproach, a good example; if she were not these things it would be necessary to invent her."[2] Europe's connection to Russia's identity, whether viewed with admiration, hostility, or ambivalence, was undisputed. It has needed inventing in every generation, and these shifting reinventions of Europe pervade Russia's intellectual history and its literary tradition.

This book is about Russian literature's continued preoccupation with the West in the initial years of the Soviet regime, from 1917 to 1934. That concern was part of a preoccupation with the current and future situations of Russia and of the individual within it. The Bolshevik Revolution cast all areas of Russian life into disorder; the decade and a half that followed was a time of reordering — of social, economic, political, and often personal transformation. The profound changes of this period were accompanied by both official and private reassessments of Russia's nature. From the country's beginnings, the West had been a major dimension of Russia's self-definition. For some post-revolutionary writers, as for their predecessors, making sense of Russia entailed looking westward as well as inward — toward some facet of the actual West or toward a more abstract, more figurative conception of the West's meaning. What the Slavophile Ivan Kireevsky had said seventy years before applies to this era:

Certainly few questions nowadays are more important than the question of the relation of Russian to Western culture. How we pose and resolve it in our minds may determine not only the dominant trend of our literature but the entire orientation of our intellectual activity, the meaning of our private lives, and the nature of our social relationships.[3]

[1]F. M. Dostoevskii, *Zimnie zametki o letnikh vpechatleniiakh*, in *Polnoe sobranie sochinenii*, 30 vols. (Leningrad: Nauka, 1972-), V, 46. The English is quoted from Feodor M. Dostoevsky, *Winter Notes on Summer Impressions*, trans. Richard Lee Renfield (New York: Criterion, 1955), p. 35.

[2]A. I. Gertsen, "Dzhon-Stiuart Mill' i ego kniga 'On Liberty,'" in *Sobranie sochinenii*, 30 vols. (Moscow: Akademiia Nauk SSSR, 1954–65), XI, 66. The translation is that of Constance Garnett (rev. Humphrey Higgins) in Alexander Herzen, "John Stuart Mill and his Book on Liberty," *My Past and Thoughts: The Memoirs of Alexander Herzen*, 4 vols. (London: Chatto and Windus, 1968), III, 1075.

[3]I. V. Kireevskii, "O kharaktere prosveshchenii Evropy i o ego otnoshenii k prosveshcheniiu Rossii," in *Polnoe sobranie sochinenii*, ed. M. Gershenzon, 2 vols.

In Kireevsky's century, as in the next, this question was posed in a great range of ways. Post-revolutionary writers, in forms as varied as the era's output, used the West to explore two interrelated issues: the identity of the individual within Russia and the identity of Russia as a nation. "Russian identity" as used in the title of this book refers to both.

These were years of ferment in literature and the arts. The experimentation of the pre-war era continued in some respects: movements flourished and faded, promoting avant-garde theories and mixing theory and practice with politics. As the twenties continued, controversies heated, to be cooled by pressure from above. The first congress of the Union of Soviet Writers, held in 1934, is a major landmark of this process. Ideologically conformist literature appeared at every stage, but it came to dominate the scene as time went on. Works involving the West lie on many points along the brilliant literary spectrum, and those I examine are diverse. They include novels, stories, and drama as well as reportage, essays, and some poetry — works popular at the time and those long unpublished (or still unpublished in the USSR). My intentions are not encyclopedic, however: I focus on works in which the West figures in a fundamental way, and which develop what I see as the topic's principal facets.

Among the fourteen writers considered are some of the period's best. With a few exceptions, these writers are of the same transitional generation: born between 1888 and 1899, they entered the Soviet era in early adulthood, beginning literary careers or developing paths already established. They are as varied as any literary generation; like other generations, though, they have a history in common. One aspect of their shared situation is the radically changing definition of their country and (for some, at least) of themselves as part of it. What was Russia coming to encompass and to exclude? The diversity of their writing offers insight into post-revolutionary intellectual history, into the perspectives from which Russia was regarded, and into the many levels of contrast and confluence that writers continued to find between Russian and Western. Their works also occasion reflection on the infinite ways the mind selects an image and refracts it into art. All of this is part of what follows. My general concern is to show how

---

(Moscow: n.p., 1911), I, 174. The English is quoted from Ivan Vasil'evich Kireevski, "On the Nature of European Culture and Its Relation to the Culture of Russia," in *Russian Intellectual History: An Anthology*, ed. Marc Raeff (New York: Harcourt, Brace and World, 1966), p. 175.

these works probe Russian identity, and how forms of the West figure in this process.

The West's many layers of meaning in Russian thought complicate and deepen my subject. A prefatory definition can indicate only the term's scope.[4] The West means, first of all, the accumulated ideas about it — assumptions and images included in every intellectual's cultural baggage. These, and some of their formulators, arise in the course of the book. Through the nineteenth century, the term *West* (*Zapad*) denoted the countries of Western Europe; it was interchangeable with *Evropa*. The United States, even after its growth from new world to world power, was set apart. America was a separate issue, still a new world compared to the old world of Europe. An additional factor enters after 1917: Europe and America are now identified with the capitalist system that Russia has repudiated. One synonym for *the West* becomes *capitalism*. Its other meanings, though, are not submerged by this one: it continues to have dimensions beyond the political and economic. Use of the term varies among writers and is sometimes vague; I have tried to clarify it throughout.

Both Western Europe and America were important presences during the early Soviet period, but concern with Europe was more prevalent and will receive more attention here. Russia's relation to Europe, not to America, had been subject to debate for centuries, and the historical concern with Europe carried over into the twentieth. It is important, too, that *Zapad* still meant the cultural heritage called Western Civilization — a heritage that Russia had in many respects shared. The degree of Russia's inclusion in this tradition remained a live issue in the twenties and thirties. The old questions persisted, now in new contexts, of whether the West encompassed Russia, a universalist Russia embraced the West, or the two were mutually foreign.

---

[4]Historical sources are cited in future notes. The following are among the many other works pertaining to the West's significance for Russia: N. Strakhov, *Bor'ba s Zapadom v nashei literature*, 3rd ed., 3 vols. (1897–98; rpt. The Hague: Mouton, 1969); Vl. Solov'ev, "Zapadniki, zapadnichestvo," *Entsiklopedicheskii slovar'*, 41 vols. (St. Petersburg: Brokhaus and Efron, 1890–1904), XII, 243–44; Aleksei Veselovskii, *Zapadnoe vliianie v novoi russkoi literature*, 5th ed. (Moscow: n.p., 1916); Prot. V. Zen'kovskii, *Russkie mysliteli i Evropa*, 2nd ed. (Paris: YMCA Press, 1955); James H. Billington, *The Icon and the Axe* (New York: Vintage–Random House, 1970); Nicholas V. Riasanovsky, *Russia and the West in the Teaching of the Slavophiles* (Cambridge, Mass.: Harvard University Press, 1952); B. H. Sumner, "Russia and Europe," *Oxford Slavonic Papers*, 1st series, ed. S. Konovalov, 13 vols. (Oxford: Clarendon Press, 1950–67), II, 1–16. Sumner writes: "In Russia, just as in the West, by the beginning of this twentieth century there was not one Europe but a competing plurality of Europes" (p. 13).

INTRODUCTION

Borders can seem as impassable as iron (in the Cold War metaphor) or as ethereal as mirages: the limits of culture look different to everyone. What does delimit one place from another? Maps unequivocally declare divisions among countries: each with one name, of one color, they stand immutable until war or politics intervenes. But societies — and thus their borders — continually evolve, as does any organic system. Only a densely layered, interpretive map can attempt to portray them at a given moment. Borders are less like fences than like rivers that restlessly change course, transforming their banks in the process.

Groups are connected by virtue of their separateness — the existence of an outer, foreign sphere enables a group to recognize itself as inner or native. But their mutual roles are more complex than this. The categories of foreign and native are not simply opposites: unlike parallel lines, they have many points of intersection. "A society," writes Lévi-Strauss, "consists of individuals and groups which communicate with one another. . . . Communication does not cease at society's borders. These borders, rather, constitute thresholds where the rate and forms of communication . . . reach a much lower level."[5] A lower level, but one driven by powerful currents. An external sphere continually affects the inner workings of a culture, serving as a stimulus of change. The nature of this interaction has been insightfully discussed by Iurii Lotman and other theorists of semiotics who have turned their attention to culture. Lotman and his colleagues emphasize the "active role of the outer space in the mechanism of culture" and the "game relationship between culture and its outer sphere."[6] What I examine is one part of this relationship: the "active role" of the West in the workings of the Russian literary imagination.

Post-revolutionary Russia is that place from which the writers studied here look out, their angles of vision variously set. In my "interpretive maps" of their works I have analyzed how they conceive of the border between Russia and the West, how they use the West to shape and shade Russia's contours, and how they explore the changing Russian definitions of foreign and native. My general term for the

---

[5]Claude Lévi-Strauss, *Structural Anthropology*, trans. Claire Jacobson and Brooke Frundfest-Schoepf (New York: Basic Books, 1963), p. 296.

[6]Ju. M. Lotman, B. A. Uspenskij, V. V. Ivanov, V. N. Toporov, A. M. Pjatigorskij, "Theses on the Semiotic Study of Cultures (As Applied to Slavic Texts)," in *The Tell-Tale Sign: A Survey of Semiotics*, ed. Thomas A. Sebeok (Lisse, Netherlands: Peter de Ridder, 1975), p. 60. The authors state as one of their principles: "The opposition 'culture-extracultural space' is the minimal unit of the mechanism of culture on any given level" (pp. 59–60).

literary juxtaposition of cultures gives this book its title. *Border crossings* should be broadly understood: the term encompasses any significant integration of the West — defined as the writer chooses — into a Russian work. Means of including the West — the use of travelers, of narrative shifts, of psychology, ideology, history — will emerge in these chapters. The writer's end, generally characterized, is to focus the reader's attention on the limits of Western and Russian — to create in the reader a mental border crossing.

How are these literary border crossings related to the actual contact between Soviet Russia and the West during the 1920s and 1930s? The West's importance to Russia was then considerable; in many sectors — economic, political, cultural — their relationship was taking on new forms. The Western presence in life is one aspect of its presence in literature; literary forms, however, never directly reflect reality. What Northrop Frye has called the two perspectives essential to criticism — "one turned toward the structure of literature as a whole and one turned toward the other cultural phenomena that form its environment" — require sensitive mediation.[7] Certainly, the concerns of writers arise from their experience — and Russia's new identity was among those subjects, in Henry James's phrase, "pressed upon the artist." But experience has many senses. Literature is also engendered by its past, by the individual writer's encounter with the literary tradition. It is shaped, too, by its internal demands. James, discussing his own frequent intertwining of Europe with his homeland, ascribes it in part to the basic artistic need of contrast. In some of his fiction, he adds, the contrast of cultures was simply "the course of the greater amusement."[8]

The distinction between Frye's approaches, both of which I employ, might be suitably stressed with the words of Iurii Tynianov. Tynianov, a pioneer of Russian Formalist theory, reminded his readers in 1922 that "there have come to be two Europes: one which we ourselves make up (and we do a good job of it — it's nice and airy), and another — which is after all the real one. The real one exists without asking us whether we want her the way she is or not; what's more, only the real one does exist — the made-up one, actually, we have only

---

[7]Northrop Frye, "The Critical Path: An Essay on the Social Context of Literary Criticism," in *In Search of Theory*, ed. Morton W. Bloomfield (Ithaca, N.Y.: Cornell University Press, 1972), p. 103.

[8]Henry James, "Preface," in *The Novels and Tales of Henry James*, 24 vols. (New York: Scribner's, 1907–09), XIV, vi.

made up."[9] The difference is obvious, as Tynianov's joking tone conveys. He mentions it, one supposes, because the distance between "the real" and "the invented" is so often underestimated. The question of their connection is raised here not only to describe my approach, but also because it is part of the book's subject The methodological faults of critics and censors did literature much damage in this period. The West was controversial territory; the writing analyzed here was read by contemporaries in both artistic and ideological terms. Literary politics therefore occasionally surfaces in my readings, along with literary history and form.

Art's conjunction with reality is reflected in the book's plan. Each of the four parts considers one aspect of Russia-West interaction; each is roughly chronological, presenting varied approaches to an issue across the period. A graph of literary forms, and one of Russia's transformation, can thus be traced in every part. The nature of this national transformation occupies Part 1 ("Russia and the West in Transition"). The works discussed look at Russia's condition relative to the West's; they question in what manner, and at what distance from each other, the two cultures are moving toward the future. This section highlights historical change; Part 2 ("Emigration: The Single Crossing") focuses on its personal dimension. Post-revolutionary emigration, as the title indicates, was a one-way journey — the barriers to communication and to return made it virtually final. Recrossing the border is a central problem of the works examined here. Their plots are propelled by the émigré's drive to bring home and self into equilibrium.

European travel had been relatively common before the Revolution. Now, with the border increasingly controlled, the experience of traversing it was sharpened. The traveler's journey is less traumatic than the émigré's, but it can raise troubling issues. Journeys of several sorts figure in Part 3 ("There and Back: Russian Travelers and the West") — fictional, actual, imagined. Shifting from Russia to the West and back, writers focused on what was native and foreign to each. Part 4 ("The Foreign Presence") approaches this question differently, looking at a reverse sort of travel: the entrance into Russia of some Western element — an idea, a person, a story — that changes the environment. The reader is led to reevaluate the meaning of Russia. The problem of who designates the native, of how Russia's borders are

---

[9] Iurii Tynianov, "O slonenke," *Peterburg*, no. 1 (1922), p. 20.

set, animates these works. Some of them focus attention on how the fundamental attributes of a culture can be redefined as alien. The border separating Russia from the West, it becomes clear here, may also be separating Russia from itself.

This possibility, explored most deeply in Part 4, is raised in the other sections as well — particularly toward the end of each. As Russia's Soviet identity became more clearly defined by experience and by the state, it was both affirmed and questioned with greater intensity. After the mid-twenties, writers were increasingly pressured to reflect the country's official image — to color in an accepted outline. The final chapter of each part turns to writing that exposes flaws in standard conceptions of Russia's borders. One sees in these works of Platonov, Olesha, Mandelstam, and Bulgakov how certain definitions of Russia can violate its native space, cutting off terrain — pieces of the past, present realities, potentials — without which Russia is incomplete. The hazards of drawing false borders — on the Western frontier or within Russia — emerges as the book's most important issue.

The body of writing studied here, created during the Soviet Union's formative years, is part of a continuum in Russian culture. Russian identity, which entered literature centuries ago, is still a current concern; Russia continues to be defined in terms of the West, both at home and abroad. Its distance from the West remains a literary issue, and it remains a political issue, an indelible feature of the post–World War II world. The international and internal borders of Russia have been understood in many senses by those within and outside them. Writers in the early Soviet period, watching Russia rapidly change shape, probed the border's meaning in ways that retain their force.

PART ONE
RUSSIA AND THE WEST IN TRANSITION

The Bolshevik Revolution ended one transitional period in Russian history and initiated another. The year 1917 came to be seen as one of the sharpest turning points in the nation's experience. Revolution is a means of radically accelerating the rate of change, and revolutionaries were determined to move into a new era. The resulting discontinuity between past and present was widely felt, and it aroused extremes of pessimism and utopianism. Across the spectrum, both among those who found the present exhilarating and those who were uneasy, eyes were turned not only to the present, but to what lay ahead. The speed of change was only one source of uncertainty: a more pressing and deeper concern was its direction.

Russia's future, a central issue in the post-revolutionary period, had been subject to much speculation in the preceding decades. The preoccupation with national transformation was no new development. As the nineteenth century progressed, debates on Russia's nature and destiny (hardly absent in earlier eras) had intensified. A profusion of ideologies — idealism, anarchism, socialism, religious faith, and liberalism among them — envisioned transforming Russia into their version of the ideal. The end of the century, in Russia as elsewhere, stirred particular reflection on what was to follow. The influential philosopher Vladimir Soloviev, after years of designing ways to reconcile the world's opposing forces, began in the late 1890s to expect an impending apocalypse. The events of 1905 — revolution, and

II

defeat by Japan — made some think him prescient. Whatever one's perspective, it was clear that more profound change was to come. Andrei Bely's novel *Petersburg* (1913-14) expressively conveys this mood, with its violent clashes of dynamism and stasis. The poet Aleksandr Blok, marking the tenth anniversary of Soloviev's death, reflected on the passing years with premature nostalgia. "Many of us today," he wrote, "are living in a state of weariness and suicidal despair; a new world is already at the door; tomorrow we will recall the golden light that gleamed on the border of two centuries, each so different from the other."[1]

The period Blok had already placed in a golden haze in 1910 has come to be called the Silver Age. It saw a flowering of the arts and an increased interchange between Russia and Europe. Russian literature, music, dance, theater, and design made a great stir abroad; while retaining their national identity, they were important to the European cultural climate. Within Russia, the influence of westernizing and nativist tendencies diminished. Many found no contradiction in pursuing both Russia's national traditions and its communality with the West. Donald Treadgold notes that in the years from 1890 to 1917 there was "a significantly new kind of cultural pluralism," in which native and Western elements developed in a "creative tension." The period was marked, he writes, by "both a proud rediscovery of the Russian past and an unhesitating meeting with the West."[2] Other historians share the view that the integration of Western thought and culture into Russian life, a centuries-long process, culminated in that time.[3]

Poets may be more effective than historians in conveying an era: in prose or in verse, the best poets can distill the amorphous into a

---

[1] Aleksandr Blok, "Rytsar'-monakh," in *Sbornik pervyi. O Vladimire Solov'eve* (Moscow, 1911; rpt. Ann Arbor, Mich.: University Microfilms, 1971), p. 103. Translations here and throughout are mine unless otherwise noted.

[2] Donald Treadgold, *The West in Russia and China*, 2 vols. (Cambridge: Cambridge University Press, 1973), I (*Russia: 1472-1917*), 217, 250, 241. See also pp. 216-42, passim.

[3] One proponent of this idea is Vladimir Weidlé, in *Russia: Absent and Present* (New York: Vintage-Random House, 1961), and other writings. Weidlé writes of the prerevolutionary years: "Never before had cultured Russia such a sense of being naturally European, of being a nation with a natural place among the nations of Europe" (p. 105). In *The Icon and the Axe* (New York: Vintage-Random House, 1970), James H. Billington also emphasizes this theme, writing of the Silver Age: "The preceding age of Alexander II and III and the succeeding age of Stalin were far more parochial. . . . But Russian thinkers in this period looked at the full spectrum of Western artistic and spiritual experience" (p. 479).

pure essence. Blok does this in his commemoration of Soloviev; for the next generation, Blok's own work was a basis for assessments of an age. Writing in 1922 on the first anniversary of Blok's death, the younger poet Osip Mandelstam identified Blok's writing with an era, as Blok had linked Soloviev to the previous one. Mandelstam highlights the mingling of the Russian and Western heritages in Blok's poetry and in the Silver Age. Blok had inherited a sense of oneness with Europe, but had also absorbed the nineteenth century's romantic nationalism; he was attuned to the myths and rhythms of both Russian and European culture. In this Blok was wholly of his time: "The domestic and the European," Mandelstam writes, "are two poles not only of Blok's poetry but of all Russian culture of the last decades."[4] The poet's gloss on his predecessor and the historian's survey offer similar views of Russia's pre-revolutionary closeness to the West.

As Russia was propelled by revolution into a new period, how was its distance from the West affected? Was the angle formed by their paths widening or narrowing? Formulating answers to such questions requires labors of definition. The terms involved — 'Russia," "West," "distance," "past," "future" — must be reduced to scale in order to be measurable. Definitions change with every sphere one enters: culture, government, and economics all demand different approaches. Given a limited field this is a manageable task: comparative data can be gathered, the past evaluated, the future projected. How does one proceed, though, with works of literature? The literary imagination may light on such data, but it respects no boundaries. The designs of every writer manipulate definitions without stating them; the "actual" and "invented" Wests of Tynianov's distinction have no precise formula of correlation. Invented Wests of great variety are developed by the writers discussed in Part 1. The Russias they create and their renderings of the West are versions of abstractions rather than precisely defined sectors. Each explores the process of transition and looks toward the stage to come; each probes the nature of Russia, using the particular West that suits his needs.

These approaches to post-revolutionary change range widely in genre and style, and include some of the period's important tendencies and extremes. Mandelstam's two essays involve a cultural and intellectual West which he considers integral to Russian national and indi-

---

[4]Osip Mandel'shtam, "Barsuch'ia nora," in *Sobranie sochinenii*, ed. G. P. Struve and B. A. Filipoff, 3 vols. (New York: Inter-Language Literary Associates, 1964–71), II, 313.

vidual identity. "Chaadaev" provides a long-range view, bringing us back to nineteenth-century conceptions of Russia's border with Europe; the later essay offers a post-revolutionary perspective on the internal West and its place in Russian life and literature. Mandelstam's essays, the only non-fiction discussed here, are distinct in another way as well: the other works considered have more to do with the contemporary West, relating its condition and prospects to Russia's. Blok polemically depicts the two in the wake of revolution and world war. Paul Valéry (like Blok, a poet who was more than poet) had written after the war that Europe was undergoing "an extraordinary shudder," a "crisis of the mind."[5] In "The Scythians," Blok presents a West afflicted with more than mental upheaval. "The Third Capital," a strangely patterned tale of European decay and Russian renascence, is Boris Pilniak's elaboration on a similar theme.

Future-building was sweetened and simplified in the rash of adventure novels that served twenties readers capitalist vice and socialist virtue embroiled in fantastic plots. Marietta Shaginian's version of the genre, a satirical entertainment called *Mess-Mend,* amply illustrates that Russian and Western developments need not be taken entirely seriously. Fantasy and ideology also combine forces in a parodied epic by Mayakovsky. The poet bashes heads as well as continents, then tossing them all into a future with no battle lines. Most works in Part I come from the early years, when the repercussions of 1917 were felt with particular intensity; the exception is Andrei Platonov's *The Hurdy-Gurdy,* which looks at national change in the quite different climate of the thirties. Blok's Russia had challenged the West to join it or be denied a future; this play explores what Russia can now offer both its own people and the West.

These literary explorations of Russia's identity and future must be placed at least briefly in the context of Marxist theory and Soviet policy. Marxism had attracted Russian intellectuals partly as the most advanced Western thought; its appeal to some was the prospect of "transforming Russia into Europe."[6] In the 1890s, writes E. H. Carr, "nothing in Russian history seemed so unimpeachably and unreservedly Western, so free of any national taint, as the Russian Marxist

---

[5]The second phrase is quoted from the title of Valéry's essay "The Crisis of the Mind," in *The Collected Works of Paul Valéry,* ed. Jackson Mathews, trans. Denise Folliot and Jackson Mathews, 15 vols. (New York: Pantheon, 1956–75), X, 23–36. The first phrase appears on p. 24.

[6]Treadgold, *The West in Russia and China,* I, 222.

movement."[7] As he points out, however, this was not wholly true at the time and was to become even less so. National roots and nationalist aims were, of course, extremely important, particularly in the Bolshevik faction that gained dominance. The many stages and varieties of Russian Marxism make generalization difficult; the dynamics of internationalist and nationalist, of gradualist and voluntarist tendencies are complex. But in general Russian Marxists before 1914 envisioned a bourgeois revolution that would advance Russia to the same stage as Europe, and a series of proletarian revolutions beginning in the most developed countries that would culminate in international socialism. National distinctions, including the relative positions of Russia and the West, would cease to be problematic. Russia's unexpected initiation of this process in 1917 and the failure of other countries to follow changed the picture. In establishing the first workers' state, Russia was leading rather than trailing the West. The success of Russia's revolution was theoretically predicated on the swift occurrence of others; after the abortive German revolution of October 1923, however, theory gave way to reality. Soviet Russia was no longer considered dependent on European socialist revolutions: those that ensued would be reversing the scheme by following Russia's model and, in a sense, "transforming Europe into Russia." From the postrevolutionary perspective, Russia was not simply participating in the West's future but defining it.

The Revolution's status as an essentially national development, rather than a prelude to world revolution, increasingly dominated Soviet policy. By 1924–25 international revolution had become not an immediate but a long-term goal, and accommodation with capitalist states was pursued in the interests of Russian security and prosperity. While Soviet relations with the West were stabilized, however, the idea that Russia had charted the course to be taken by the West — and the world — was still an article of faith. The link between this attitude and Slavophile views of Russia's mission to revive the West has often been noted. But Party leaders were split in this regard: for Bukharin, a principal architect of policy at this time, nationalism was a danger rather than an attraction.[8] Shifts and conflicts among the leadership

[7]E. H. Carr, "'Russia and Europe' as a Theme of Russian History," in *Essays Presented to Sir Lewis Namier,* ed. Richard Pares and A. J. P. Taylor (London: Macmillan, 1956), p. 386.

[8]See Stephen F. Cohen, *Bukharin and the Bolshevik Revolution* (New York: Alfred A. Knopf, 1974), pp. 187–88.

can be traced in the records of Party and Comintern congresses: they need not be chronicled here. Internal differences notwithstanding, Party positions on the nation's identity and destiny emerged as national definitions. The blueprints of Russia's connection to the West and path toward the future, revised in the course of the twenties and thirties, were prominently displayed.

Russian thinkers had been occupied throughout the nineteenth century with developing proposals of their own. Russia's greatest novelists, particularly Dostoevsky, made national identity a focal point of their work.[9] The tsarist state, of course, had its own formulas: their inadequacy, not their absence, impelled people toward others. But the imperial formulas represented centuries of interplay between history and innovation, and were, after all, imperial. The Revolution was in theory a collective endeavor, a mass reassessment of goals. Russia's identity, it seemed, needed no further illumination. Fortunately, however, solved problems have always invited further solution. The changing features of Russia and the West continued to raise questions and stimulate the imagination. Among the works discussed below — Mayakovsky's and Shaginian's, for example — some take no issue with official answers. But the number of artistic solutions to a given problem is infinite, and literary forms are involved here as well as political ones. The drama of transition inspired enthusiastic and troubled participants alike to try a hand at the director's art.

---

[9]Michael Holquist analyzes Dostoevsky's novels as a merging of the search for national and individual identity in *Dostoevsky and the Novel* (Princeton, N.J.: Princeton University Press, 1977).

I

THE OPEN SEA
Preserving Unity with the West

Osip Mandelstam, "Chaadaev" (1915) and "On the Nature of the Word" (1922)

No body of writing better evokes the post-revolutionary experience of transition than the poetry and essays of Osip Mandelstam. His most powerful works concern the corrosion of the links that bind one to language and to history. Mandelstam, the best Russian poet of this century, is among those of his generation who assumed Russia's closeness to the West. But never in Russia was this an assumption so deep and widespread as to be unspoken. The Russia-West relationship remained an issue to ponder, as Mandelstam does with varying explicitness in his prose. The West of which he writes, in works treated here and in Part 3, is more a set of ideas than a place. When Mandelstam considers Russia's future in connection with the West, he has in mind not the contemporary geopolitical West, but the internal West that forms part of what is Russian.

In a book that dwells on what distinguishes Russia from the West, it is useful to start by recognizing that to be separate (i.e., individual) is not necessarily to be separated. The two essays discussed below stress both Russia's uniqueness among nations and its unity with Western culture. In "Chaadaev" (1915) Mandelstam explores the identity of the Russian nation in relation to the West, linking this to the identity of the Russian individual. "On the Nature of the Word" (1922) concerns the West and the identity of Russian literature; this essay also intertwines the definitions of self and country. In both

works, Mandelstam's use of history brings present and future more
clearly into focus.

The nineteenth-century thinker Petr Chaadaev is renowned for
history's most impassioned warning of Russia's estrangement from the
West. His eight "Philosophical Letters," written largely between 1826
and 1831, are credited with changing the course of Russian intellectual
history. The First Letter, which caused such fireworks on its publication in 1836 that no others appeared in his lifetime, contains
the blazing accusation that "we are neither of the West nor of the
East, and we possess the traditions of neither. Somehow divorced
from time, we have not been touched by the universal education of
mankind."[1] Chaadaev saw Europe moving steadily forward in history, propelled by the force of its traditions; Russia was standing
still, growing "physiologically," but spiritually only a child. After
Chaadaev, it was imperative to define Russia's identity in terms of the
West. His ideas became a measure against which one judged others. In
confronting this part of Russia's heritage, Mandelstam was joining a
long line of worthy predecessors.

Among his contemporaries Chaadaev had generated more con-
troversy than converts. His statement of the case was too extreme and
idiosyncratic to be embraced entire. While it fueled the debate between Slavophiles and Westernizers that dominated mid-nineteenth-
century intellectual life, Chaadaev was not claimed by either side.
Westernizers, for one thing, could not accept his emphasis on the
historical role of Roman Catholicism; Slavophiles scorned his dis-
missal of Russia's past. Pushkin, long his friend and admirer, also
voiced strong objections to Chaadaev's view of the past. "As for our
history being nil, I absolutely cannot be of your opinion," he wrote to
him frankly. "Are the awakening of Russia, the development of its
power, its march toward unity . . . — is all this to be not history, but a
pallid and half-forgotten dream? . . . And (cross your heart) do you
find nothing impressive in the present-day situation of Russia, nothing
which will strike the future historian? Do you believe that he will place
us outside Europe?"[2] Pushkin's implicit negative answer is in a larger

---

[1]*Sochineniia i pis'ma P. Ia. Chaadaeva*, ed. M. Gershenzon, 2 vols. (Moscow: n.p.,
1913–14), I, 77. The appearance of this edition may have sparked Mandelstam's interest
in writing about Chaadaev. The translation is that of Mary-Barbara Zeldin in Peter
Yaklovlevich Chaadayev, *Philosophical Letters and Apology of a Madman* (Knoxville:
University of Tennessee Press, 1969), p. 34. Further citations are to this edition.
[2]Pushkin to Chaadaev, 19 October 1836, in A. S. Pushkin, *Sobranie sochinenii*, ed.
D. D. Blagoi et al., 10 vols. (Moscow: Khudozhestvennaia literatura, 1959–62), X, 308.

sense affirmative, in that he sees no contradiction between valuing both Russia's past accomplishments and its growing closeness to Europe. Aleksandr Herzen, whose own life so involved Russia's relation to the West, was also deeply impressed and provoked by the First Letter. He later summarized its impact in these well-known words: "It was a shot that rang out in the dark night; . . . whether it was news of the dawn or news that there would not be one — it was all the same: one had to wake up."[3]

The young Mandelstam, though several generations removed from the initial stir, approached Chaadaev with striking immediacy and intimacy. This early essay show that the shot of Herzen's metaphor was still resounding. "The trace left by Chaadaev on the consciousness of Russian society," Mandelstam begins, "is so deep and indelible that one involuntarily wonders whether it was drawn by a diamond across glass."[4] The mark on Mandelstam's mind was broad as well as deep. His essay is comprised of three dimensions: Chaadaev's theoretical West, Mandelstam's interpretation of how Chaadaev viewed the West, and the author's personal formulation of how Russia and the West are connected.

Chaadaev's experience is placed before us as well. Mandelstam evocatively sketches his long European journey of 1825–26. The most important aspect of this trip is its closure. Chaadaev left Russia, we are told, intending to remain abroad. His return, Mandelstam implies, demonstrates his belief in Russia's connectedness to the West, and in Russia's unbounded possibilities. Earlier travelers to Europe had stayed because they found vitality and by comparison saw stasis at home. Chaadaev is contrasted to them as "the first Russian who, in

---

Translation cited from *The Letters of Alexander Pushkin*, trans. J. Thomas Shaw, 3 vols. (Bloomington: Indiana University Press, 1963), III, 780.

[3]A. I. Gertsen, *Byloe i dumy 1852–1868*, in *Sobranie sochinenii*, 30 vols. (Moscow: Akademiia Nauk SSSR, 1954–65), IX, 139. The translation is that of Constance Garnett (rev. Humphrey Higgins) in Alexander Herzen, *My Past and Thoughts: The Memoirs of Alexander Herzen*, 4 vols. (London: Chatto and Windus, 1968), II, 516. An important discussion of Chaadaev's thought in relation to nineteenth-century Russian writers is in Michael Holquist's *Dostoevsky and the Novel*, pp. 14–20.

[4]Osip Mandel'shtam, "Petr Chaadaev," in *Sobranie sochinenii*, ed. G. P. Struve and B. A. Filipoff, 3 vols. (New York: Inter-Language Literary Associates, 1964–71), II, 326. Parenthetical references in the text are to this edition. The article first appeared, under the title "Chaadaev," in *Apollon* 6–7 (1915): 57–62. My translations of Mandelstam, here and throughout, draw heavily on those of Sidney Monas in Osip Mandelstam, *Selected Essays*, ed. Sidney Monas (Austin: University of Texas Press, 1977), and of Jane Gary Harris and Constance Link in *Mandelstam: The Complete Critical Prose and Letters*, ed. Jane Gary Harris (Ann Arbor, Mich.: Ardis, 1979).

actual fact, ideologically, had lived in the West and found the road back. His contemporaries felt this instinctively and valued terribly Chaadaev's presence among them" (p. 333). We imagine an intense, larger-than-life figure stepping firmly across the border and showing that to be committed to Russia was to make a choice to develop oneself.

The last point requires explanation, and to explain it is to get at the heart of Mandelstam's meaning. Chaadaev argued that while historically Russia has been excluded from many achievements of the past, it is freer of the constraints the past can impose. He presents Russia's historical poverty as a rare opportunity, a chance to cover a tabula rasa with new forms of writing. "We never lived under the domination of historical necessity," he writes. "Let us not today deliver ourselves up to a sullen inevitability which we never knew. . . . Let us be aware that there is no absolute necessity for us . . . that it is given to us to measure every step we take."[5] Russia was free to choose its future because it had thus far stood apart from history. Mandelstam defines this as the chief virtue Chaadaev recognized in Russia, explaining: "For Chaadaev, there was only one gift that Russia had: moral freedom, the freedom of choice. Never in the West had it been realized in such majesty, in such purity and fullness" (p. 333).

In what sense does Mandelstam term this freedom to choose a "moral freedom"? Partly in the sense that the nation has not yet compromised or limited itself. Chaadaev's "Letters" help further clear the path toward an answer. The philosopher deals with both the individual mind and the national, believing that "nations, although composite beings, are, in fact, like individuals, moral beings, and that consequently an identical law governs the mental life of each."[6] This idea is important to Mandelstam's essay, though he never states it. It is present in the parallel he subtly draws between the nation's freedom to choose its future and the individual's freedom to choose his life. If Russia is free to fill its blank page of history, he implies, so each Russian is free to make his own imprint on the earth. This is not a logical connection but a metaphoric one. Mandelstam is not saying that the Russian is inherently freer to define his identity than a native of any other country. Rather, he means that history places before the

---

[5]"Apology of a Madman," in *Philosophical Letters and Apology of a Madman*, p. 175. While Mandelstam, like many others, discounts the sincerity of the "Apology," it is helpful in interpreting Mandelstam's essay.

[6]Letter Six, in *Philosophical Letters and Apology of a Madman*, p. 114.

Russian an image of freedom writ large. The historical openness of Russia offers a model in terms of which each person can view his individual history.

Mandelstam modulates most audibly between the key of history and the key of the individual in three closing paragraphs. They are preceded by a one-stroke dramatization of the significance of Chaadaev's return from the West. Chaadaev's contemporaries, Mandelstam writes, "could point to him with superstitious respect, as once to Dante: 'He was there, he saw — and came back' " (p. 334). A change of key signature is then signalled by a grammatical shift, as the third-person past yields to the first-person present. Chaadaev fades; the author's time takes shape:

> And how many of us have spiritually emigrated to the West! How many are there among us who live in unconscious duplicity, whose bodies are here, but whose spirits have remained there!
>
> Chaadaev signifies a new, deepened understanding of nationality as the highest flowering of individual personality, and of Russia as the source of absolute moral freedom.
>
> Having allotted us inner freedom, Russia presents us with a choice, and those who have made this choice — they are genuine Russian people, wherever they may attach themselves. But woe unto those who, after circling about their native nest, weaken and turn back! (p. 334)

Now Mandelstam asserts Chaadaev's meaning for this generation. Those who have "spiritually emigrated to the West," who live divided, are those who fail to understand that Russia need not be thought of as separated from the West. They assume that one must head westward, mentally if not actually, in order to participate in a culture that has a past and future. Mandelstam is arguing that living wholly in Russia, one can live fully — connected to Europe, and attuned to the possibilities within oneself. Chaadaev revised the definition of Russian national and personal identity: to be Russian, after his symbolic return from the West, does not mean to be cut off, but to be able to reach anywhere.

In "Chaadaev" Mandelstam finds his own way of describing Russia's unique, open identity — the quality that Dostoevsky and others, from their various perspectives, had called Russia's universalism. Mandelstam terms Chaadaev's thought "national-synthetic," explaining: "A synthetic nationality does not bow its head before the fact of national self-consciousness, but rises above it in sovereign personality, unique in its own nature and therefore national" (p. 333). The implication is that Russia should be understood as such a nation — developing in its own way, but with unlimited access to all that has been habitually defined as foreign.

Mandelstam's rhetoric elevates and clouds his meaning as he draws to a close. The above-quoted final paragraph challenges each person to make use of his inner freedom, and proposes that to do so is to internalize the essence of being Russian. The "choice" Russia presents is not a choice between two or more defined things; it is not a matter of selecting, for example, a "Russian" identity or a "European" one. To choose is to accept the challenge of individual freedom that is each Russian's heritage. Beyond this Mandelstam makes no prescriptions: his definition of nationality does not stipulate that one literally stay within Russia's borders, geographic or intellectual. The decision to be made is a resolve to understand (with Chaadaev) that neither Russia nor the individual is already defined, already enclosed. Those who do so, writes the poet, "are genuine Russian people, wherever they may attach themselves."[7]

What of the parting judgment against those who do not? They "emigrate spiritually to the West" because they lack the will and depth to reach beyond categories. Distancing themselves from the native place, they perceive only outlines of the life within. Mandelstam's final words may sound isolationist and chauvinist, but in the context of the essay they are not. He expresses in "Chaadaev" an internationalism grounded in individualism.

Chaadaev ended the "Philosophical Letters" with a utopian vision of a universal union of peoples and souls. He describes this fusion as "the final phase of human nature, the resolution of the drama of the universe, the great apocalyptic synthesis."[8] Mandelstam does not propose an image of the future, but his concern with Russia's future development is evident. His ending, in contrast to Chaadaev's cosmic one, provides a microcosmic view of the future. He fixes on its most basic component: the internal makeup of the individual on whom Russia's course depends.

---

[7]The link between Mandelstam's definitions of his personal identity and of Russia's is explored in Gregory Freidin's excellent article, "The Whisper of History and the Noise of Time in the Writings of Osip Mandel'shtam," *The Russian Review* 37, no. 2 (1978): 421–37. Freidin writes: "If there were to be a place for Mandel'shtam in Russian culture, it had to be within that intellectual tradition which emphasized the universality of mankind's destiny and did not set Russia apart from the West" (p. 428).

[8]Letter Eight, in *Philosophical Letters and Apology of a Madman*, p. 160.

The centrality of the individual runs through Mandelstam's prose, whether the object of discussion is language, literature, or history. His writing on Acmeism, the literary movement he helped create, brings out one aspect of this issue. One of the movement's underlying principles was that language is autonomous, responsible not to some transcendent scheme of possibility but to reality alone. This view of language extends also to the individual: as language denotes things and not symbols, so the individual stands only for himself. In "The Morning of Acmeism," Mandelstam states this with mathematical simplicity, citing the law of identity: "A = A: what a splendid theme for poetry."[9] The essay announces the dawn of a literary era, challenging the premises of Symbolism and Futurism. "On the Nature of the Word," written a decade later, is a broader commentary on transitions; it elaborates on Acmeism's meaning in light of changing historical and literary conditions. The advent of a new political era required that Russian literature be reexamined. Assessing it from this post-revolutionary perspective, Mandelstam argues that the principles of Acmeism are still vital, in both senses of that word — alive and indispensable. "Acmeism is not only a literary, but also a social phenomenon in Russian history," he writes. "With it a moral force was reborn in Russian poetry. . . . Until now, the social pathos of Russian poetry has risen only to the conceptual level of 'citizen'; but there is a higher principle than 'citizen' — the concept 'man.' In distinction to the old civic poetry, the new Russian poetry has to educate not only the citizen, but also the 'man.' "[10]

Mandelstam had written that Chaadaev's mark was as deep and indelible as if cut by diamond on glass. "On the Nature of the Word" puts this image to other use. Here it describes not the impact of an exceptional individual, but the strength of identity each individual possesses. In a revolutionary age, when life's contours are being reshaped, individuals must remember and believe in their own power to mark existence. "Everything has become heavier and more massive," writes Mandelstam; "thus man, too, must become harder, because

---

[9]"Utro Akmeizma," in *Sobranie sochinenii,* II, 366.
[10]"O prirode slova," in *Sobranie sochinenii,* II, 300. First published as a brochure (Kharkhov: Istoki, 1922). The closeness between Mandelstam's interpretation of Chaadaev and his poetics is evident if we note another definition of Acmeism, this one attributed to him. Anna Akhmatova recalls that Mandelstam, asked in the thirties to define Acmeism, termed it "a longing for world culture." Akhmatova's memoir is quoted in Clarence Brown's *Mandelstam* (Cambridge: Cambridge University Press, 1973), p. 136, an invaluable source.

man should be harder than anything on earth, and should regard his relation to the earth as that of diamond to glass" (p. 300). The metaphor has the individual marking the world with strong strokes. In this era, such marks may not be indelible. The speed of change now is swift, and its direction difficult to gauge. Each gust of historical wind tosses time farther and cuts the earth deeper (deeper than the single diamond's trace). My image derives from Mandelstam's: "No doubt it would be an exaggeration to consider each year of our present history a century, but something in the nature of a geometric progression, a regular and natural acceleration, may be noted in the stormy discharge of the accumulated and growing potentials of historical force, historical energy" (p. 283). The individual, the artisan of life and of language, is in for buffeting.

"Language" is a key term in Mandelstam's appraisal of the problem, as the essay's title indicates. He considers language not as an empty system of signs, but as a carrier of a nation's identity, the principal means by which a people defines itself. The central characteristic of the Russian language is what Mandelstam calls its "Hellenism." This denotes not classical culture per se, but the values Mandelstam sees embodied in it. They are those same beliefs in the sanctity of literature and of the individual described above. Hellenism is anti-utilitarian, opposed to using man or language to some external end. It champions life on a human scale, and in Mandelstam's poetic definition, the home is a dominant image: "Hellenism means . . . the humanizing of the surrounding world, warming it with the most delicate teleological warmth. Hellenism is any stove near which a man sits, treasuring its warmth as something related to his inner warmth" (pp. 295–96). It is equivalent to humanism, and when Mandelstam writes elsewhere of "the European humanistic heritage," he is referring to the same thing. In this usage, "European" is inclusive of "Russian" — Russia is part of that heritage, just as it is "Hellenic."[11]

Mandelstam claims, further, that the Russian language not only belongs in this category, but exemplifies it. Russia is more than connected to the West: through its language, Russia has internalized the roots of Western culture. His explanation of how this came about is

---

[11]While Mandelstam uses "Europe" in this sense in various writings, the specific reference is to his "Gumanizm i sovremennost" (1923), *Sobranie sochinenii*, II, 394–96. There are many discussions of Mandelstam's Hellenism. One that focuses on his poetry and view of language is Victor Terras, "Classical Motives in the Poetry of Mandel'stam," *Slavic and East European Journal* 10, no. 3 (1966): 251–67.

one of those bold schematic statements that reveal more about a writer's imagination than about history. It conveys the idea without striving to be literal, and conjures up some engraving of an episode from classical myth. "Russian is a Hellenic language," he writes. "Due to a whole complex of historical conditions, the vital forces of Hellenic culture, having ceded the West to Latin influences, and having lingered only briefly in childless Byzantium, rushed to the bosom of Russian speech and communicated to it the self-confident secret of the Hellenic world view" (p. 287). Whereas earlier religious thinkers and empire-builders had anointed Russia the "Third Rome," successor to fallen Byzantium, Mandelstam presents Russia as a kind of "Third Athens" (my term, not his). But he is not proposing a new theory of historical linguistics or national destiny. The Russian language, he explains, is linked with "Hellenic philological culture not etymologically and not literarily, but through a principle of inner freedom that is equally inherent in them both" (p. 288). In the context of the essay, the poet says this of Russia not to grant it a privileged place, but because the autonomy of language now needs emphasizing. He says it, too, simply because it is his language and the medium of his poetry. Its definition is therefore inseparable from how he defines himself.

The phrase "inner freedom" had appeared earlier in "Cha-adaev," where Mandelstam calls inner freedom a part of each Russian's heritage. Here he makes a similar point about the heritage of Russian language and literature. They, unlike Chaadaev's historical Russia, have a coherent past interrelated with that of the West. Chaadaev himself is rebuked in "On the Nature of the Word" for lacking a philological perspective. Judging him from this angle, Mandelstam finds a serious flaw: "Chaadaev, when he contended that Russia had no history, that is, that Russia belonged to an unorganized, unhistorical cultural system, omitted one circumstance — and that is language" (p. 289). The poet-philologist cannot pardon the philosopher's disregard of the word, the unit of history that to Mandelstam mattered most.

"Chaadaev" ends in a swift flourish: "But woe unto those who, having circled about their native nest, weaken and turn back!" Concluding the later essay, Mandelstam looks forward more expansively. Without mentioning the word "revolution," he poignantly describes what faces the literature which the essay defines: "The age will quiet down, culture will fall asleep, the people will be reborn, having given its utmost to a new social class, and this whole current will draw the fragile boat of the human word out into the open sea of the future, where there is no sympathetic understanding, where dreary commentaries replace the fresh wind of the enmity and sympathy of one's contemporaries" (p. 300). In any age, the future may promise cold waters and posterity may cast a stern shadow. Mandelstam is not expressing a writer's routine anxiety in the face of the future, however: he has already told us that this is not a routine age. The choices made now are unusually important, and the future unpredictable. The "human word" headed across hazardous seas holds the view of language and of the individual that Russia shares with the oldest of Western cultures. The task of the poet in this transitional period, Mandelstam suggests, is to develop culture in a way that will ensure the survival of these values intact. The writer should cultivate Russian literature's broad roots — roots sunk deep in the past it shares with Western literature as a whole. Language, like the Egyptian funerary boat to which he likens it, must carry the necessities of daily life on their journey toward the future reader, "so alien and so precious" (p. 300).

This metaphor of culture sailing into the unknown belongs to literature's crowded log of time-traversing ships. One such ship that Mandelstam calls to mind is in Pushkin's narrative poem "Autumn (A Fragment)."[12] In the final stanzas, the poet turns from the glowing woodlands to the more vivid landscape of his mind. The last full stanza, which describes how thought becomes art, must be quoted together with the final, intentionally dangling line:

XI

And thoughts seethe boldly in my mind,
And weightless rhymes run forth to meet them,
And fingers beg for pen, the pen for paper,
One minute more — and verse will freely flow.
So slumbers motionless a ship in stillest waters,
But hark — the sailors suddenly rush out, they crawl
Up, down — and the sails are filled, they swell with wind;
The colossus moves and cleaves the waves.

XII

It sails. Where then are we to sail? . . .

---

[12]A. S. Pushkin, "Osen' (Otryvok)" (1833), in *Sobranie sochinenii*, II, 379–83.

The self-absorbed, inspired poet abruptly turns to the reader. In the final line, the metaphoric ship has two meanings: the private poem in progress and the common enterprise of living. The ending suggests that time, like language, is a difficult medium in which to move. How is one to set the course, and how fully can one control it? In the context of the 1920s the question seems perfectly at one with Pushkin's preceding account of writing, because the issue of where the nation was headed so preoccupied writers of the period. Both Pushkin's lines and Mandelstam's passage make a connection between creating literature and creating the future. Pushkin's link is vague; Mandelstam says in his essay that in creating art, as in forming the common future, the individual should be the measure of all things.

Mandelstam imagines Chaadaev's mind lit up by one idea: "In the West there is unity!"[13] Chaadaev, that is, saw Europe as a harmonious and growing civilization propelled by a coherent tradition which excluded Russia. Mandelstam holds that Russia is joined with the West at the most fundamental level, and that Russia has internalized the West to form a unity of its own. In his writing, Russia's link to the West is not a literary theme or political issue, but an approach to man and to literature that makes possible the best in both. As the post-revolutionary era began, he was concerned with how Russia's relationship to this West might change. His hope was that it would not change, that Russia's inner unity would survive the transitional years to nourish the distant future.

---

[13]"Petr Chaadaev," p. 328.

2

THE BARBARIAN LYRE:
Challenging the West

Aleksandr Blok, "The Scythians" (1918)

One recognized marker of the post-revolutionary transition was the death in 1921 of Aleksandr Blok. When the celebrated poet died, he was widely felt to have been a casualty of that "open sea" of historical experience that Mandelstam describes. Blok was regarded, and saw himself, as a member of a transitional generation. With his passing, a prominent bridge between two periods was gone. His death occasioned many evaluations of his career and of the era he was prematurely leaving. A year later, looking back on these reactions and on literary life since Blok, the younger poet Mandelstam wrote feelingly of the obligation to see Blok clearly, "to fight the optical illusion of perception, with its inevitable coefficient of distortion."[1]

The difficulty of seeing Blok without distortion is due not only to the wide attention focused on him, but also to a great poet's depth and breadth. Blok, born in 1880, was a magnetic figure to the generation that followed the course of his poetry, drama, essays, and personal life. It may seem odd that Blok, well-known before Mandelstam had entered adulthood, should follow him in this discussion. Mandelstam belonged to a literary generation that grew up in, and moved on from, the Symbolist movement of which Blok was a part.

---

[1]Osip Mandel'shtam, "Barsuch'ia nora," in *Sobranie sochinenii*, ed. G. P. Struve and B. A. Filipoff, 3 vols. (New York: Inter-Language Literary Associates, 1964–71), II, 312.

The chronology of composition and of historical situation guides here, rather than that of careers. Blok's "The Scythians" appeared between Mandelstam's two essays, three months after the Revolution. It is not representative of Blok's poetic oeuvre or outlook — no single poem can be. He published little in his last years, and much of his writing after 1917 deals with the transition to the "new world" whose approaching shadow he had long seen. This poem is Blok's dramatization of Russia and the West embarking on that transition. In his last writings, Blok came to regard the Revolution's aftermath with pessimism; "The Scythians," however, is not in this category. It is a utopian outburst written at a critical time — a time when Blok's was a voice much listened to. "The Scythians" presents the Revolution as a turning point in Russia's relationship with Europe, and is probably the best-known portrayal of how the Revolution cast Russia and Europe in new roles.

In the essays discussed above, Mandelstam writes of the West in terms of the past and future of life and literature in Russia. Blok's sphere in "The Scythians" is political as well as cultural, encompassing the pasts and futures of nations — of Europe and of the nation it must now look to. In the voice of a passionate pamphleteer, Blok warns the West that it cannot survive its present crisis without heeding Russia.

"The Scythians," written in late January 1918 and printed a few weeks later, is a topical poem: it relates to the continuing world war, to the breakdown of Russia's separate peace negotiations with Germany, and to Europe's failure to support the Revolution. In literary terms, it refers to the past rather than the present, echoing earlier Russian poetry about Russo-European and Russo-Asian tensions.[2] Its antecedent closest in time is Soloviev's poem "Panmongolism" (published posthumously in 1905), the opening lines of which form its epigraph.

"Panmongolism" is a prediction of apocalypse, a warning to Russians that they are not an invincible Third Rome, but that Mongol hordes threaten them with annihilation. Blok foresees this fate for the West, but "The Scythians" is not simply a reworking of Soloviev with

---

[2]R. V. Ivanov-Razumnik, the central figure of the Scythian group, analyzes connections between Blok's poem and others in "Ispytanie v groze i bure," in his *Vershiny: Aleksandr Blok, Andrei Belyi* (Petrograd: Kolos, 1923), pp. 187–203. Among the poems mentioned are Pushkin's "Klevetnikam Rossii" and "Borodinskaia godovshchina," Tiutchev's "Na vziatie Varshavy," and several by Soloviev. The essay, written in April 1918, also explains Ivanov-Razumnik's understanding of the term "Scythian."

Europe replacing Russia as the imperiled place. One difference is that Soloviev speaks only of Russia, while Blok's depiction of an Asian menace involves both Russia and Europe. Soloviev suggests no way of averting Russia's tragedy; Blok offers Europe an alternative to destruction. Soloviev warns his country that its time in history is over, while Blok proclaims to Europe that Russia's great hour has come — and that it can be a time of European rebirth as well.

The Mongols massed for attack in "The Scythians" are more metaphoric than Soloviev's; as in the earlier poem, these Eastern hazards to civilization are put in historical perspective. In the past, Blok reminds Europe, Russia has protected it from the onslaughts of westward-moving barbarians. He is not suggesting that such a threat now literally exists: destruction by Mongols is a melodramatic metaphor for the historical process of European decline and fall. This decline has long been in progress, suggests the poet, but Europe has failed to recognize the signs. Now it is dying a death as final and frightening as savage immolation. Russia, responsible in the past for Europe's survival, can help it now as well — but only if Europe recognizes how to achieve renewal.

What accounts for Russia's immunity from apocalypse? It is strong not only because it is historically young, but also because it is an alloy of two elements: European cultivation and intellect, and the passionate energy of the East. Blok proclaims Russia's universality in stanzas that begin with an assertion of deep-seated Europeanness:

> We love all things — the fire of cold figures
> And the gift of divine visions,
> We grasp all things — the sharp Gallic wit,
> And the gloomy Germanic genius . . .
>
> We remember all things — the hell of Parisian streets,
> And Venetian coolness,
> The distant fragrance of lemon groves,
> And the smoky hulks of Cologne . . .[3]

These lines are not addressed to Europe alone. As Mandelstam points out, Blok is amending the Russian "deflection from the unity of European culture"[4] — correcting those contemporaries and predeces-

---

[3]Aleksandr Blok, "Skify," *Stikhotvoreniia, Poemy, Teatr,* 2 vols. (Leningrad: Khudozhestvennaia literatura, 1972), II, 196–98. In all quotations from the poem, ellipses are the poet's.

[4]Mandel'shtam, "Barsuch'ia nora," p. 313.

sors who had been so devoted to finding Russia's national identity that they neglected its communality with Europe. The poem does stress Russia's inner Europeanness, but it stresses the nation's unrestrained, elemental spirit and strength with even more vehemence. Having resolved any doubt of Russia's Westernness, the poet spotlights its opposite facet. The images that follow shock not only in themselves, but because they fall right after the majestic European cathedral. "We love the flesh — its taste and color," Blok proceeds, "And flesh's suffocating mortal smell. . . ." That contrast indicates the breadth attributed to the nation of "Scythians." This term, which represents Russia's identity by serving as the title, warrants a closer look.

Historically, the Scythians were the first known dwellers in southern Russia, a Central Asian people who founded an empire north of the Black Sea lasting from roughly the eighth to the second centuries B.C. As used figuratively in Russian to describe a person, "Scythian" can connote unrestraint and passion, backwardness and barbarism. In Russian intellectual history, particularly in the nineteenth century, it was used on occasion to contrast Russians with the less fiery, more rational Europeans.[5] One must also mention the loose-knit literary-philosophical group that called itself "the Scythians," active for a few years after 1916, among whose affiliates were Bely and Blok. As linked with this group, the term "Scythian" connotes vitality, creativity, and independence, not barbarism. The views of all affiliates were diverse; generally, though, they believed in the renewing potential of revolution and "hoped that the ideal Scythian — the independent and creative individualist — would emerge out of the Revolutionary strife and lead the way to a new communal era." The utopian future they envisioned, writes one scholar, is "based on creativity (art), individualism (man), and international harmony (Russia and the world)."[6] All this is part of the poem's background; what kind of Scythian, though, emerges from the poem itself?

Blok's Scythian has a collective rather than an individual face. The poem is structured on a polarity between "we" and a plural "you." Thus Blok dwells on the "Asian" qualities that distinguish the nation from Europe, including its readiness to act. "Yes, we are Scythians! Yes, we are Asians," cries the opening quatrain, "With slanted and greedy eyes!" The words seem calculated to intimidate the West

<hr>

[5]Stefani H. Hoffman cites the usage of Pushkin and Herzen in her fine and thorough "Scythianism: A Cultural Vision in Revolutionary Russia" (diss. Columbia University, 1975), pp. 29–30.
[6]These are among Hoffman's characterizations of the Scythians (pp. 33, 211).

into listening. It appears, too, that Blok's depiction of Russia plays on a European misperception of his country, as though Europe has seen only Russia's "un-European" side. The repeated "Yes" confirms the addressee's opinion; the poem endorses this definition and embellishes it, exaggerating Europe's assumptions to demonstrate that Russia is indeed primitive and fierce, and that its present role results precisely from that youth and vitality. The idea that Blok is arousing Europe with its own words is supported by a related diary entry of this time in which he writes: "We are barbarians? Very well then. We'll show you just what barbarians are."[7]

While Russia in the poem has "barbarian" qualities, it is not the antagonist here but a potential savior. It could cause destruction not by offensive action, but by refusing to intervene in Europe's defense. The Scythians are clearly set apart from the figurative Mongol threat, which stands for the future that Europe seems headed for. As forceful as the collective speaker's assertions of will are its appeals that the "old world" "come to its senses" before decline becomes irrevocable. Three of the nineteen stanzas are entreaties, offering a future beyond the morass of Europe's continuing war (which, it must be recalled, European writers recorded in terms at least as strong as Blok's). Europe is urged to summon up its wisdom and answer correctly the riddle the sphinx of history poses. Should it choose the right path at this turning point, Russia will welcome it to the task of creating a new era; should it fail, Europe, not Russia, will be to blame. The duality of Russia — its life-giving and unsuppressable nature — is summed up by the poem's final phrase, in which a "barbarian lyre" summons Europe to a bright, harmonious future.

The "barbarian lyre" seems a contradiction in terms, an oxymoron. How can the most peaceful of instruments be played by a savage musician? One thinks of the lyre as companion to a single artist, an image that brings into the poem the creative individual who occupied the Scythian group's ideal future. In the poem's context, the lyre is a collective voice issuing a whole people's call to a "fraternal feast." Given its usage, the phrase relates to Blok's ideas about the "spirit of music" that animates every group on the ascendant in history. He explains in "The Collapse of Humanism" that every dominant culture carries within it a "spirit of music," which is taken over by the culture that succeeds it. The young culture may embody an-

---

[7]Blok, diary entry for January 11, 1918, in *Sobranie sochinenii*, 8 vols. (Moscow-Leningrad: Khudozhestvennaia literatura, 1960–63), VII, 317.

tithetical values, but it nevertheless is the only source of progress. It is not paradoxical, he writes, "that the barbarian masses turn out to be preservers of culture, commanding nothing more than a spirit of music, in those epochs when a civilization that has lost its wings and fallen silent becomes the enemy of culture, despite the fact that it has at its disposal all the factors of progress — science, technology, law, etcetera."[8] If one looks only at the national, Russian context, the carriers of music are the forces of revolution, displacing the old culture, in which Blok includes himself. As he says in the essay (first made public as a speech to his peers), the "wild chorus" of the masses "is openly hostile to what has been instilled in us by a humanistic European upbringing and education in the past century."[9] The internal Russian split between a westernized intelligentsia and the people is only one of the West-East rifts Blok hoped would soon be resolved. The international arena of "The Scythians" has Russia as a whole in the role of the primitive force that may seem bent on destroying culture, but is actually making its continuation possible.

That future culture, the poem implies, should not exclude all elements of the old world. In "The Scythians," Europe is offered the possibility of renascence if it will accept the end of its era of dominance.[10] This appeal to the old world is similar to Blok's urging the Russian intelligentsia to "listen to the Revolution!" (in an important essay written the same month).[11] The stance proposed in that essay is more specific than the action prescribed in the poem. The word "revolution" is not mentioned here, and it is unclear how Europe should accomplish what the speaker advocates. Heeding Russia's appeal to "Come to us!" seems to entail endorsing its course and working with it to create a new order, recognizing that history has arrived at a stage that demands and promises much.

---

[8]Blok, "Krushenie gumanizma," in *Sobranie sochinenii*, VI, 111.

[9]Ibid., p. 112.

[10]The idea that European dominance was ending was widely expressed by both Europeans and non-Europeans around this time. One Russian thinker whose writings on this idea are relevant to "The Scythians" is Nikolai Berdiaev. In *The New Middle Ages* (1924), he wrote: "The most powerful feeling produced by the World War is the realization that this war marks the end of Europe as a monopolizer of culture, and as an isolated province of the globe claiming to be the universe." Quoted in Prot. V. Zen'kovskii, *Russkie mysliteli i Evropa*, 2nd ed. (Paris: YMCA Press, 1955), p. 270. Translation is Galia S. Bodde's in V. V. Zen'kovskii, *Russian Thinkers and Europe* (Ann Arbor, Mich.: J. W. Edwards/American Council of Learned Societies, 1953), pp. 185–86.

[11]Blok, "Intelligentsiia i revoliutsiia," in *Sobranie sochinenii*, VI, 20.

The consequences for Russia if Europe refuses are not dire. As a synthesis of Western and Eastern qualities, Russia will survive regardless of Europe's fate. The implication is clear, however, that Russia prefers a future made in common with the West to one made beside its ruins. Despite the bombastic descriptions of the Scythian nation, the ideal presented in the poem is internationalist. Images of international harmony are not drowned in the other rhetoric. The Scythians insistently call to Europe: "Come to our peaceful embrace! / Before it is too late — sheathe the old sword, / Comrades! We will become brothers!" Images like the last, and like the final quatrain's "fraternal feast of labor and peace," are reminiscent of the poems and songs of the international socialist movement. In its use of national categories and of metaphor, though, the poem's vision of the route to utopian internationalism is far from Marxism. This is not class conflict, but a border crossing of Europe to Russia that can effect a synthesis of West and East on a higher level than is possible within Russia alone. In proposing that Europe "come to us," Blok is trying to efface the border, to end their separation. The "light from the East" that others of this time and before saw emanating from Russia can provide the spark.[12] Blok's depiction of Russia, as we have seen, is quite different from Soloviev's in "Panmongolism," where Russia's light is waning. It is closer in spirit to Soloviev's earlier writings on unifying East and West. Blok admired the philosopher as a visionary; in "The Scythians" he plays the role of seer himself, promising a harmonious future if Europe will cross over to it.

---

[12]Of the examples of this idea in literary history one should cite Dostoevsky, whose 1880 speech commemorating Pushkin presents Russia's universality and mission in spiritual terms. An exultant Dostoevsky proclaims: "Oh, the peoples of Europe have no idea how dear they are to us! And later — in this I believe — we, well, not we but the future Russians, to the last man, will comprehend that to become a genuine Russian means to seek finally to reconcile all European controversies, to show the solution of European anguish in our all-humanitarian and all-unifying Russian soul . . . and finally, perhaps, to utter the ultimate word of great, universal harmony." In F. M. Dostoevskii, "Pushkin (Ocherk)," *Polnoe sobranie khudozhestvennykh proizvedenni*, ed. B. Tomashevskii and K. Khalabaev, 13 vols. (Leningrad: Gosizdat, 1926–30), XII, 389–90. Translation quoted from F. M. Dostoievsky, "Pushkin (A Sketch)," in *The Diary of a Writer*, trans. Boris Brasol, 2 vols. (New York: Scribner's, 1949), II, 979–80.

3

ICE AND ICON
Spengler in Russia

Boris Pilniak, "The Third Capital" (1923)

The two basic terms in the political formulas of the day, "we" and "they," fit a variety of categories — ideological, class, national. Blok's essay "The Collapse of Humanism" shows the chameleon quality of the first person plural. The pronoun both distinguishes the Russian intelligentsia from the masses and denotes a national collective. Toward the end of his essay, Blok turns from the part to the whole. Seemingly contradicting the assurances of Russia's European nature in "The Scythians," he lyrically describes what separates Russia from Europe. "We have no historical recollections," he writes, "but great is the memory of the elements; our expanses are still fated to play a role of greatness. We have listened thus far not to Petrarch and not to Hutten, but to the wind rushing across our plain; the musical sounds of our cruel Nature have always resounded in the ears of Gogol, of Tolstoy, of Dostoevsky."[1] He even more bluntly contrasts Russia's potential with Europe's in an elliptical diary entry: "Europe (her theme) — is *art and death*. Russia — is life."[2]

Blok uses the terms "culture" and "civilization" in this essay in the sense detailed by Spengler in *The Decline of the West* (1918). (Civilization, in Spengler's definition, is the final stage of a culture, its

---

[1]Aleksandr Blok, "Krushenie gumanizma," in *Sobranie sochinenii*, 8 vols. (Moscow-Leningrad: Khudozhestvennaia literatura, 1960–63), VII, 114–15.

[2]Blok, diary entry for January 11, 1918, in *Sobranie sochinenii*, VII, 318. Emphasis in original.

ossified form.) The poet's depiction of Russia as a young culture excluded from the decline of European civilization is also found in Spengler's writing: he asserts in *Prussianism and Socialism* (1919) that "'Russianism' is the promise of a future culture as the evening shadows grow longer and longer over the Western world."[3] This idea, of course, has a long history in Russian thought. Spengler's theory of historical cycles owes much to Danilevsky's *Russia and Europe* (1869); his views on Russia rely heavily on Russian fiction, particularly Dostoevsky. But while the idea of a vital Russia replacing a dying Europe has many Russian sources, its discussion after the Revolution often focused on Spengler's treatment of the issue. Numerous articles addressed Russia's current situation with reference to Spengler's theories in general and his fragmentary remarks on Russia in particular.[4]

The intensity of interest in Spengler's thought was due more to its implications for the future than its interpretation of the past, though the two are hardly separable. In describing Russia's past interaction with Europe, Spengler is as doctrinaire as the firmest Slavophile. In the introduction to *The Decline of the West,* he objects to the term "Europe" partly because its use has led to the false assumption that Russia and Western Europe are joined in a whole. Spengler regards the reforms initiated by Peter I as a mistaken imposition on Russia of an artificial history. His perspective, while it has much in common with those of Russian thinkers, is clearly a foreigner's. He is a patronizing observer: he acknowledges that as one of the "late, urban, and intellectually mature members of a wholly different culture" his understanding of an "inscrutable" Russia can only be subjective. And subjective it is, as a sample illustrates: since Peter, he writes, a "childlike, inarticulate, fearsome people has been

---

[3]Oswald Spengler, *Preussentum und Sozialismus* (1919; rpt. Munich: C. H. Beck, 1924), p. 93. The English is quoted from Oswald Spengler, "Prussianism and Socialism," in *Collected Essays,* trans. Donald O. White (Chicago: Henry Regnery, 1967), p. 122.

[4]These include, in addition to the articles cited below, the following: A. M. Deborin, "Gibel' Evropy ili torzhestvo imperializma," *Pod znamenem marksizma,* no. 1 (1922) (rpt. in his *Filosofiia i politika* [Moscow: ANSSSR, 1961], pp. 108–29); V. Dodonov, "Predchuvstviia i grust'," *Zapad,* no. 2 (1922), pp. 30–32; P. Preobrazhenskii, "Osval'd Shpengler i krushenie istiny," *Pechat' i revoliutsiia,* no. 1 (1922), pp. 58–65; N. Vegov, "Budushchee Zapadnoi Evropy," *Zapad,* no. 3 (1922), pp. 24–31; V. Nemchinov, "Esteticheskaia teoriia obshchestva (O. Shpengler)," *Sibirskie ogni,* no. 1–2 (1923), pp. 148–68. In *Krasnaia nov',* no. 2 (6) (1922), there appeared three essays on Spengler under the heading "*Zakat Evropy*": Karl Grasis, "Vekhisty o Shpenglere," pp. 196–211; V. Bazarov, "O. Shpengler i ego kritiki," pp. 211–31; and Sergei Bobrov, "Kontuzhennyi razum," pp. 231–41.

confused, wounded, tortured, and poisoned by having forced upon it the patterns of a foreign, imperious, masculine, and mature 'European' culture."[5] This view of Russia's past determines Spengler's prediction of the fate of Bolshevism. As an attack on the westernized state, the Revolution has been supported by the masses; because Marxism is itself fundamentally Western, however, it will eventually be destroyed by the masses. Religion, not Bolshevism, will come to dominate Russia's future, "for what this townless people yearns for is its own life-form, its own religion, its own history."[6]

Russian Marxists as well as non-Marxists differed with Spengler on many grounds. His poor understanding of what Russia had in common with Europe was faulted, as was his pessimistic judgment of contemporary Europe. It may be pleasant to dream of a Western fall and a renaissance from the Russian East, wrote one scholar, but right now the reverse seems more reflective of reality: "'Cursed Europe' is living still, while we . . . are dying out."[7] Some of the debate was sparked by a 1922 collection of essays on Spengler edited by the religious philosopher Nikolai Berdiaev (expelled from Russia the same year).[8] In his contribution, Berdiaev uses Spengler as a text for his ideas on Russia's potential to revive both itself and Europe. He approvingly points out Spengler's suggestion that a new Russian culture is replacing a dying West, but differs sharply with Spengler on Russia's spiritual distance from Europe. Russia holds the key to the future because it understands both West and East: its universalism enables it to save both. Such passages in Berdiaev remind one of "The Scythians." Berdiaev's faith in history and religion are one: he presents a view of Russia's destiny that relies not on a theory, but on a belief in Russia's spirit. Within Russia lies a "mystery," he concludes, which will have a decisive influence on the world.[9]

Spengler's theory, an attractive vehicle for journalists and

---

[5]Spengler, "Prussianism and Socialism," p. 123.

[6]Spengler, *The Decline of the West,* trans. Charles Francis Atkinson, 2 vols. (New York: Alfred A. Knopf, 1937), II, 196.

[7]Pitirim Sorokin, "Nichalo velikoi revizii," *Vestnik literatury* (Petrograd), no. 2–3 (38–39) (1922), p. 3. Ellipsis in the original.

[8]These four essays were published in a volume entitled *Osval'd Shpengler i Zakat Evropy,* ed. N. Berdiaev (Moscow: Bereg, 1922). The title piece (pp. 5–33) is by F. A. Stepun. The others are S. L. Frank, "Krizis zapadnoi kul'tury," pp. 34–54; N. A. Berdiaev, "Predsmertnye mysli Fausta," pp. 55–72; Ia. M. Bukshpan, "Preodolennyi ratsionalizm," pp. 73–95.

[9]Berdiaev, ed., p. 72. On Spengler and members of the Berdiaev circle in Berlin see the excellent study by Robert C. Williams, *Culture in Exile: Russian Emigrés in Germany, 1881–1941* (Ithaca, N.Y.: Cornell University Press, 1972), pp. 245–52, 316–17. Williams discusses the idea of a "light from the East" on pp. 242–75.

scholars of various persuasions, also left its mark on Russian fiction. One of the most interesting literary juxtapositions of a renascent Russia and a decaying West is Boris Pilniak's extended story *(povest')* "The Third Capital," published in 1923.[10] Pilniak refers to Spengler, but has ideas of his own as well. His story conveys both faith in Russia and a belief in fiction — in the need to look beyond facts. Contemporary Europe and Russia are both shown in crisis. But while Pilniak paints a dark picture of the Civil War, he finds hope for Russia, though not for the West. Blok's suggestion in "The Scythians" that Russia can help Europe avert its crisis is not echoed here. In "The Scythians," the present upheaval in both places opens the possibility of eliminating the border between them. The border in "The Third Capital," however, can be crossed but not transcended: its sharp delineation will continue. Pilniak's Europe is marooned in Spenglerian ice, its life cycle come to an end.

Pilniak gained prominence with the publication in 1922 of his first novel, *The Naked Year.* The qualities associated with his prose are all present here, among them ornamentalism, shifting points of view, word play, and lyricism. In some respects derivative of Bely, Pilniak recalls him in more than style. Like Bely's, his writing sometimes focuses on Russia's inner conflict between its Eastern and Western identities. In *The Naked Year* the Revolution is invoked as a triumph of Russia's native Easternness, a healthy force that will purge Russian culture of its corrupting European elements. The idea that Russia's

---

[10]Both the title and genre warrant comment. The former (which was later changed to "Mat'-machekha") is not referred to in the text. It is presumably an allusion to the concept of "the third Rome." The work was first issued in full, as "Tret'ia Stolitsa," in the anthology *Krug,* bk. 1 (1923), pp. 199–295. Future references are to Boris Pil'niak, *Sobranie sochinenii,* 8 vols. (Moscow-Leningrad: Gosizdat, 1929), IV, 109–227. The title in this edition is "Mat'-machekha." In his dedication (to Aleksei Remizov) Pilniak refers to the work as a *povest'.* Viktor Gofman, expressing the widespread view that clear distinctions among genres are absent in Pilniak, finds no reason why *The Naked Year* should be termed a novel while "The Third Capital" (which is approximately the same length) is not. ("Mesto Pil'niaka," in *Boris Pil'niak. Stat'i i materialy,* in *Mastera sovremennoi literatury,* 3, ed. B. V. Kazanskii and Iu. N. Tynianov [Leningrad, 1928; rpt. Ann Arbor, Mich.: Ardis, n.d.], p. 10.)

Contemporary critics devoted some attention to the work, but in more recent criticism it receives brief mention, if any. Early articles of interest, in addition to those cited elsewhere, include: V. Pereverzev, "Na frontakh tekushchei belletristiki," *Pechat' i revoliutsiia,* no. 4 (1923), pp. 127–33, and Viktor Shklovskii, "O Pil'niake," *Lef,* no. 3 (7) (1925), pp. 126–36. My own interpretation is developed in more detail in "Pil'njak's *The Third Capital:* Russia and the West in Fact and Fiction," *Slavic and East European Journal* 22, no. 1 (1978): 39–51.

Westernization has ended is distilled in one character's pronouncement that "the Revolution has set Russia in contrast to Europe."[11]

The image of an awakened Russia standing in opposition to an increasingly moribund Europe is sketched in *The Naked Year*, but not developed. It arises again in the 1925 novel *Machines and Wolves*. The West figures here as the realm of industrial progress, and the question is raised whether Russia, after a revolution that Pilniak portrays as anti-European, is to betray its recaptured roots and yield to the essentially Western machine.[12] As in *The Naked Year* (and in his 1930 novel *The Volga Flows into the Caspian Sea*), the author's chief concern is Russia's post-revolutionary experience. The current state of Europe remains tangential.

Pilniak visited Europe in 1922 and 1923, and European settings surface occasionally in his fiction. "The Third Capital" is the only one of his works that places Europe in a central role, and that dramatizes both its condition and that of Soviet Russia. He is quoted as having written it with the European reader in mind, "right after returning from Europe — using raw material."[13] It merits attention not only as a neglected work of a major writer, but also for its development of the contrast between Europe and Russia present elsewhere in Pilniak. Here his anatomy of Russian life continues, but his field of vision is broader. He moves beyond the Revolution's effect on Russia's inner makeup to consider how Russia as a whole now relates to Europe. The opposition dominating "The Third Capital" is not internal but international. It is an opposition more complex than it first appears, developed by setting, character, and incident, and also conveyed through style and symbol.

Pilniak's approach to what separates Russia from Europe involves stylistic as well as geographical borders. The boundary between Russia and Europe is firm throughout; other conventional markers are, however, continually disregarded. Pilniak was termed the twen-

---

[11]Boris Pil'niak, *Golyi god* (1922; rpt. Chicago: Bradda, 1966), p. 101. Pilniak also expressed such views in non-fictional form. See, for example, his article "Zakaz nash," *Novaia russkaia kniga*, no. 2 (1922), pp. 1–2.

[12]Pilniak resolves the issue by suggesting that technology need not be viewed as Western, and thus can become one dimension of Russia's new identity. Gary L. Browning develops this conclusion in "Civilization and Nature in Boris Pil'njak's *Machines and Wolves*," *Slavic and East European Journal* 20, no. 2 (1976), 155–66.

[13]These words are quoted by N. A. Kovarskii in his essay "Svidetel'skoe pokazanie," in *Boris Pil'niak. Stat'i i materialy*, p. 88. No source is indicated, and I have been unable to locate one.

ties' most characteristic writer because his prose exemplified experimentation with form and the collapse of generic boundaries.[14] "The Third Capital" conforms to this image: its seemingly disparate components include fictional material and sections tending to journalism. Like other early works of Pilniak, it was regarded as an anarchic mass of fragments, "each striving for autonomy."[15] But although it is fragmented, its segments are drawn into a coherent whole. Their unity can be understood through the roles played by "fact" and "fiction." These terms function not only as stylistic markers: they relate also to key elements in Russian and Western existence.

One central fiction links Russia and the West, spotlighting their differences. It involves two characters: the Russian Emelian Emelianovich Razin and one "mister Robert Smith, an Englishman, a Scotsman" (p. 120). The story of Smith and Razin, who are emblematic of the bourgeois European and the post-revolutionary Russian, spans nearly the entire work. Though often interrupted, it is the only strand of "The Third Capital" with an exposition, conflict, and resolution — the only complete plot. Pilniak states in an opening section that there are no characters but "Russia, Europe, the world, faith, unbelief" (p. 112); these men illustrate the "characters" in action.

Razin is clearly a namesake of both the eighteenth-century Cossack rebel Emelian Pugachev and his seventeenth-century predecessor Stenka Razin. This Razin, however, is no peasant leader of mass movements: the name grants him attributes that he at first appears to lack. He is an intellectual, a philologist who now serves as secretary of a district department of education. He feels an allegiance to the past, but is part of the Revolution's bureaucracy. Razin spends his nights closeted with books in one of those decaying provincial houses that recur in Pilniak's writing. What he has in common with his forbears is an act of banditry: he lures Smith to the woods, shoots him in the back, and robs him. Elsewhere Pilniak identifies *"razinovshchina"* and *"pugachevshchina"* with the pre-Petrine, purely Russian peasant spirit that is resurfacing in the Revolution. By thus naming his character, the author links him to this mentality and asserts his Russianness; by making him an intellectual, he endows Razin with reason as well as instinct. The tension between a rational and an elemental Russia,

[14]Gofman, "Mesto Pil'niaka," pp. 7–9.
[15]Iurii Tynianov, "Literaturnoe segodnia," *Russkii sovremennik*, no. 1 (1924), p. 305. Tynianov uses this phrase to characterize several works by Pilniak, "The Third Capital" among them.

40

which in other works Pilniak presents through multiple characters, is embodied here in one figure, a variant of Blok's Scythian. Russia's dualism is internalized in Razin, and he confronts the West as a composite — scholar, bureaucrat, and outlaw.

Razin is not embittered by the Revolution, but he cannot tolerate the economic privations it brings. This leads him to make a trip to Europe, an episode that is briefly and elliptically related. After three months abroad, he returns with goods to use and sell. Blok writes of the Russian's natural belonging to all that comprises Europe; Razin, encountering Europe after Civil War Russia, finds the gap too great to grasp. Blizzards rage over Russia, but as Razin moves westward the meteorological and social climates grow increasingly mild. On returning he becomes disoriented, the features of Russia and Europe confused in his mind. If Razin's sanity has been shaken by the contrast between Russia and Europe, the experience has also heightened his perception. His apprehension of Russia's situation is now unbearably acute. Frustration drives him from the provinces to Moscow, where he encounters and eventually murders Smith. At his trial, he makes it clear that his motive was not ideological, but economic. Razin robs Smith for the same reason that he goes abroad: both incidents show a desperate Russia driven to plundering Europe.

But the Europe depicted by Pilniak, for all its mildness of climate, is itself in a state of crisis. Spenglerian strains issue from the narrator, from paraphrase of contemporary observers, and from several characters, including Mr. Smith.[16] Smith is painted as the typical British capitalist; in Russia on business, he lives in colonialist luxury. But he is not complacent: he is aware of, even obsessed with, his impending death and that of his culture. In letters and inner monologues, he ruminates on the decline of civilization in Europe and its rebirth in Russia.

This theme is introduced as early as the first page, where the narrator sets the scene by declaring: "Lent of the eighth year of the World War and of the death of European culture (according to

---

[16]Pilniak represents a long passage on the effect of the world war on Europe as an address by Pitirim Sorokin. (The first professor of sociology at the University of Petrograd, Sorokin emigrated to Europe in 1922, and in 1923 came to the United States.) The source of this passage is not clear. Some of the ideas and phrases appear to be borrowed from Sorokin's *Sovremennoe sostoianie Rossii* (Prague, n.p., 1922), pp. 12–14, although Sorokin's subject here is the impact of the Revolution on Russian society. Sorokin's article on Spengler is cited above; in his later writings he devotes much attention to the crisis of the West.

Spengler) — and the sixth Lent — of the Great Russian Revolution."
Time is figured in terms of both European civilization and Russian, as
if they existed in different dimensions. The contrasting time frames are
valorized: Europe's is a countdown toward death, a coda; Russia's is a
prelude to a new age. In the opening lines, Pilniak has already
suggested the possibility of Russia's renascence, of the achievement of
the Third Rome alluded to in the title.

Rebirth often seems overshadowed, however, by descriptions of
Russia's present misery. Europe and Russia, despite the opening contrast and references to Spengler, have an important similarity: both are
moribund. Razin has no vision of a brighter future. His statement to
the court begins: "I request that I be shot. I am dead anyway"
(p. 211). Europe, in the person of Smith, is dying because its time has
come; Razin's Russia is being ravaged by the aftereffects of revolution.
The idea that they are experiencing parallel deaths runs through "The
Third Capital."

The account of Smith's and Razin's worlds and of their relationship, fragmented though it is, points to a way of ordering other parts
of the work.[17] The remaining sections cannot be categorized as readily.
They leap from provincial towns to European capitals, from the stone
streets of Tallinn to the North Pole. We see exiled officers, Paris dan-
dies, drunken peasants. These episodes might be described, borrowing
one critic's phrase, as a "literary inventory."[18] But they need not be
regarded as a series of unconnected units.

They fall into two groups: the sections set in Russia tend to
resemble non-fiction, while those dealing with non-Soviet existence
have an affinity with fiction.[19] I use the term "non-Soviet" because the
work's contrasts involve more than Russia and Europe. There are

---

[17]These include excerpts from Ivan Bunin's "The Gentlemen from San Francisco"
(1915) and Vsevolod Ivanov's "Hollow Arabia" (1922). The use of passages from other
fiction (including his own) is frequent in Pilniak, and often noted with disfavor by
critics. (See, for example, Tynianov in "Literaturnoe segodnia," p. 303.) Though at
times Pilniak abuses this practice, it functions here effectively and to a definite end: the
pair of excerpts furthers the contrast between the dying West and suffering Soviet
Russia that the Smith-Razin fiction introduces. While Bunin describes a scene of Western decadence and excess, Ivanov details starvation and allegations of cannibalism
during the Civil War. These two bits of fiction complement the skeletal plot.
[18]Gofman, "Mesto Pil'niaka," p. 10.
[19]This identification of "non-fictional" with Soviet and "fictional" with foreign
relates to two major prose trends of the twenties. One is "factography" ("literatura
fakta") — writing that eschewed the literary and claimed a commitment to "naked
material." The other, represented in the extreme by then popular translated novels, is a
polar tendency relying on dynamic plots and exotica. Pilniak employs both kinds of
prose, mixing the exotic and ornamental with the documentary, in many of his works.

three principal locales: Western Europe, the Baltic (largely Tallinn), and Russia. The events in Tallinn primarily involve Russian émigrés, and thus might be placed on the "Russian" side of an opposition. But Russia in "The Third Capital" is specifically Soviet, and the Estonian capital is clearly foreign ground (as it had been in fact since 1918). The Baltic countries' Western roots are emphasized: they have escaped "soviets, devastation, and famine . . . because they do not have the Russian national soul, the Russian-sectarian hypnosis" (pp. 163–64). On looking beyond the story of Smith and Razin, one sees that "The Third Capital" is shaped not only by an opposition between Russia and Europe, but also by a distinction between the new world of Soviet Russia and everywhere else: Europe, émigré Russia, and the Russian past.

The more "fictional," non-Soviet sections are partially executed plots that represent a variety of styles: there are echoes of Jules Verne, of Turgenev, of Bely.[20] They include the stories of Smith's brother Edgar on a doomed polar expedition; of Smith's wife, who after an affair with Edgar is leading a luxurious life in Paris; of double agents, depravity, and romance in Tallinn. Scenes of exploration, adultery, and adventure are played out by characters who are individualized and who intermittently reappear. The fragments situated in Russia are less extended, and resemble journalistic vignettes or anecdotes rather than fictional episodes. These Soviet incidents range from the amusing to the grotesque. Pilniak tells of a switchman who walks the tracks with the Gospels in his bag and the *ABC of Communism* open in his hand; of a swindler who sells a peasant an electric lamp, claiming that he need simply nail the plug to a wall; of a famine-stricken custodian who eats his wife and then goes mad. The characters may be named, but they are nevertheless without identity. Each is an isolated case, described simply and then dismissed.[21]

While the foreign characters seem more fictionalized than documented, Pilniak's treatment of the West includes some journalistic narrative as well. Descriptions of Europe develop the picture of a civilization in crisis: its nightclubs and morgues become metaphors for its condition. They have in common an agglomeration of unclothed

---

[20]Shklovsky (in the above-cited article, p. 127) notes in Edgar Smith a resemblance to the hero of Verne's *The Adventures of Captain Hatteras.*

[21]Some differences between "The Third Capital" 's foreign/fiction and Soviet/nonfiction elements might be illustrated by comparing two sections: one set among Russian émigrés, the other in Razin's hungry town. The former depicts a girl named Liza Kalitina, whose family has resettled in Tallinn and who leads a comfortable, carefree life. By naming her after Turgenev's heroine in *A Nest of Gentlefolk,* Pilniak is gesturing

bodies, no longer human. A naked woman dances expressionless to the "naked rhythm of violins," while in the morgues of "Rome — London — Vienna — Paris — Berlin" there lies "a young woman, her left breast cut off, a piece of breast — meat — lies next to her on the zinc" (p. 160). The sensuality associated with the foreign — with Russians abroad, Smith's wife, bygone Russian winter nights — is shown here in a grotesque, perverted form.

The characterization of Western behavior as destructive and deviant is furthered in a passage describing the guillotining of a certain Landru, attended by thousands of Parisians. A Frenchman named Henri Landru was indeed executed in 1922, for the bizarre murders of ten women and a boy. Pilniak neither refers to the crime and trial (which had been widely publicized), nor proposes a connection with Russian life. A comparison is prompted, however, by the numerous references to cannibalism in Russia. In one striking scene a Soviet peasant soldier, welcoming a group of expatriate Russians returning to their homeland from America, bluntly informs them that "in the Volga region people are eating each other." He continues: "B-but, — comrades, — that doesn't scare us, because we are in power, we are our own masters" (p. 132). The cannibalism in Russia is treated as a fact of life, a terrible but instinctive act. Landru's preying on humans is the criminal, perverse behavior of a rare individual. It stems from a diseased imagination (the realm of fiction), rather than from the reality of starvation. Soviet life in this work is generally ruled by exigency, and a contrast between excess and need is one feature of the non-Soviet/Soviet dichotomy. The distinction between fiction and fact described above is not only stylistic: it also involves a distinction between a West largely oblivious of its impending crisis and a Russia where crisis is being universally experienced.

The meanings of fact and fiction are amplified in several sections that together form the work's conclusion. Razin, who has become Smith's interpreter, accompanies him to a performance held by "the Indian yogi Ben-Said." Pilniak describes the traditional performances of such magicians, who for centuries had traveled across Russia mys-

---

toward nineteenth-century values. Liza is life-loving and pure; her portrait is created through ornamental description, rhythmic narrative, and dialogue. There is also a Soviet Liza in the novel, whose story is both a substantive and stylistic contrast. This young girl is defiled rather than loved, and she is described briefly and colloquially. Liza Kalitina, the epitome of innocence, has in the second Liza an antithesis — a Soviet counterpart who prostitutes herself to stave off starvation. Both Lizas are Russian, but they are foreign to each other, literally and figuratively. Kalitina, a relic of an earlier era, has nothing in common with contemporary Russian life.

tifying audiences with feats like fire-swallowing and walking on nails. This one is of a different breed. He begins by informing the audience "that he, Ben-Said, was no Ben-Said and no Hindu, — but a peasant from Samara province . . . that he would now demonstrate the methods of Indian magic and would prove that they had nothing whatever to do with any mysterious power but were only tricks, sleight of hand, training and endurance, — that previously magic had been used by the powerful of the earth to keep the masses enslaved in ignorance" (p. 215). The new era's Ben-Said has no use for fictions: he is devoted to revealing the reality they mask. His importance is suggested by Smith, who is struck by the sensation that this yogi, refusing to fictionalize himself and exposing falsehood, is "the key to understanding Russia and the Russian Revolution" (p. 217).

The peasant-yogi's mentality is consistent with Pilniak's portrayal of Soviet existence. The lives of those in Russia have been stripped of illusion. Some people recognize the impossibility of evading reality; some, like Ben-Said, have purposefully chosen not to obscure it. Reality's harshness has brought others, like Razin and the cannibal custodian, to madness: unable to lessen hardship physically, they have mentally escaped it altogether. Ben-Said's story is a key to Pilniak's Russia, because it illustrates the absence of fiction that marks the characters' experience and the author's style.

The last section set in Russia dramatizes the qualities of starkness and extremity associated with Russia throughout. The narrator, now in the first person, brings us on a spring day to an old church, where valuables are being collected in order to buy food for the starving. Among the ornaments dismantled is the silver mounting on an icon of the Madonna and Child. The mounting, tarnished and wax-encrusted, covers much of the painting. When it is removed the figure comes alive in a new image: "The Madonna seemed bared, brought closer, she had come, had drawn near, leaned down . . . protecting all those mourning and being born, she was the key to all Russian revolutions and revolts" (p. 225). This incident, like Ben-Said's performance, involves a turning from fiction to reality. Like the magician, the Madonna of the new era is unadorned, divested of mystery. But for Pilniak she is an object of worship in this state as well: she represents the promise of a healed, renewed Russia. An earlier passage describes Russia as "this fearful, incredible country, where they have cannibalism and a new religion" (p. 172). A major element of this "new religion" is faith in the future. The Madonna does not symbolize Russia's modern role as a "third capital" of civilization, in the way that the Church embodied Russia's status as the Third Rome of Christendom. Pilniak does not glorify Russia; rather, he introduces the Madonna to show that Russia's hope is justified. Belief in the future is the one "fiction," the one transcendent, remaining to the Soviets — and it is a "fiction" that the West can maintain only in vain.

The barrenness of the West's future is illustrated in the following and final section of the work. It returns to the polar expedition of Edgar Smith, now hopelessly icebound. Captain Smith and his dwindling crew continue to follow the same kind of strict daily routine that has earlier been attributed to English life. Here the rigidity of that life is brought to an extreme. The parallelisms that pervade "The Third Capital" leave their mark on its concluding pages. The two final scenes — the transfigured Russian Madonna in springtime and the impassive Briton trapped forever in a field of ice — must be regarded as the final players in the Russia-West drama.

The images of spring and winter also mark the courses of world cultures in *The Decline of the West*. The West, here and in Pilniak, is arriving at the end of its life cycle, marooned in eternal winter. Spengler describes the final stage of a culture as a freezing of forms, "the thing-become succeeding the thing-becoming, death following life, rigidity following expansion, . . . petrifying world city following mother earth."[22] One recognizes the role of these opposing terms in "The Third Capital." Russia, though it has undergone a kind of death, is a culture in the ascendant, with other life cycles to come.

What makes this renewal possible, in Pilniak's view, is not only the force of history, but the force of faith. In Spengler's theory, rising nations are "possessed of the stuff of which cultures are made: creative spontaneity and religious devotion."[23] While Pilniak stresses the Soviets' stark confrontation with reality, he also shows them looking beyond it. "Russia lives by the will to wish and the will not to see," Smith reflects; "this lie I consider a deeply positive phenomenon, unique in the world" (p. 219). Soviet life, in a view that seems attributable also to the author, has become permeated by lies in order to make living possible. Faith sustains Russia — but a faith that exacts a price. What characterizes the mass of Russians is not only fact, but also a kind of fiction: the necessary fiction of the visionary. Russia has the "religious devotion," the "will to wish and the will not to see,"

---

[22]Spengler, *The Decline of the West*, II, 31.
[23]The formulation is that of Erich Heller, in "Oswald Spengler and the Predicament of the Historical Imagination," *The Disinherited Mind* (New York: Farrar, Straus and Cudahy, 1957), p. 183.

that enables it to look with hope toward the future.

The optimism expressed in "The Third Capital" was evidently not forceful enough to convince some readers of its orientation. Pilniak seems antagonistic towards Europe, wrote Viacheslav Polonsky, then *Novy mir*'s editor, but could he be hopeful about Russia while portraying it so negatively? Aleksandr Voronsky also objected to Pilniak's ambiguous treatment of Russia, advising that a writer who deals with political issues is obliged to put his thoughts in order.[24] Neither critic mentions a twice-repeated passage near the end in which Pilniak addresses the matters of intention and interpretation. He disavows any claim to accuracy by confessing that he has consciously engaged in distortion, that "of course: all this is untrue, unhistorical, all this is only a key which unlocks the romantic in history" (p. 225). The author's admission indicates that his conception of "The Third Capital" involves the same tension between fact and fiction that pervades the work.

Pilniak notes a conflict between the roles of chronicler and poet elsewhere as well. Introducing his American travels in *O.K.* (1933), he waxes lyrical about the world's division into East and West. He then interrupts in the third person to restrain himself, asserting his reportorial persona: " — and the writer was thinking all this untruthfully, because to think thus is romanticism [*romantika*], characteristic of writers, but wholly unnecessary."[25] Unnecessary, perhaps, in a work that purports to be documentary. But this kind of vision is necessary to Pilniak in "The Third Capital" as a means of countering the reporter's evidence. Pilniak can depict the future positively because he enlists the aid of *romantika,* showing both Russia's reality and her promise. Blok wrote in his diary, quoted above, that Europe's theme is death, while Russia's is life. Much in this story's portrayal of Russia supports the view of some Spengler critics that Russia is the moribund party. "The Third Capital" as a whole, however, illustrates Blok's aphorism.

---

[24]Viacheslav Polonskii, "Shakhmaty bez korolia (O Pil'niake)," *Novyi mir,* no. 10 (1927), p. 179; Aleksandr Voronskii, "Literaturnye otkliki," *Krasnaia nov',* no. 2 (12) (1923), p. 338. Voronsky objects not only to the distorted picture of Europe and Russia, but also to the relation that obtains between them in the work. He cites one instance in which a character, with no apparent rebuttal from the author, describes Europe's dependence on a newly dominant Soviet state. A peasant who lectures returning expatriates at the border credits Russia with having given Europe the Third International, thus holding the key to Europe's future. Voronskii protests the inaccuracy of this formulation, stressing the historically integral relationship between Russia and the West.

[25]Boris Pil'niak, *O'Kei: Amerikanskii roman* (Moscow: Federatsiia, 1933), p. 16.

4
MARXISM AND MAGIC
Fantastic Transitions

Vladimir Mayakovsky, "150,000,000" (1920)
Marietta Shaginian, *Mess-Mend, or a Yankee in Petrograd* (1924)

Critics found "The Third Capital" objectionable on several grounds, among them its treatment of Europe as a monolith. The gloomy capitalist was all very well, but where were the progressive forces of Europe, the proletariat and revolutionaries? Aleksandr Voronsky states the issue plainly: "There are two Europes in Europe: the author has hardly taken note of the second Europe, the Europe of workers' blouses, of revolts, strikes, and uprisings."[1] The role of this "second Europe" is indeed small. We briefly see Europe's alienated calling for the Third International, but Pilniak does not pursue the idea of a divided West ready for revolt. Like Blok in "The Scythians," he focuses on national rather than class distinctions. Internationalism as envisioned in "The Scythians" involves Europe and Russia as a whole, not a joining of their proletariats; Pilniak writes of the dying West without specifying that only its exploiting class is doomed. Except for a bit of rhetoric, he draws no connection between the European supporters of the Third International and the revolution in progress in Russia.

Such connections were broadly drawn, however, in much other Soviet writing of the early twenties. Even after 1925, when the doctrine of "socialism in one country" made international revolution a less vital issue, the Soviet government continued to pronounce the

---

[1]Voronskii, "Literaturnye otkliki," *Krasnaia nov'*, no. 2 (12) (1923), p. 336.

sickness of the capitalist West and the nearing triumph of its proletariat. The West's internal class struggle and the conflict between the
bourgeois West and socialist Russia became fixtures in Soviet fiction.
Both national and class divisions figure in such writing. Western
capitalism, resisting revolution where it should next occur, and Soviet
Russia, proof that proletarian victory is possible, are contending for
the prize of the future. A spate of satirical, futuristic, and adventure
novels in the twenties proceeded from the assumption that Russia was
moving toward a utopian future that would include the West, if only
its reactionary forces could be crushed.

Most works in this category are popular fiction, aimed at a mass
audience. Though some are tedious and silly, the more serious treatments of transition should be seen against the background of this
sensationalist literature. It is significant as a whole, an index of both
literary and political trends: some writers' attraction to fast-moving,
fantastic techniques, and the need to transmit ideology in palatable
form. These works reduce the complexities of change to facile solutions, pulling puppet strings and tossing about people, countries,
and continents. This is a literature of "good guys" and "bad guys," in
which the victory of the former is assured by political theory. The
battle was not to be left entirely in history's hands, however. Socialism
might be destined to triumph everywhere, but its development was
subject to manipulation. Change could be speeded or subverted. History could be plotted (as governments and parties were in fact doing),
and writers had their own ideas about plotting it.

While these fictions of Russian and Western transformation are
ideologically predictable, their action is highly improbable. As one
Soviet scholar understatedly comments: "The true causes of socio-
historical processes flickered extremely faintly through a cascade of
self-sufficient adventures."[2] The road to utopia, though, has rarely
been depicted realistically. Pilniak in "The Third Capital" points out
his deviation from historical analysis; such statements are unnecessary
in this fiction, because the action they depict is so blatantly unrealistic. They concern transition as a historical process, but give su-

---

[2] L. F. Ershov, "Satiriko-iumoristicheskaia povest'," in *Russkaia sovetskaia povest'
20–30-kh gg.*, ed. V. A. Kovalev (Leningrad: Nauka, 1976), p. 355. Another useful essay
in this collection is A. F. Britikov, "Detektivnaia povest' v kontekste prikliuchenche-
skikh zhanrov," pp. 408–38. Other commentaries on popular fiction involving Russia
and the West include: S. Dinamov, "Avantiurnaia literatura nashikh dnei," *Krasnoe
studenchestvo*, no. 6–7 (10–11) (1925): pp. 109–12, and A. Vulis, *Sovetskii satiricheskii
roman: evoliutsiia zhanra v 20–30-e gg.* (Tashkent: Nauka, 1965), pp. 48–63.

pernatural causes precedence over historical ones. Imagination rules. Transition in Russia and the West is treated as a game in which both participants have weapons more powerful than socio-historical forces. Revolutionary change, which was proving confusing in Russia and stalled in the West, is alternately helped and threatened by the fantastic. Elements of science fiction, detective fiction, and utopian fiction are mixed together; incredible human and technological powers are deployed. The devices used might collectively be labeled "magical" — "magic" understood as the opposite of the progression of events ordained by Marxist-Leninist theory.

The authors of such entertainments include the obscure and the prominent. Some unfold more surprises than others. Those works with titles like *Death Rays* (1925) and *Appetite of the Microbes* (1927) promise few. Lavrenev's *The Fall of the Republic of Itl* (1925) thinly veils capitalists and communists in imaginary names. (The forces of the northern land of Assor [an approximate reversal of *"Rossiia"*] oust the colonial regime of Nautiliia [a take-off on England] in the distant country of Itl.)[3] Ilya Ehrenburg in *The D.E. Trust* (1923) shows a divided West destroying itself. The novel concerns an American plot to destroy Europe: as if bored with all the talk of Europe's decline, Ehrenburg decides to kill it off.[4] Ehrenburg (whose cynicism about both Russia and the West will be discussed in Part 3) takes none of this seriously. His parodic writing was in turn parodied by Valentin Kataev in *Ehrendorf Island* (1925). Another of Kataev's novels, *The Sovereign of Iron* (1925), plays with detective fiction: one of the heroes is Stanley Holmes, nephew of Sherlock.[5] Kataev and Ehrenburg are remembered for their other, superior writing; the same is true of

---

[3]The novels named are the following: N. A. Karpov, *Luchi smerti* (Moscow-Leningrad: Zemlia i Fabrika, 1925); A. Shishko, *Appetit mikrobov* (Moscow-Leningrad: Molodaia gvardiia, 1927); B. Lavrenev, *Krushenie respubliki Itl'* (Moscow-Leningrad: GIZ, 1926). Others which might be mentioned are A. Irkutov and V. Verevkin, *AAAE* (Moscow: Mospoligraf, 1924) and L. Nikulin, *Taina seifa* (Moscow: Puchina, 1925).
[4]The first edition (to which I did not have access) is Il'ia Erenburg, *Trest D. E. (Istoriia gibeli Evropy)* (Berlin: Gelikon, 1923). The British scholar Robert Russell observes that in its original form the novel is unusual in its pessimism toward Soviet Russia's future as well as toward the West's. Ehrenburg "makes no important distinction between European Russia and the rest of Europe on the one hand, or between emergent Siberia and the other surviving world powers such as America and Africa on the other." In Russell's "Red Pinkertonism: An Aspect of Soviet Literature of the 1920s," a paper presented at the eleventh annual convention of the AAASS, New Haven, October 1979, p. 10. This excellent paper places the genre in a broad context.
[5]Valentin Kataev, *Ostrov Erendorf* (Moscow: Gosizdat, 1925); *Povelitel' zheleza* (V. Ustiug: Sovetskaia mysl', 1925).

Viktor Shklovsky and Vsevolod Ivanov, co-authors of the adventure serial *Mustard Gas* (1925).[6] The entertainment value of their story is part of its plot. This saga of a future capitalist scheme to destroy Russia and Asia is ultimately revealed to take place in 1925 in the mind of one Petrov, a bored young Russian provincial. Petrov has been holding the villagers enthralled with tales of false Tarzans in London, fraudulent prophets in New York, improbable Chaplin movies and Chinese barbers in Siberia, flaming arrows over Moscow, and a devastating gas destined for the proletariat. All of this, and much more, is interwoven into dozens of sub-plots. At the end the invented story penetrates the frame, and Petrov finds himself attacked by the weapon of his own imagination. Shklovsky, a master at analyzing literary devices, uses them indiscriminately: *Mustard Gas* is virtually an encyclopedia of adventure episodes. Here, as in most of these works, ideology is upstaged by action and undercut by irreverence. Any proletarian, pro-Soviet sentiments become tinged with the satire that colors everything else.

The West and Russia are not always placed in opposite corners of the ring. Russia may be generalized into a proletariat from which national identities are erased. Mayakovsky's *Mystery-Bouffe,* written in 1918 to celebrate the first anniversary of the Revolution, is one example of pure internationalist class struggle. The lines are clearly drawn between exploiter and exploited (here "the clean" and "the unclean"), and their conflict swiftly and painlessly resolved. This is an apocalyptic leap into the future. The old world is flooded and the ruling class easily overthrown; the earth reemerges, magically scrubbed clean into a proletarian paradise. The proletariat, throughout the play, identify themselves with no nation. Russia plays no spe-

---

[6]V. Ivanov and V. Shklovskii, *Iprit* (Moscow: Gosizdat, 1925), vyp. 1–9. As indicated, the novel was issued in nine installments. The first installment, written by Shklovsky, appeared in *Lef*, no. 3 (7) (1925), pp. 70–76. Shklovsky's note prefacing the excerpt explains that they intended to depart from adventure novels of the sort being written by Shaginian and Kataev by integrating factual material into the plot. The novel's execution is remote from the authors' intention: as Shklovsky goes on to confess: "I am not entirely satisfied with the novel, since parodic-ironic material took up a good part of it" (p. 70). A good description of the novel is found in Richard Sheldon, "Viktor Borisovič Shklovsky: Literary Theory and Practice, 1914–1930" (diss. University of Michigan, 1966), pp. 208–12. I have been unable to discover details of Shklovsky and Ivanov's collaboration. In his memoir of Ivanov, "Vsevolod Ivanov," in T. A. Ivanova, ed., *Vsevolod Ivanov —pisatel' i chelovek,* 2nd ed. (Moscow: Sovetskii pisatel', 1975), pp. 8–26, Shklovsky does not mention *Iprit*. According to one scholar, Ivanov was ashamed of the novel. See L. Gladkovskaia, "Put' iskanii," in Vsevolod Ivanov, *Sobranie sochinenii,* 8 vols. (Moscow: Khudozhestvennaia literatura, 1973–78), I, 21.

cial role in leading them toward the utopian future. Only the Russian merchant, one of the wiliest of "the clean," asserts his nationality. He reacts with outrage to the catastrophe, perceiving himself unjustly threatened because he is not considered European. Assuming that the East alone is marked for destruction, he protests that he does not belong to it. "Honored sirs, this is outrageous!" he blusters. "Do you take me for Asia?"[7]

Mayakovsky's other fantasy of class struggle, the narrative poem "150,000,000" (1920), is a national as well as proletarian epic. Here, and in Shaginian's novel *Mess-Mend, or A Yankee in Petrograd* (1924), it is the Russians who lead the way to communism. Having begun its own transition to utopia, Russia moves the West toward the same goal — in Mayakovsky through destruction, and in Shaginian through inspiration. In "150,000,000" Russia transforms the West by force, through the strength of the Russian proletariat and the revolutionary impulse it arouses in nature; in *Mess-Mend* Russia helps subvert the West by the power of its example. The United States, rather than Europe, represents the West in both. America was a useful antagonist because it was more exotic and remote to readers (a more distant kingdom, as befits a fairy tale) and because it embodied capitalism at its healthiest. As such it provided a sharper contrast to Russia and a more formidable adversary. But as Mayakovsky and Shaginian demonstrate, no bastion is too formidable for the imagination. The poem and novel between them provide a sample of devices for magical transitions in Russia and the West.

In the matter of imagination, Mayakovsky was not outshone by his contemporaries: his poetry expanded the possibilities of language. Some of his poems about the impact of a changing world on the individual are more lasting than this poem about people changing the world. But "150,000,000" has some of the linguistic exuberance of Mayakovsky's best writing. He sets in motion what one of the poem's ninety-seven neologisms calls "resounding-legged gymnasts of words."[8] This poem parodies the *bylina* (the Old Russian epic song),

[7]Vladimir Maiakovskii, *Misteriia-Buff*, in *Polnoe sobranie sochinenii*, 13 vols. (Moscow: Khudozhestvennaia literatura, 1955–61), II, 176. Two versions of the play were written, in 1918 and 1921. The first, which premiered on 7 November 1918, is quoted here.

[8]Vladimir Maiakovskii, "150,000,000," in *Polnoe sobranie sochinenii*, II, 113–64. The phrase quoted, *"slov zvonkonogie gimnasty,"* is in line 416. Citations in parentheses are to lines in this edition. The number of neologisms was calculated by Assya Humesky, *Majakovskij and his Neologisms* (New York: Rausen, 1964), p. 251.

and in it Mayakovsky mixes lofty and telegraphic language, poetic formulas and slang.

The final scene of "150,000,000" shows a mass celebration in a future world without national boundaries. On a flowering square that was once part of the Sahara, earth-dwellers are joined by fellow citizens of the cosmos to commemorate those who made possible their utopia. Mayakovsky catalogues the preceding sacrifice and struggle in a requiem; the concluding lines describe his poem as "a bloody Iliad of revolutions," "an Odyssey of the hungry years." His universal scenario and use of the plural "revolutions" suggest that the poem does not hail the Russian people alone. The opening, however, better expresses the spirit of the work as a whole. Post-revolutionary Russia is the setting; among the snatches of dialogue emerging from the din are the following exclamations (rhymed in the original, as is the entire 1708-line poem): "Dear old Russia is finished! / They've done in the poor thing! / We'll find a new Russia. / One that's world-wide!" (lines 56–59). The world utopia envisioned is to be formed by extending the borders of Russia to the globe's limits. "150,000,000," while paying deference to the spirit of internationalism, glorifies Russia's role in making the West safe for socialism.

The paraphrase of Woodrow Wilson is apt because a grotesquely caricatured Wilson personifies Russia's adversary in the poem. In a burst of hyperbole Mayakovsky describes his dazzling, futuristic Chicago headquarters, his limitless flesh, and his entourage (which includes Whitman in a smoking jacket). But although Wilson is placed in the most American of settings, his nationality is not essential to his identity. The section concludes with a note that this gluttonous tyrant might be any of the leaders of his class. Wilson is not lampooned primarily as an American, but as the architect of a Western plan for world harmony.

The protagonist, as befits a *bylina,* is a modern warrior-prince, a proletarian hero named Ivan. He is an entirely national figure, very different from the non-aligned workers of *Mystery-Bouffe.* Mayakovsky first published this poem anonymously, a device calculated to support the opening assertion that the 150 million citizens of Russia are its author. Ivan, like the ostensible author, is the nation incarnate. His supernatural origins and magical achievements parody the *bylina* tradition. All Russian nature and humanity coalesce into a hero of mythic proportions, with arms the length of the Neva. The narrator has already announced his mission: "Today / we will

fling Russia / to paradise / beyond the rainbow chinks of sunsets"
(lines 197–200). He continues, in his tireless circus-barker style:
"Unassisted / right before your eyes / today / we / will / make /
miracles" (lines 289–94).

And Ivan goes off to make them. Striding over to America, he
challenges Wilson to "a championship of the world class struggle"
(lines 1212–13) to resolve whose plan for the future will prevail.
Wilson combats the enemy with what Mayakovsky calls a "ven-
omous host of ideas" — "democratisms, / humanisms — / on they
come / isms upon isms" (lines 1495–99). Neither these nor the clouds
of pestilence he unleashes can protect Wilson from a fully mobilized
Ivan. Ivan's cause, though defined as a Russian mission, is not defended only by Russian forces. Here, as in *Mystery-Bouffe* and elsewhere in Mayakovsky, the world's inanimate inhabitants are on the
side of revolution. Paving stones fling themselves through diamond-
bright store windows, telephone poles and skyscrapers revolt, water
rises up out of the ocean. (There are renegades: the Petrograd Admi-
ralty does "wall-to-wall" battle with a recalcitrant Louvre.) Wilson is
reduced to ashes, and the future materializes, entering like an off-stage
maiden whom Ivan has rescued from the dragon. The "maiden"
image is mine, not the poet's. His future, entirely unmaidenly, bellows
forth the championship's outcome like a trillion trumpets: "The future is here! / The future is the winner!" (lines 1586–87).

It is worth noting that Mayakovsky's fantastic Wilson is not all
that far from political rhetoric of the day. The poem was written
during 1919–20; final proofs were approved in November 1920.
Addressing the Second Congress of the Comintern in August of that
year, Trotsky offered the following description of one menace to
Soviet success: "Wilson, the American provincial, carrying the highly
rated dollar not only in his pocket but also on his forehead, had made
up his mind that his fourteen points should become the new Gospel of
the world. He had, however, come up against the English fleet and
against something more formidable, viz., Soviet Russia and Communism, and the vexed American apostle went back to the White
House at Washington, to his Mount Sinai."[9] Trotsky's version has the

---

[9]From Trotsky's speech at the final joint session of the Second Congress of the
Communist International, the All-Russian Central Executive Committee, the Moscow
Soviet, the All-Russian Council of Trade Unions, and the Factory Committees, August
7, 1920. Excerpted in Xenia Joukoff and Harold H. Fisher, eds., *Soviet Russia and the
West, 1920–1927: A Documentary Survey* (Stanford, Calif.: Stanford University Press,

essentials of Mayakovsky's: caricature, confrontation, and superior Soviet strength. The differences are of degree. The former Commissar of Foreign Affairs, then Commissar of War, was in no position to charge Mount Sinai. The poet playing at war commissar can dispense with strategy and resolve the conflict in a flash. Literary transition to the future requires no more than a bit of magical footwork.

The realm of capital is vanquished in "150,000,000" through Russia's efforts, not the international proletariat's. This may in part explain Lenin's aversion to the poem; his other objections are easy to imagine. Lenin was no lover of avant-garde art, and a prize fight between a Russian giant and a Western buffoon was hardly his idea of what lay ahead.[10] Lenin presumably cared about works like this because struggle with the capitalist West, as a prime task of the young Soviet government, was felt to require correct literary expression. A Party leader of more literary bent, Bukharin, proposed one suitable form in a *Pravda* article of 1923.[11] Bukharin called for writers to adapt to their purposes the detective novel of the sort popular before the Revolution. The exploits of detective Nat Pinkerton and his men, a frequent subject of such novels, gave a name to a genre — "the pinkerton." Pinkerton's agency had tracked down subversive workers; suggesting that battles between proletarian virtue and capitalist vice be waged on this model, Bukharin dubbed the new genre "the red pinkerton."

His advocacy of the genre seems largely attributable to its proven mass appeal. The regime was concerned both with promoting literacy and with using literature as an ideological tool; this was an easily comprehensible, engaging form. The respective aims of communism and capitalism were clear enough: what they needed to suc-

---

1957), pp. 41–42. Trotsky later called the poem's caricatures of Wilson and Chicago "bohemian silliness." See his 1924 *Literature and Revolution* (Ann Arbor: University of Michigan Press, 1960), p. 153.

[10]In a note to Lunacharsky, Lenin chides the Commissar of Education for voting to publish such "flagrant stupidity and pretentiousness" in what Lenin considered a large edition. The note concludes with an uncomradely suggestion that Lunacharsky "be flogged for futurism." (Mayakovsky had presented Lenin with a copy of the poem signed "with comfutist greetings" — an amalgam conveying the poet's joint allegiance to communist ideology and futurist art.) See note from Lenin to A. V. Lunacharskii, May 6, 1921, in N. I. Krutikova, ed., *V. I. Lenin o literature i iskusstve,* 5th ed. (Moscow: Khudozhestvennaia literatura, 1975), pp. 483, 780.

[11]This article, mentioned in many sources, does not appear to be included in the most comprehensive bibliography of Bukharin's writings, Sidney Heitman's *Nikolai I. Bukharin: A Bibliography* (Stanford, Calif.: Hoover Institution, 1969).

ceed as fiction was intrigue. Plotted simply, as in "150,000,000," the story had drama but little dramatic interest — the outcome was clear from the start. Commissar of Education Lunacharsky, defending the poem to Lenin, pointed out that Mayakovsky's readings of it were a great success, "even among workers."[12] But whatever the mock epic's appeal, it did not approach the enormous success of the "red pinkertons" that followed. Their plots invested the conflict with excitement and attracted the reader with the promise of a good read.

Marietta Shaginian's *Mess-Mend, or a Yankee in Petrograd* is one novel directly inspired by Bukharin's article. *Mess-Mend* was among the most popular works of its kind, and served as a model for other revolutionary adventure fiction.[13] It was published serially in ten pamphlets with lurid come-on covers (photomontages by Rodchenko).[14] The name on those covers was not Shaginian's, however: it belonged to "Jim Dollar," identified in an editorial foreword as an American proletarian writer. This fiction was transparent, but there was some uncertainty as to the actual author. In a 1926 article explaining her work Shaginian dispels all the rumors, including one that Jim Dollar was Bukharin himself.[15]

If there were doubts about the author, there were none about the heroes. The enemy is international capital, particularly its American variant. Here it faces two sorts of antagonists, active and passive. The American proletariat, not the Russian, actively pursues capital's fall. Russia's role is unaggressive but decisive: its attraction for talented Americans presents the greatest threat to capitalism and provides the novel's central mystery.

---

[12]Note from Lunacharskii to Lenin, undated (but apparently May 6, 1921), in Krutikova, ed., *V. I. Lenin o literature*, p. 483.

[13]A. F. Britikov is among those who make this point (see "Detektivnaia povest'...," p. 425).

[14]Dzhim Dollar [Marietta Shaginian], *Mess-Mend, ili Ianki v Petrograde. Roman-skazka* (Moscow: Gosizdat, 1924–25). This version is included in the author's *Sobranie sochinenii*, 4 vols. (Moscow: Khudozhestvennaia literatura, 1935), III. In 1956 she issued a revised version, which also appears in the most recent *Sobranie sochinenii*, 9 vols. (Moscow: Khudozhestvennaia literatura, 1971–75), II. Shaginian explains in a preface to the 1956 version that the revision largely entailed clarification and emphasis of the novel's two main tendencies: "the parodic, directed against the imperialists, and the romantic, glorifying the international proletariat" ("Predislovie avtora," in the later *Sobranie sochinenii*, II, 235). The first edition makes the reader's detective work more difficult. As Shaginian explains, in the twenties readers liked having to figure out gaps in the plot.

[15]Marietta Shaginian, "Kak ia pisala *Mess-Mend*," in *Sobranie sochinenii* (1935), III, 375–82.

The mystery surrounds one Jeremiah Rockefeller (named Morlender in the revised edition), a world-famous inventor. The later change of name is an improvement, because the character is the best of inventors, not the most powerful of capitalists. That role is played by his employer and collaborator, Kressling, who sends him on a month-long trip to Russia. Alarmed by the tone of Rockefeller's letters, Kressling secretly summons him home. His report confirms Kressling's fears: the inventor has been impressed by Soviet achievements and worker control, and is eager to have his patents benefit the Soviets as well as the West. Kressling, obsessed in particular with Rockefeller's current project (an unspecified device that could give Kressling control of the world), deems him too dangerous to leave at large. He imprisons Rockefeller, spirits him out of the country, and disseminates the story that he has been murdered by the Soviets in Petrograd. This deception has two purposes. It allows Kressling to assume control of the patents, and it enables him to incite Rockefeller's son Arthur to vengeance. Kressling and his allies (who include a multinational assemblage of exiled aristocrats and monarchs) send the son to Petrograd disguised as an American communist named Vasilov. His mission: to blow up strategic factories and arrange the destruction of the Soviet leadership. After more than fifty chapters of incredible escapes, murders, and feats of information-gathering, Arthur proves to be his father's son. He is even more excited than his father by what he sees in Russia, and resolves to stay on and cast his lot with the Soviet future.

The American writer Lincoln Steffens declared on returning from Russia in 1920, "I have been over into the future and it works."[16] The same sentiment might be applied to young Rockefeller. Russia in the novel has not been propelled instantly into the future, but it is right on course. The post-revolutionary ordeal has been weathered with few scratches. A chapter in which Arthur alias Vasilov tours a centerpiece of Soviet industry is called "Mister Vasilov in Wonderland." The factory is Soviet society in microcosm. Technology is not the only thing transformed: the workers, now their own masters, radiate perfection and happiness. Overwhelmed by their expertise and the surroundings, Arthur exclaims: "Utopia!" "Exactly," answers his guide, "we have set ourselves the task of bringing about utopia."[17] Like Alice, Rockefeller is more and more amazed by each sector of Wonder-

---

[16]Quoted in *The Autobiography of Lincoln Steffens* (New York: Harcourt Brace, 1931), p. 799.

[17]Shaginian, *Mess-Mend,* in *Sobranie sochinenii* (1935), III, 253.

land he visits. In the West, the passageway to Wonderland is blocked by the capitalist system; Arthur realizes that the best way to get there is Russia's route.

Arthur's conversion comes about through no effort on the Soviets' part. They engage in none of the scheming rampant in the novel. Russia appears unthreatened by the West, sure of its ability to thrive regardless of what transpires there. The counterplot to Kressling's plan is masterminded and executed by Americans, principally his own employees. The workers (to continue the "Wonderland" metaphor) are busy looking for ways to reach the rabbit hole. Their leader is a tall, fair-haired master craftsman appropriately named Mick Thingsmaster, who combines the qualities of Sherlock Holmes, Robin Hood, and Edison. Led by Mick, they foil the capitalist plot through their extraordinary command of the physical world. They penetrate walls, travel on power lines with the speed of electricity, make secret movies of enemy meetings. In all this they are helped by a network of workers who belong to a secret union called "Mess-Mend" (Shaginian picked the words from a dictionary). Every object they produce is marked with a tiny "MM" sign and is specially made to serve the anti-capitalist cause. Shaginian wrote later that the novel illustrates a doctrine of her own devising: "The worker can conquer capital through his secret power over the creations of his hands, over things."[18] In other words, capitalism's downfall will be the skill developed by workers in serving it.

Capitalism is at its strongest in America, and its workers are technological wizards and super-sleuths. Their wizardry is matched by that of Kressling's best agent, the Houdini-like hypnotist Grigorio Chiche. In this confrontation of fantastic powers, of course, Chiche's black magic loses to the white magic of Mick and his merry band. Soviet Russia is on the sidelines, a challenge to the capitalists and proof to the workers that they can succeed.

What of the thwarted, but still otherwise unshaken Western establishment? The prognosis for the West, implicitly pessimistic, is made explicit in one of the book's most ridiculous formulations. Jeremiah Rockefeller's closest friend, an elderly Dickensian doctor named Lepsius, has been collecting data throughout the novel for a scientific breakthrough. He finally reveals the object of his research, and his results, in a dramatic scene at an international congress in

---

[18]Shaginian, "Kak ia pisala *Mess-Mend*," p. 377.

Petrograd. Lepsius announces that the reactionaries of the world, however powerful they may be, are biologically doomed. The spines of capitalists and aristocrats, he has found, are slowly degenerating from vertical to horizontal — a development correlated with their social devolution from civilization to bestiality. (Rodchenko's cover montage for this installment shows a dinosaur — the eventual form, presumably, of those ill-fated exploiters.) The decline of the West is literally on its way, and the only escape is to join the proletariat. The outlandishness of Lepsius's theory is an index of the novel's seriousness: all this is clearly the stuff of humor. The West is subverted by fantastic means, and is being attacked from within by even more improbable forces. If proletarian magic doesn't get it, biology will. Shaginian's version of Social Darwinism is another fantastic device to speed the transition to utopia. As in "150,000,000," magic upstages Marxism.

Mess-Mend's critics faulted it partly on those grounds: its ideological message was infected by the fantasy pervading the novel. One reviewer called the portrayal of the proletariat a reactionary travesty, noting that "Jim Dollar turns the workers' organization into a secret society of masons, with secret masonic signs." He conceded, though, that the book was hard to put down.[19] Shaginian does include a rationale for her departure from realism. The "publisher's" biographical sketch of the ostensible author emphasizes that he had no literary education, but grew up enthralled by movies. Since the sensationalist movies that inspired Dollar were far from realistic, he does not aim for verisimilitude. The device of a non-Russian, non-realist author gives Shaginian license in depicting both the West and her own country. She does not step beyond the bounds set by ideology: *Mess-Mend* as a whole affirms that the portrayal of Soviet Russia as a new world is based on fact, not fantasy.

Russia's transition from revolution to utopia is not wholly a

[19]G. Fish, untitled review of *Mess-Mend, Zvezda*, no. 3 (1924), p. 314. The novel was staunchly defended, however, by the chief editor of *Gosizdat*, N. L. Meshcheriakov. In his preface to the first edition, he writes that the novel's fantasy matches the fantastic nature of the epoch. "This is a novel of our time," he continues, "when monumental events pass before us with purely cinematographic speed." See Shaginian, *Sobranie sochinenii* (1935), p. 107. In "Kak ia pisala *Mess-Mend*," p. 377, Shaginian is impatient with those who found her approach to a serious topic frivolous. "Don't forget," she reminds the critics, "that this is a parody. *Mess-Mend* parodies the West-European form of the adventure novel, parodies, and does not imitate it, as some critics mistakenly think. But it is the fate of many books to begin in jest and to finish in earnest."

matter of magic in *Mess-Mend*. In its attention to Russia's technological progress, it resembles the later production novels that measure national growth in terms of industrial output. (One such novel, discussed in Part 4, is Valentin Kataev's *Time, Forward!*) But the 1930s works, however unrealistic they may be, do deal with some of the problems of building utopia. *Mess-Mend* does not: Shaginian's Russia, transformed by fantastic means, is proceeding toward the future with extraordinary ease. The leap from past into future is not complete, as it is at the end of "150,000,000": this is a Wonderland still in motion. The capitalist West is not instantly leveled by a mythic hero. In essence, though, Mayakovsky and Shaginian are not too far apart. Both use established popular genres (one ancient, one recent) to dramatize the Marxist destinies of socialism and capitalism. The extraordinary forces in the Old Russian epic parodied by Mayakovsky are comparable in function to the mental and technological magic that Shaginian borrows from the detective genre and from science fiction. In these works and others like them change is easily accomplished, the product of what Pilniak, concluding "The Third Capital," calls "the will to wish."

5

WANDERING TOWARD THE FUTURE
Russian and Western Illusions

Andrei Platonov, *The Hurdy-Gurdy* (1932–35)

Popular literature, as we have seen, resolved the question of where Russia and the West were headed. Through the limitless resources of fantasy, it expressed the limitless possibilities of Russia. Reality, however, revealed possibility's limits. As the Revolution receded into the past, it grew increasingly clear that the transitional period would be an extended one. The New Economic Policy of 1921–28 was an acknowledged "step backward" — a retreat to make "two steps forward" possible, but a retreat nonetheless. Compromises in economic and foreign policy were accompanied by a general lowering of expectations. The change of outlook during NEP has been called a psychological as well as a material necessity: "It was psychologically impossible," writes one historian, "to maintain the exalted mood of faith and enthusiasm in which present turmoil and horror could be welcomed as the birth-pangs of the new world of the future." By the mid-twenties, there had been a shift of emphasis "from visionary utopianism to hard-headed realism."[1]

The period of the first and second five-year plans (1928–37) might be characterized as combining the qualities of utopianism and realism. Socialism was not imminent, but it could be quantified, temporally and materially. The vision, in official rhetoric, was still uto-

---

[1] E. H. Carr, *Socialism in One Country 1924–1926*, 2 vols. (London: Macmillan, 1958–59), I, 23.

pian, but its attainment required sweat and sacrifice wholly of this world. Enormous industrial projects and ambitious production goals brought a superhuman dimension to the task. Unstinting effort and unshakable idealism were held sufficient to build the future. The faster they were generated, the sooner it would arrive.

The literature of industrialization is considerable: most of the writers who continued to publish during the thirties made at least one contribution to the genre. Marietta Shaginian turned from socialist fantasy to the not unrelated genre of socialist realism, publishing *Hydrocentral* in 1934; Boris Pilniak revised his controversial tale *Mahogany* (1929) into the five-year plan novel *The Volga Flows into the Caspian Sea* (1930). Sholokhov, Leonov, Kataev, and Ehrenburg were among the many respondents to literature's "social command." Most treatments of national progress concern both technological and psychological change. Their literary value is in some measure a function of how profoundly they interrelate the two. Too many writers accepted the assumption that mind and matter could change at the same rate. And too many took for granted the direction of change, more concerned with its quantity than its quality.

Andrei Platonov is one writer who during the thirties continued to probe the relationship between politico-economic and spiritual development. Plagued with reprimands and publication difficulties during much of his career, Platonov has gained the recognition he deserves only since the 1960s. His prose of the twenties and thirties shows his deep interest in technology and psychology, and includes some of the best writing on Russia in transition. He is a masterful creator of dreamers and wanderers, craftsmen of the hand and of the mind. Platonov's most powerful works show seekers of happiness who fail — or are forced — to confront what separates their dreams from reality. Much of his writing is set in provincial Russia and Soviet Central Asia, remote from centers of policy or production. Whatever meaning life is given by the state and society penetrates incompletely here. One might best capture the environment of Platonov's fiction from an aerial perspective. Mapped from above, it would reveal groups and lone individuals making their way across a harsh landscape toward an unmarked ideal, the rough terrain obscuring from view both other travelers and what lies ahead.

What these seekers find seldom matches their expectations. In Platonov's novel *The Foundation Pit* (1929) the worker-protagonist Voshchev pointedly raises the relationship between spiritual and material goals.[2] Fired for daydreaming, Voshchev argues to an official that his thoughts will eventually increase production. He is working out a plan to create happiness: emotionally fulfilled people, he reasons, will work more productively. The official is unconvinced by his reversal of the Marxist dictum that existence determines consciousness, and Voshchev sets off to continue his search for spiritual contentment. The construction site he comes upon is a place of dying, not building. Society, as viewed here in microcosm, is proceeding toward neither spiritual nor material well-being. In the novella *Dzhan* (1936) the interaction of emotional and social existence is also problematic.[3] The Moscow-educated Chagataev leads the half-dead remnants of his nomadic ancestral people across the wilderness, bringing them finally into society's care. Though their physical needs are met for the first time in their lives, they soon disperse, silently and spontaneously. They seem unwilling to see life as a collective, forward-moving endeavor. Soviet society is shown here as humane and progressive; the youngest member of the group remains, reclaimed to life. But the haunting ending, the slow stream of people setting out, each for his private wilderness, demonstrates the difficulty of creating a collectively defined future.

Platonov most profoundly explores conceptions and realities of change in his novel *Chevengur*, written in 1927–28.[4] *Chevengur* concerns the nature of Russia's transition, via revolution, from past to future. Its setting is unspecified but evident: rural Russia around the end of the Civil War. The protagonists are more deeply naïve than Platonov's other visionaries: they believe that to declare a new world is to create it. They enact a revolution in miniature, driving out and massacring the "bourgeoisie" of the village of Chevengur. Satisfied

---

[2]Andrei Platonov, *The Foundation Pit/Kotlovan*, bilingual ed., trans. Thomas P. Whitney (Ann Arbor, Mich.: Ardis, 1973). Anthony Olcott notes that the novel (still unpublished in the Soviet Union) was probably written in 1929. See his excellent and informative "Andrej Platonov: The Citizen-Artist" (diss. Stanford University, 1976), p. 123.

[3]*Dzhan* was written after Platonov's visits to Central Asia in 1934 and 1936, but was first published in *Prostor*, no. 9 (1964). Anthony Olcott mentions that Platonov's original ending, which remains unpublished, was cut by the editor. The complete ending evidently suggests even more strongly than the published version that one can change the world only on a small scale. See "Andrej Platonov: The Citizen-Artist," pp. 195–204.

[4]Andrej Platonov, *Chevengur* (Paris: YMCA, 1972). The date of composition is suggested by Anthony Olcott in the foreword to his translation, *Chevengur* (Ann Arbor, Mich.: Ardis, 1978), pp. xv–xvi. The translation is the only complete edition of the novel, which remains unpublished in the Soviet Union.

that an era has been ended, they go to sleep expecting communism to rise with the sun. The rest of the novel follows the disjunction between their expectations and the dusty, violent shambles of reality. Their attempt to make the new world appear reminds one of the reliance on magical means of transition in popular literature. Platonov's satire, however, is of a different stamp. Mayakovsky's announcement at the end of "150,000,000" that "the future has arrived" is a comic simplification of the historical process; in *Chevengur* the summary declaration of the future is at once comical and tragic. Sasha Dvanov, the novel's chief hope, has devoted himself to finding a new life beyond the present. After Chevengur's failure he turns to a more certain path to the beyond, reenacting his father's suicide in a lonely lake. The earthly "other world" has proven impossible to reach.

Platonov sees the confusion over when the troubled present will yield to a bright future as a persistent problem in Soviet life. The failure to understand change does not fade when the era of socialist construction replaces the days of revolutionary romanticism. *The Hurdy-Gurdy* (1932–35), a play set in 1931, contains another Platonovian innocent who believes in socialism's imminent arrival. He is an anachronism, still possessed of an earlier era's utopianism. The play follows his initiation into reality, but its scope is broader than this. It is among Platonov's few works (excluding his war stories) that concern both Russia's future and the West's. *The Hurdy-Gurdy* questions Russia's ability to change either itself or the West, and casts earlier approaches to this subject in a new light.

Alyosha, the clear-eyed innocent, is entranced by the beauty and potential of technology. His vision is international: he dreams of a dirigible that will symbolize humanity's forward flight. This conveyance to the future "will rise up above the needy earth, above the third international, it will descend and the hands of the world proletariat will touch it. . . . "[5] Thus inspired, Alyosha travels through the Russian countryside to spread his vision and wait for socialism. His companion is an adolescent girl named Miud, one of Platonov's wise and stubbornly logical children. Her name, the acronym for Interna-

---

[5] Andrei Platonov, *Sharmanka* (Ann Arbor, Mich.: Ardis, 1975), p. 35, ellipsis in the original. References in parentheses are to this edition, which is the only one in Russian. See the translation by Carl R. Proffer, *The Barrel Organ*, in Andrei Platonov, *Collected Works* (Ann Arbor, Mich.: Ardis, 1978), pp. 159–222. The title is given as "*The Hurdy-Gurdy*" (a better translation) in Simon Karlinsky's fine essay, "Andrei Platonov: 1899–1951. An Early Soviet Master," *The New Republic*, March 31, 1979, pp. 25–30.

tional Youth Day, is another expression of belief in a universal utopia. Alyosha and Miud describe themselves as cultural workers sent on this mission by their collectiye farm, but they seem rootless and unique. Their culture brigade is completed by a robot of Alyosha's invention called Kuzma. Alyosha has designed the slogan-spouting machine as a tool to educate the masses for socialism. With Kuzma and a hurdy-gurdy (or "barrel organ") to enlighten and entertain, Alyosha and Miud proceed across what the stage directions call "the empty bright world."

The first scene finds them at a stopping point, weary of the journey whose end they believe in but cannot see. In their surroundings and conversation is a desolation of the sort that pervades *Waiting for Godot.* Beckett's characters are more passive: they wait rather than wander. But their dependence on Godot, whom they cannot recognize, is reminiscent of the trust in socialism in Platonov's play. Miud and Alyosha are waiting for socialism, whose shape they imagine but have not yet seen. Vladimir and Estragon aim toward nothing but keeping their appointment with Godot, although Godot eternally promises to come "tomorrow." Their recurrent questioning of what will happen recalls Platonov's opening lines:

MIUD. Alyosha, I've grown tired of living on this earth.
ALYOSHA. Don't worry, Miud, soon there'll be socialism — then everyone will turn happy.
MIUD. Me too?
ALYOSHA. You too.
MIUD. And if something makes my heart start aching?
ALYOSHA. Well, then it'll be cut out, so as not to bother you.
    Pause. Miud sings wordlessly. Alyosha looks off into the distance. [p. 7]

Alyosha and Miud envision socialism as a point they will come to, a state of being awaited so long that it must be close ahead. Their conception of making the transition into the future is contrasted with that of a grotesque pair of European future-builders. The play's Westerners, one Stervetsen and his daughter, appear as if conjured from the landscape. They have come to Russia not to see the future or help build it, as did so many foreign visitors, but to appropriate it. Stervetsen, a Danish professor and food-production specialist, proposes to buy the superstructure of Soviet society and bring it back to Europe. His offer is a parody of Soviet efforts to spread socialism to the West. Stervetsen evidently thinks that instead of bothering to plot world revolution, the Comintern can simply hand over Russia's superstructure — and even receive foreign currency in exchange. Since the Soviets already have the base on which socialist society depends, he reasons, they will quickly develop another superstructure to replace the old one.

Through Alyosha, Platonov discredits the belief that Russia will soon find its own salvation in socialism; through Stervetsen, he discredits the idea that Russia can save the West. Stervetsen mouths ideological clichés in a fractured Russian even stranger than the often awkward idiolects of Platonov's characters. "We in Europe have a lot of lower matter," he explains, "but the fire has gone out in the tower. The wind blows right into our weary heart — and above it there is no superstructure of inspiration" (p. 12). Platonov's judgment of this figure is embodied in his name — a Scandinavian suffix added to a Russian term for a nasty, base individual. Why is a believer in Russia's achievements thus reviled? The author ridicules him, it seems, because of his naïveté: he has confused rhetoric with reality, and believes that money can turn the former into the latter. Stervetsen's conviction that Russia can revive the West is foolish; Alyosha's unsatisfied faith in his own country is tragic. Both are disillusioned in the course of the play, their respective hopes for the future destroyed by the reality of contemporary Russia.

Reality enters in the form of a frequent target of satire: the greedy, manipulative bureaucrat. *The Hurdy-Gurdy* exposes not only the simplistic notions of progress held by individuals, but also the official Soviet program for progress. Stervetsen is not pictured in the offices of Moscow, where his mission would be welcomed and directed through the proper channels. Platonov drops him in a remote cooperative that illustrates the economic problems of the early thirties. Its officials are caricatures, their conversations ludicrous compendiums of bureaucratese and slang. The foreigners' first encounter is with Alyosha and Miud, who scorn the offer to exchange money for ideology. Miud quickly sees that their plan, like the new clothes of the fairy-tale emperor, has no substance. "Alyosha, but how can they buy an idea," she wonders, "when it's inside the whole body?!" (p. 13). Stervetsen's arrival at the cooperative, however, is met quite differently. He has come at a difficult time: food supplies are low, and the officials are complaining that if only they could requisition a foreign scientist, he would be able to turn their inedible resources into food. Stervetsen enters, the apparent answer to their needs. But rather than use his expertise for the common good, they proceed to swindle him for their personal enrichment.

The central problem in this cooperative is feeding the populace, and nourishment is a key metaphor in the play. The nourishment the system fails to supply is clearly spiritual as well as physiological. Platonov, who in other works deals feelingly with the attachment between man and machine, here satirizes the notion that technology can transform and sustain society. The cooperative's chairman, Shchoev, stages a demonstration of "the food of the future" to impress his visitors with the fruits of the superstructure that can be theirs. This scene must rank among the more revolting feasts in literature. With no food left to distribute, Shchoev directs the preparation of burdocks, nettles, bird droppings, locusts, and other local resources, and has them served by rigged-up wooden machines with levers and conveyor belts. The machines and their products are a crude come-down from the massive, futuristic food service devised by bustling food chief Andrei Babichev in Yuri Olesha's *Envy* (1927). Platonov's bureaucrats use technology to distract attention from what it produces. But despite the disgusting meal (which leaves the citizens convulsed in nausea), the European has lost none of his enthusiasm. He repeats the offer, his broken Russian adding to its absurdity: "We would greatly desire, you will gladden all Pan-Europe, if you will release to us the hot spirit from your state superstructure" (p. 40). Shchoev feigns reluctance, wanting to establish the most advantageous terms. He agrees to sell only pieces of the superstructure. The Westerner had envisioned a mission to bring the future to Europe; he ends up acquiring as many Party directives as two suitcases of foreign clothes can buy.

Even this preposterous foreign professor eventually realizes that his plan is misguided. Alyosha's pursuit of socialism also crumbles, his days of spreading song and ideology ended. His "iron man" gets farther and farther out of control, developing a cynical, opportunistic voice of his own. The dismayed Alyosha is denounced for a crime that one character calls having "oversimplified our ideology" (p. 52). Alyosha's invention, then, has caused his downfall. The corruption of Kuzma shows that ideas are dangerously vulnerable to distortion.

The abstractions purveyed by Alyosha and Kuzma are preserved, however, in the mind of Miud. The play's ending finds the young girl leaving the now dismantled cooperative, heading off alone to resume her journey. She is observed by the two Europeans, who are now aware that they have bought worthless scraps of bureaucracy, not building blocks of a new West. Their laconic comments on Miud's departure recall the opening scene, but the echo is not exact. The play's "Godot," its off-stage objective, has significantly changed in shape. Miud's song in scene one contrasts sharply with her traveler's song at the end. The earlier lyrics describe a confident journey to a destination that is known and named: "Down the hard, cheery road / We barefooted walk along — / We've only to go a bit farther: / Our happy home is built" (p. 8). In the final song, the waiting home becomes "unknown freedom"; the nearly attained goal is now "a distant land." The happy travelers of scene one's song are now described as a group of aliens, "comrades only of the wind" (pp. 58–59). As Miud disappears into the distance, the Westerners see that the leveled settlement, its inhabitants lying silently face-down on the ground, is the only "superstructure of the soul" they will find. The last words of the play, spoken by the daughter, suggest that Russia's failure is Europe's loss as well. Only the wisp of spirit represented by Miud, the Westerner realizes, is worth bringing back to "weeping Europe."

The categories and characters in this play are simple: few ambiguities are generated. The failed settlement is razed to make way for a natural gas drilling field; workers energetically move in. This is progress of a sort — but the plan makes no provision for the displaced residents' future. Two levels of change are at issue here — the national and the human. For Platonov's dreamers, they are inseparable: the national revival they seek is tied to spiritual renewal. Only this, suggests Platonov, can provide a foundation for Russia's future. Nothing less than this can legitimate a Russian claim to inspire the West.

The folly of believing in instant transitions is illustrated in Platonov's novels; *The Hurdy-Gurdy* shows that utopia may not draw any nearer with time. In the play, fifteen years after the Revolution, we see the weaknesses of Russia and Europe in defining and implementing their goals. Although Russia is reputed to have reached the final stage of history, the play lampoons the belief, humorously but sincerely presented in *Mess-Mend,* that she can serve as an inspiration to the West and a model for its future. Platonov's Westerners believe Russia to be the source of Europe's future civilization; Blok's "Come to us," ringingly intoned in "The Scythians," reverberates here as a hollow echo. The West does turn to Russia, as Blok calls on it to do. What it finds is closer to black comedy than to a "fraternal feast of labor and peace." Platonov looks beyond rhetoric to find that Russia has nothing but rhetoric to offer. The keeper of Russia's hopes for the future ends the play still wandering in transition.

The young girl's unswervable faith in her ideal recalls the icon of the caring Madonna that closes Pilniak's story. Though their dissimilarities are many, both parting images are alike in their singularity, in standing out from their surroundings as the sole embodiments of faith in the future. From the desolation of the provinces, in both works, emerges a sign that the future may hold renewal. This possibility has a much stronger presence in "The Third Capital": there optimism is substantiated by the era's newness, and by contrast with the freezing-over West. Pilniak's romantic nationalism leads him to project an ideal onto reality — to imply a future ahead that will justify the present. Promise lies not in the floundering individuals who form the story's documentary montage, but in the people as a whole. The source of optimism in Platonov's play is the reverse: the Soviet experiment's idealism has faded to illusion, and nothing holds promise but a single individual — a naïve and powerless one, who pursues what by the end of the play seems a futile quest. The watching West is not more moribund than this — just foolish in its own illusions.

These works vary so widely in form and intent that comparisons are tricky. As the preceding analyses show, the West and Russia's futures fit differently in the structure of each. Looking back, one might view the treatments of Russia in transition as uniquely designed portraits in motion, each showing a face of the present that looks ahead. Blok's all-encompassing national spirit beckons Europe with its barbarian lyre; in Pilniak the gloomy Razin is an unstable alloy of reason and rebellion; Mayakovsky's Ivan, a warrior-prince in the mold of the square-jawed proletarian of the poet's posters, crusades into the sunrise. The national drama, not individual existence, is the common concern of these works: in some, the individual is absent or secondary. The country's changing identity dominates: all in Russia pass through the transforming machine of revolution, variables in the same equation. The West, too, is used as a national whole, an adjacent mass whose form and direction help shape one's perspective on Russia.

Mandelstam's essays have introduced a differently conceived West: they present the West's relationship with Russia in an intellectual, not political, context. The border between them is historical, yes, but also psychological — a matter of perspective. "Chaadaev" stresses the need to regard the identity of self and country as open, to see

Russia as unique, but connected with the West; "On the Nature of the Word" makes it clear that the heritage of humanism is central to Russia, and must remain so if life and literature are to thrive. The individual life should stay in the foreground as the present is turned to future. "Everything has become heavier and more massive," wrote Mandelstam in 1922; "thus man, too, must become harder, because man should be harder than anything on earth, and should regard his relation to the earth as that of diamond to glass."[6] In his metaphor, each person has the power to engrave his own path on earth. But in any era, and especially at a time of conflict, larger forces may encroach on one's efforts, and the individual may find himself at odds with history.

The sense of Europe as a culture and a heritage, as a set of ideas rather than a set of current events, will arise again as we continue. So also will the association of the West with the primacy of art and of the individual. The link between personal and national identity may be strained in times of broad and rapid change; people may be estranged from events around them. This gap becomes literal if one permanently departs. Many did cross the border after 1917, most of them heading west. The West, in fiction concerning the emigration, presents a personal alternative as well as a national one. The experience of post-revolutionary transition was one fertile literary subject; another way for writers to explore individual and national change was to consider the possibility of complete estrangement — emigration.

---

[6]Osip Mandel'shtam, "O prirode slova," in *Sobranie sochinenii,* ed. G. P. Struve and B. A. Filipoff, 3 vols. (New York: Inter-Language Literary Associates, 1964–71), II, 300.

PART TWO
EMIGRATION: THE SINGLE CROSSING

The post-revolutionary emigration, the first wave of three within this century, is the story of a disparate group of individuals. About a million Russians left their homeland between 1917 and 1922, the vast majority never to return. They settled in places as diverse as Shanghai and Sofia, but the major centers of emigration in the twenties were Berlin and Paris. Some émigrés had followed the retreating Germans in 1918; most left with the defeated armies of the Civil War; others were expelled or departed later. Relative to the population, the number who left were insignificant — less than one percent. But among them were people prominent in all spheres of Russian life, from politics to the arts. The emigration's effect on the country was disproportionate to its size: it was an important facet of the transition from pre-revolutionary to Soviet Russia. Since it was centered in Europe, it became a focal point of Russian thinking about the West.[1]

European travel was so common before the Revolution that distinctions between foreign residence and emigration were sometimes

---

[1] The number of émigrés by 1922 is given as 860,000 in Paul Tabori, *The Anatomy of Exile* (London: Harrap, 1972), p. 182. In 1932 the Special Refugee Committee of the League of Nations calculated the total emigration to that date as 844,000. See Roland Gaucher, *Opposition in the USSR 1917–1967*, trans. Charles Lam Markmann (New York: Funk and Wagnalls, 1969), p. 123. It is impossible to establish an exact figure. Robert C. Williams writes in "'Changing Landmarks' in Russian Berlin, 1922–1924," *Slavic Review* 27, no. 4 (1968), p. 581, that "in 1921 the Russian diaspora numbered close to three million refugees."

vague. Russians abroad (except for political exiles) could fully maintain their ties with home, and could return at will. After 1917 contact was more difficult: the human and written traffic across the Soviet border grew increasingly controlled. Emigration was now a more clear-cut category, though ambiguities remained in the early years. It was not always easy to distinguish permanent sojourners abroad from temporary ones. One unknown variable was the longevity of the Soviet regime. Initially, optimistic opponents of the Bolsheviks maintained hope that the regime would fall, enabling them to return. But that hope soon began to seem illusory. It was evident by 1922 that the only real route back was through acceptance of the new state—a position adopted by members of the Smena Vekh (Change of Landmarks) movement. The movement's name, which has also been translated as "Changing Directions," indicates its mission: to encourage émigrés to support and return to Soviet Russia. Not many did; Aleksei Tolstoy was the most prominent writer among them. Other émigré movements also directed attention homeward. The Eurasians (who saw Russia as a compound of Asia and Europe) held that the world's salvation was rising in an East whose heart was Russia. Their 1921 manifesto was entitled *The Way Out to the East*. Most émigrés, however, forced either "to find a 'way out to the East' by returning home or to 'go West' into permanent emigration and statelessness," took the latter path.[2] The departure from home was soon widely acknowledged to be a one-way journey.

The graphic representation of Part 1 of this book might be two lines, vertical arrows representing the paths of Russia and the West toward the future. To continue the geometric scheme, picture Part 2 as a single horizontal arrow pointing westward, its shaft stretching from Russia into Europe. This line marks the passage into emigration, and it has no parallel opposite pointing the way back. That route of return must be envisioned as an imagined one, a dotted line that would not support a traveler. The exit westward was a crossing fraught with anxiety: one could not count on doubling back.

As one might expect, the condition of emigration surfaced frequently in émigré fiction. The early prose of Vladimir Nabokov, who left at twenty in the 1919 Crimean evacuation, includes some of the

---

[2]Williams, " 'Changing Landmarks'," p. 582. Williams examines the Smena Vekh, Eurasian, and Scythian groups in *Culture in Exile: Russian Emigrés in Germany, 1881–1941* (Ithaca, N.Y.: Cornell University Press, 1972), pp. 252–81. Gleb Struve discusses these movements and chronicles twenty years of émigré literature in *Russkaia literatura v izgnanii* (New York: Chekhov, 1956).

best-known examples. The riches of Nabokov's first stories and novels are not reducible to the theme of émigré rootlessness: only a fiery stare unmindful of their other layers would attempt to thus melt them down. What Nabokov called an "animal aching yearn for the still fresh reek of Russia"[3] is only evident at times, and it takes on strange forms. The idea of returning along the shaky dotted line figures, for instance, in *Glory* (*Podvig*, 1931), where the hero challenges his will and the possible by contriving to surreptitiously recross the border for a day. A surrealistic, uncontrollable return in "The Visit to the Museum" (1939) suggests that if one probes the pre-emigration past, one may find oneself hurtling through history into another version of one's life.

One émigré journalist, assessing the first period of life in emigration in 1925, wrote that thoughts and dreams of return, "physical and 'spiritual,' the pull 'from the gut' and 'from the head'... are 'immanent' to emigration, 'eternal' for it, *never* die out *in any emigration*" (his emphasis).[4] A poignant expression of the pull homeward is in some émigré poems of Marina Tsvetaeva. The poignancy is hard, not gentle: Tsvetaeva is a poet of strong will and strong voice, a poet whose work bears scars of the unresolved struggles in her mind. (Her eventual return, tragically, proved to compound them.) She asserts independence of ties to any place or era in "Homesickness! Long ago...," written in 1934 Paris. In the final stanza, as though exhausted by the effort, she modulates her claim: the poem ends with a fragmentary hypothetical phrase which hints that the sight of a rowanberry tree — a traditional emblem of Russia and of life — would suffice to restore her stranded self.[5]

To mention such writers as Nabokov and Tsvetaeva is to be tempted into digression. The writing of those who lived in emigration is certainly a fruitful source. But it would take a different book to investigate it — one not limited, as is this one, to perspectives from the Soviet side of the border. The emigration marked not only its partici-

[3]Vladimir Nabokov, *Speak, Memory: An Autobiography Revisited*, rev. ed. (New York: G. P. Putnam's Sons, 1966), p. 281.
[4]Mark Vishniak, "Na rodine i na chuzhbine (Piatiletnie itogi)," *Sovremennye zapiski* 26 (1925), p. 393. This, the most prominent of émigré periodicals, is a fascinating source on the European emigration.
[5]Marina Tsvetaeva, "Toska po rodine! Davno...," in *Izbrannye proizvedeniia*, ed. A. Efron and A. Saakiants (Moscow-Leningrad: Sovetskii pisatel', 1965), pp. 304–5. Tsvetaeva lived abroad from 1920 to 1939; she committed suicide two years after her return. The most complete account of her career is Simon Karlinsky, *Marina Cvetaeva: Her Life and Art* (Berkeley and Los Angeles: University of California Press, 1966).

pants: it also figures in the writing of some who remained. The assumption that writers draw material from personal experience may as often be disproved as validated: what can only be imagined has its own attraction. Perhaps in part because they had not experienced emigration, some Soviet writers set off on paper.

Western Europe had long served Russians as a home-in-exile (and had most recently been the planning ground of the Revolution these émigrés were rejecting). For many émigrés, Europe's geographic and cultural proximity, its freedoms, and its familiarity made it the obvious destination. Russians had commonly visited, studied, and conducted business there. Yet as time passed, the growing difficulty of traversing the border in either direction widened the felt distance between Europe and what was now Soviet Russia. As Henry James (quoted earlier on this subject) says in explaining his "international" fiction, contrast is a fundamental tool of the artist. "On the interest of *contrasted* things," writes James, "any painter of life and manners inevitably much depends" (his emphasis).[6] Literary treatments of emigration bear this out. Soviet writers focused more intently on the distance between Europe and Soviet Russia than on their closeness. Emigration was attractive terrain because it was antithetical to home. The situation of leaving provided a context for exploring the situation of staying. Their differences were not necessarily framed in "Russian versus Western" terms. The main axis of contrast in some works is better labeled "home — gone" or "native — foreign." In some cases, foreignness is the most significant feature of the fictionalized émigré environment; in others, aspects of the West are important to the characters' experience and the author's design.

Emigration was an extremely sensitive political issue, as it continues to be. Constraints on publishing were operative from the beginning of the Soviet regime, and sympathetic treatments of emigration were not likely to be printed. Soviet fiction concerning this issue, predictably, does not yield a bell-shaped curve of orientations. There are, to be sure, simplistic works that condemn emigration as traitorous and that satirize despicable or pitiful Russians abroad; others use it as an exotic backdrop for intrigue. Shaginian's novella *The Saga of a Society Lady* (1923) fits the former category; some works of Aleksei Tolstoy, like his novel *Black Gold* (1931), fit both. But the more profound dimensions of leaving Russia were not always submerged in ideology. Emigration figures in more valuable and varied works than

---

[6]Henry James, "Preface," in *The Novels and Tales of Henry James,* 24 vols. (New York: Scribner's, 1907–09), XIV, vi.

these, including those to which we now turn: Shklovsky's journalistic novel *Zoo, or Letters Not About Love* (1923), Pilniak's story "The Old Cheese" (1923), and two plays — Mikhail Bulgakov's *Flight* (1926–28) and Iurii Olesha's *A List of Assets* (1931).

By any stylistic measure these writers would stand far apart. Their works show a range of approaches to emigration across the decade. The connection between personal identity and the national future is raised in all of them; they have in common, too, a concern with emigration's permanence and the possibility of return. Few of the characters are free of the need to turn around. The desire to counter departure by retracing one's path is an insistent dream in *Flight*, a nostalgic thought in Pilniak, an ideological dilemma in Olesha, and a personal and literary strategy for Shklovsky.

Having excluded the writing of émigrés, I at once proceed to bend the rule: *Zoo* was written in Berlin, shortly before the author, a temporary émigré, returned to Russia. It was published both at home and abroad, however, which cannot be said of *Flight*. Bulgakov's play was neither printed nor staged in his lifetime. Its title refers to one form of emigration — the most prevalent during the Civil War, when it is set. In *Flight* the West plays a minor role: the protagonists never sufficiently release themselves from Russia to accept a link to another place. Pilniak also interrelates the Civil War era with the émigré's loss of home, while orchestrating images of East and West. His story, like *Flight*, concerns in part the difficulty of separating oneself from the past.

Zoo and *A List of Assets* focus on emigration as it affects the artist. Olesha uses emigration as a means of raising questions about the artist's personal and civic life. The autobiographical novel written in exile, curiously, treats that condition less literally than Olesha's play. Emigration and the West in Shklovsky are literary tools, part of a network of metaphors and devices. Olesha, who wrote that his play was about "the Europe of the spirit" rather than about Europe itself, actually merges the two.[7] His Europe is both a state of mind and the stage for a political melodrama. The play's use of melodrama is revealing of the climate in which it was written. After the early twenties, emigration denoted not the hasty exodus of thousands but the conspicuous, premeditated act of a few.

---

[7] Iurii Olesha, "Tema intelligenta," *Stroika*, no. 3 (1930), p. 16. An abridged version of the article appears in Iu. Olesha, *P'esy. Stat'i o teatre i dramaturgii* (Moscow: Iskusstvo, 1968), pp. 262–65.

6

THE LOSS OF HOME

Mikhail Bulgakov, *Flight* (1926–28)
Boris Pilniak, "The Old Cheese" (1923)

The literature of the Civil War period, like much war fiction, has less to do with warfare than with the passing of an era. A major concern of early Soviet fiction is the destruction of the past and the gestures made to forestall it. Change was in progress on two levels (not as separable in reality as on paper): private and domestic life, and the life of the nation as a whole.

The former is fiction's more customary province. The loss of one's personal past, and particularly of home, the place where one most fully belongs, often figures in fiction set between 1918 and the early twenties. The best treatment of the Civil War, Isaac Babel's *Red Cavalry* (1926), includes trenchant studies of the destruction and attempted preservation of home. The story cycle opens in the pillaged house of Polish Jews and moves through a succession of desolate domestic settings — Gedali's dusty shop, the sacked castle of Bere-stechko's count, a landowner's bloody parlor, inhabited by his still alive but now mad wife. One story tells of the young Cossack Prishchepa who, seizing fate himself, ravages his childhood home in a frenzied but purposeful ceremony of destruction. Unable to preserve the past, he chooses to kill it — a strategy also used in Evgenii Zamiatin's "The Cave." Set in freezing and hungry post-revolutionary Petrograd, the story shows the painfully strong drive to survive and to maintain even a shell of home around oneself. That drive, however powerful, cannot suffice: the same writer's "In Old Russia," a nostalgic tale of timeless

79

folkways, tells why. Private life takes place in a larger arena than the domestic circle. In the story's preface, history is inexorably moving through a dense forest that symbolizes the Russian past, and the time has come for a new and unknown stage: "The forest is no more, it was devoured by fire: stumps, ash, soot. Perhaps illimitable fields will be plowed here, perhaps some new, unheard-of wheat will ripen . . . perhaps a city will grow up — alive with ringing sound and motion, all stone and crystal and iron — and winged men will come here flying over seas and mountains from all ends of the world. But never again the forest."[1]

Fiction dealing with emigration during those years is a subcategory of contemporaneous literature — sharing some common characteristics, set apart by others. The past's departure is intensified in this fiction: to the loss of the personal past is added that of country, the larger stage of one's life and expectations. How well the place of emigration can serve as an adopted stage is unknown. In "emigration" (as distinct from "émigré") fiction, this destination may have a distinct nationality, or it may be experienced simply as "non-Russia" — a polar and alien place. The works examined in this chapter provide contrasting examples. Two East-West contrasts shape Pilniak's story: a tension between Europe and Russia felt by the émigré and an internal tension between Russia's Eastern and Western elements. The Europe-Russia contrast in *Flight* is less significant: most of the characters mentally divide the globe into "Russia" and "everywhere else." Their concerns are personal — not with the lost country, but with the lost site of the self, the domain emblematized as one character's haunting streetlights, another's green-shaded lamp.

A year before starting *Flight*, Bulgakov had published a novel called *White Guard* (adapted for the theater as *The Days of the Turbins* [1926]). While both works are set during the Civil War, *White Guard* never leaves the domestic setting. The paired novel and play movingly portray history's assault on equilibrium. Although the Turbins are tragically affected by the war, their family and home remain a bastion of security, a kind of fairy-tale pot that faithfully yields whatever is needed. In *Flight* Bulgakov removes his characters from their

---

[1] Evg. Zamiatin, "Rus'," in *Sobranie sochinenii*, 4 vols. (Moscow: Federatsiia, 1929), IV, 121–22. The story was first published as a separate book: *Rus'* (Petersburg: Akvilon, 1923). My translation relies somewhat on that in Yevgeny Zamyatin, "In Old Russia," in *The Dragon: Fifteen Stories*, trans. and ed. Mirra Ginsburg (Chicago: University of Chicago Press, 1976).

native environments, focusing on those who fled the lives they wanted to preserve. These lives are never shown: the play begins in transit and ends on the brink of return. Here, and in Pilniak's story, the attachment to the past is doubly broken. Two borders separate the characters from home: the border of time, and the border they have crossed into exile.

In the fall of 1921, when the action of *Flight* concludes, the thirty-year-old Bulgakov was himself experiencing an emigration of sorts. It was then that he moved from Kiev to Moscow to begin his writing career in earnest. His self-description bears some resemblance to that of a refugee: "At the end of 1921," he writes in a brief autobiography, "I arrived in Moscow with no money and no belongings, to stay there forever."[2] By 1928, when he completed *Flight*, Bulgakov had triumphed in the Moscow theater and had three plays running simultaneously — *The Days of the Turbins*, *Zoya's Apartment* (1926), and *The Crimson Island* (1927). The latter two are topical, satirizing respectively the underworld antics of NEP and theatrical censorship (of which Bulgakov was a frequent victim). *Flight*, however, is removed in time and place from Moscow of the late twenties. It is also distinct in form: the eight scenes, grouped in four acts, are designated "Dreams." Bulgakov thus indicates his intention to go beneath the surface of experience and discover interior reality.

The term "Dreams" also dispels any expectations of the play's historical accuracy — though the basic situation is accurate enough. *Flight* involves a climactic stage of the Civil War. It follows the experiences of several civilians and White officers who join the evacuation of Wrangel's army from the Crimea in late 1920. None of the protagonists comes south intending to emigrate: the officers expect to resist the Reds, and the civilians have not planned beyond the White-controlled Crimea. Each successive dream moves them farther from their intentions and from home. Acts 1 and 2 take place near and in the Crimea; acts 3 and 4 are set in Constantinople, and briefly in Paris, in the summer and fall of 1921. All the protagonists emigrate, but only some are willing to make that status permanent. The calculating Korzukhin and the pragmatic Liuska accommodate comfortably to circumstance; the feisty Major General Charnota, while remaining abroad, anticipates a nomadic future. The play's controversial ending

---

[2]Quoted by Pavel Markov in his introduction to Mikhail Bulgakov, *P'esy* (Moscow: Iskusstvo, 1962), p. 6.

focuses on the three who plan to return: tormented General Khludov and the romantic leads, Golubkov and Serafima. After a year-long drift away from Russia, through Sevastopol, Constantinople, and Paris, there begins a movement back — to Constantinople, and toward home.

General Khludov is the play's greatest creation, the one who must have absorbed Bulgakov most. He is marked by two forces that animate Bulgakov's fiction: the power of illusion and the grip of conscience. Khludov (based on the White General Slashchov) has terrorized his prisoners and subordinates, leaving a trail of corpses across the Crimea. Driven by the growing hopelessness of the White position, he strikes out at all in his way. He finally goes too far: the outspoken orderly Krapilin, the last man Khludov orders hanged before the evacuation, haunts him from that moment as a grisly conscience. The last victim claimed by Khludov is himself. In his relentless pursuit by conscience he seems a precursor of Pontius Pilate in *The Master and Margarita* — another despot fallen captive to a lowly truth-teller whose fate he controlled. In Bulgakov's novel, Pilate dreams of his victim for more than nineteen centuries until he is released from guilt by the novel's hero. In *Flight,* with no supernatural forces to rely on, Khludov seeks his own solution. For him return to Russia is a means of reconciling with Krapilin's ghost — not because entering Soviet Russia will vindicate him, but because he will surely be killed at once. Thus he will find rest, sharing the fate of his victims.

Serafima and Golubkov are drawn back to Russia not to confront the past but to recover it. Sergei Pavlovich Golubkov is one of those privileged young Petersburg men who function in Russian literature as a sort of litmus paper: take one educated, self-absorbed young man, lower him into a given medium, and watch him react. His identification with a type is explicit: he introduces himself as the son of a prominent idealist professor. Golubkov's own commitment to the life of the mind distorts his vision of the events and ideas around him. In a period of political polarization, he is startlingly aloof from causes. He travels south from Petersburg not because he objects to the Bolshevik takeover, but because conditions there have made it impossible for him to work. The nature of his work is not specified, but it is presumably some scholarly endeavor unrelated to contemporary reality. Golubkov is not entirely passive: his departure is an attempt to control his life. He soon realizes that the currents of the time are far more powerful than he, but he persists in trying to regain control. Golubkov's first lines, which open Dream One, foreshadow the difficulty he will have. The farther he gets from Petersburg, he tells Serafima wonderingly, "the more incomprehensible everything around us becomes."[3]

Stronger than Golubkov (whose love she comes to reciprocate) is Serafima Korzukhina, wife of Wrangel's Assistant Minister of Commerce. Serafima boldly accuses Khludov of brutality and rebels against her interrogators. But she reacts to events rather than shaping them: she is no more able than Golubkov to gain control of her life.

The individual's impotence before history is expressed not only by the play's action, but also by its form and staging. It is in the nature of dreams to be beyond one's control, to descend and depart without warning. The dreamer is cast unprepared into unfamiliar territory. For all their bizarreness, dreams can be more vivid than waking life, investing details with significance and stretching the senses. The numerous and specific stage directions convey Bulgakov's images of his Dreams. The realistic settings — a monastery church, a railway station, streets, rooms — are sharply seen and heard for a time and then fade out of focus. Each scene begins in darkness or waning light and ends with envelopment in darkness. There is something hypnotic about the flow of one Dream into the next; the cycle seems impossible to stop. The ending of Dream Five marks this most explicitly: "The dream suddenly disintegrates. Darkness. Silence descends, and a new dream flows on" (p. 182).

The sense of submission to time is particularly strong in the three Constantinople scenes. The glow of the sunset and music of the street dominate the air, making the individual ineffectual in their midst. Serafima and Golubkov, reunited at the end in Constantinople, decide to break out of this atmosphere and return to Russia. Their resolve is strengthened by the seeming unreality of what they have been through. Overwhelmed by the sensation of living in a dream, they want to extend the figurative meaning of "dream" to a literal one. If it seems never to have happened, perhaps it never has. Their transition from a figurative to a literal understanding of "dream" can be measured by Golubkov's opening and closing lines. In Dream One, listening to the chanting monks in the catacombs below, Golubkov

---

[3]Mikhail Bulgakov, *Beg*, in his *P'esy*, p. 127. Page references cited in the text are from this edition. My translations of *Flight* borrow heavily from those of Carl R. Proffer and Ellendea Proffer in *The Early Plays of Mikhail Bulgakov*, ed. Ellendea Proffer (Bloomington: Indiana University Press, 1972). Ellendea Proffer's introductions to the plays provide valuable material on Bulgakov's career in the theater.

comments that his recent experiences sometimes seem to him like a dream. His last lines, and those of Serafima, are an attempt to force that semblance of dreaming into actuality. "None of it happened, none of it," he assures Serafima, "it was all delirium. Forget it, forget! A month will pass, we'll make it, we'll return, and then the snow will fall, and will cover our tracks . . . " (p. 214). In his wishful thinking, their departure from Russia can be wiped out: their return can take them back not only across space but across time. Control having escaped them, they try to recover it through imagination.

Golubkov and Serafima never regard emigration as a state in which one can have a real life. There is home — Serafima's snow-covered Karavannaia Street and Golubkov's lamp-lit study — and there is the shadowy, shifting outside world. It makes no difference where one is within that non-Russian realm. Serafima's husband, the manipulative Korzukhin, takes the opposite view, exchanging his Russian past for a life in Europe. Korzukhin is an extreme version of Talberg in *White Guard*, another pragmatic, unloved husband who ends in emigration. He is a modern caricature of the Europeanized Russian, but quite similar to his predecessors in eighteenth-century satire. Korzukhin's transformation into Parisian émigré reminds one of the landowner Firiulin in Iakov Kniazhnin's comic opera *Misfortune from a Coach* (1779). Disdaining all things Russian, Firiulin decides that by redefining his possessions as "French," he can transcend his lamentably Russian environment. Thus he rewards his steward Klimentii by dubbing him "Clément" and decrees that the bold peasant Lukian shall let nothing but French cross his lips. Korzukhin also works at redefining himself, and persists in denying his wife's existence, even in the safety of Paris. Firiulin-like, he gives his Russian servant a French name and proscribes the use of Russian. The experience of Charnota's mistress Liuska/Lucie also suggests that one can thrive in emigration only by shedding one's identity. Liuska becomes disgusted with the squalor and instability of Constantinople and goes to Paris, exchanging Charnota for Korzukhin. She conceals her past from Korzukhin and conforms to the order of his household by adopting a French name.

The single scene set in Europe is a farcical portrayal of European emigration. There are many comic touches in *Flight*: exploiting the dream's characteristic hyperbole, Bulgakov intensifies the play's humor and its pathos. Dream Seven, in Korzukhin's Paris mansion, is the most broadly written, full of theatrical clichés. Bulgakov may have

THE LOSS OF HOME

his admired Molière in mind, although parts of the scene are common to a multitude of comedies. It opens with Korzukhin's dressing-down of a servant, and moves from his paean to money through a ruinous card-game, ending with the appearance of the humble lady lover in upper-class disguise. On one level, the scene is a comic confrontation between a rich villain and a pair of allies—the ingenuous lover (Golubkov) and the rogue (Charnota). Why does Bulgakov thus caricature the only Russians able to establish a life in Europe? He means perhaps not to ridicule that category of Russians but to indicate the absence of satisfactory alternatives for the émigré. The examples of Korzukhin and Liuska suggest that settling abroad entails self-distortion and self-deception. The only way to have a future in emigration is to purge oneself of everything Russian, including one's former (but frustratingly present) self. The hyperbole of Dream Seven (the penultimate scene) suits the play's rhythm: it highlights the émigré's essential homelessness, thus setting the stage for the lovers' decision to go back to the only authentic home there is.

The Central Repertory Commission's May 1928 resolution banning *Flight* lists its ideological flaws, which include the motivation for the returns to Russia. Later that year, literary and theater figures gathered at the Moscow Art Theater to discuss revisions that might satisfy the commission's objections. Several speakers, among them Maksim Gorky, argued that no changes need be made: Gorky praised the play as a "superlative comedy" and predicted phenomenal success. Vladimir Nemirovich-Danchenko, one of the theater's founders and directors, ended the session by announcing that he still felt one criticism was justified: the treatment of Serafima's and Golubkov's return. "The motives for their return must be explained," he said. "One wants the feeling attracting them to their homeland to be more clearly defined. The interest of émigrés in what is happening here has to be emphasized."[4] To do this, he argued, would entail only minor revisions.

---

[4]Abridged texts of the commission's resolution and of the Moscow Art Theater discussion are in *Neizdannyi Bulgakov, Teksty i materialy*, ed. Ellendea Proffer (Ann Arbor, Mich.: Ardis, 1977), pp. 84–87. Gorky's remarks appear on p. 86, and Nemirovich-Danchenko's on p. 87. Plans to produce *Flight* were revived in 1929 and 1933, but permission was not forthcoming. (See Ellendea Proffer's introduction to *Flight* in *The Early Plays of Mikhail Bulgakov*, p. 161.) The play was first produced in 1957. A. Colin Wright discusses *Flight*'s historical sources, production history, and interpretation in *Mikhail Bulgakov: Life and Interpretations* (Toronto: University of Toronto Press, 1978), pp. 124–40. I had access to Wright's book after completing my

Bulgakov's unwillingness to rewrite the ending — or any of the play — is one index of the falsity of this final point. Such a revision of the ending would distort the émigré state of mind that Bulgakov seeks to convey. The couple know that Russia has changed, that the past departs whether one emigrates or not. They have seen Russia in revolution, but they can now believe in the possibility of reclaiming the past because they are removed from home. It is important to Bulgakov's use of the dream form that the lovers neither oppose nor embrace the Soviet regime, but appear almost oblivious of it. The strength of their desire to return may seem to imply enthusiasm for the Soviet regime, but it does not.[5] An ideologically acceptable ending, as Nemirovich-Danchenko pointed out, would entail approval, or at least acknowledgment, of the future planned by the Soviets. But Soviet Russia hardly exists in the play: the Bolsheviks figure only as a military threat. Serafima and Golubkov anticipate resuming their personal lives, not committing themselves to their country. Emigration for them was a personal matter; return, too, is unmotivated by ideology. Any revision of the ending faithful to Bulgakov's conception would have to express Serafima's and Golubkov's detachment from all possible destinations — Europe, Constantinople, Soviet Russia — and their tie only to the narrow sphere of their personal surroundings.

A revision expressive of the original would also have to retain its ambiguous final word. Aroused by the image of home, Serafima cries: "Let's go! The end!" This is a literal and unsatisfactory translation: the word "*konets*" can also be rendered "it's over" or "it's finished." The speaker appears to mean that the unreal life of their flight has ended, but the word has other overtones. This is the "end" of flight because they are reversing direction, but it is an entry into another unknown. The ending's ominous ring is reinforced by the play's epigraph, taken from Vasilii Zhukovsky's poem "A Singer in a Camp of Russian Soldiers" (1812). The three lines used by Bulgakov read: "Immortality is a calm, bright shore; / Our path is a striving toward it. / Let him rest, who has ended his flight!"[6] In Zhukovsky the word

---

own work on the play. Harold B. Segel discusses the treatment of emigration in *Flight* and other plays of the period in his useful *Twentieth-Century Russian Drama: From Gorky to the Present* (New York: Columbia University Press, 1979), pp. 170–74.

[5]On this point I differ with Ellendea Proffer, who writes that "the return to the fatherland of Khludov, Serafima, and Golubkov rings suspiciously like a socialist-realist ending" (Introduction to *Flight, The Early Plays of Mikhail Bulgakov*, p. 163).

[6]The poem, "Pevets vo stane russkikh voinov," can be found in V. A. Zhukovskii, *Sobranie sochinenii*, 4 vols. (Moscow-Leningrad: Khudozhestvennaia literatura,

"*beg*" ("flight") means "the race of life," not the act of fleeing; the "end of flight" in the poem is death. There is a double meaning, then, in Serafima's assertion that their flight is done. One should not read her words solely through Zhukovsky's metaphor and regard them as the playwright's death sentence. "*Konets*" can be interpreted as the end, not of the lovers' actual lives, but of the past they envision as still real. The line that completes Zhukovsky's quatrain, omitted by Bulgakov, is relevant here as well. Rest if you have traversed the road, says the poet, but continues: "You, travelers, have patience!" Bulgakov's characters will need that, and more, to make the crossing back from emigration.

◆　◆　◆

The word "*strannik*," translated above as "traveler," is Zhukovsky's designation for the person with part of life's path still ahead. It can also mean "wanderer," and it is in this usage that we find it in a 1922 poem by Anna Akhmatova. The opening line serves as its title; the first of four quatrains reads: "I am not with those who left the land / For enemies to tear apart. / Their coarse flattery I do not heed, / To them I will not give my songs."[7] Akhmatova's scorn for the émigrés is mitigated by pity. Their action is traitorous, but its consequences for them are severe. The poet feels pity "As for the prisoner, for the ill." Shifting to direct address, she intones: "Dark is your path, wanderer, / Of wormwood smells your foreign bread." The second half of the poem is a proud description of those who, with the poet, stayed in Russia and destroyed what remained of their youth. Nothing in the conflagration around them eases their sacrifice except the conviction that they are right, and that history will justify them.

"The Old Cheese," written a year after Akhmatova's poem, is in some ways a prose gloss on the poetic text: it dramatizes the contrast between the émigré's lot and that of the stoic who remains. The story's

---

1959–60), I, 149–67; the lines quoted are on p. 164. The ending of *Days of the Turbins* points to the same sort of ambiguity: Studzinsky closes the final scene by calling the Red victory "for some a prologue, but for others — an epilogue."

[7]Anna Akhmatova, "Ne s temi ia, kto brosil zemliu," *Stikhi i poemy*, ed. V. I. Zhirmunskii (Leningrad: Sovetskii pisatel', 1976), p. 152. The poem is dated Petersburg, July 1922. Amanda Haight gives a translation and discusses Akhmatova's decision not to emigrate in her *Anna Akhmatova: A Poetic Pilgrimage* (New York: Oxford University Press, 1976), pp. 74–76. My translation draws somewhat on hers.

title is the name of a London pub where part of it is set; Pilniak included it in a slim collection called *English Stories* (1924), a product of his recent travels.[8] *Flight* begins on a dark, turbulent threshold of Russia, and the Constantinople to which it proceeds is only another kind of border existence. Pilniak alternates between two more stable points: 1922 London and the Russian interior four years earlier.

The story concerns a Russian family on the steppe beyond the Volga in the fall of 1918. Five people live on the isolated farm: the widowed mother is an entomologist; her sons (one of them an artist) tend the farm with their wives. They are obviously not natives of the region but amateur farmers, intellectuals whose experience is not limited to the steppe. The Revolution has not brought them here — they have come sometime before it, and regard it as a progressive but distant development. "There is a revolution in Russia," one writes, "all the roads are deserted, only very rarely does a Kirghiz horseman appear for a moment on the horizon and then vanish beyond the ravines; no one visits us and we visit no one" (p. 9). Their domestic peace is tragically interrupted by a group of those silent Kirghiz. Suspicious of the settlers, perhaps aroused by the Civil War's disruption of their own lives, the horsemen raid the farm, killing the men and raping the women. The pregnant Olga miscarries; Maria, the other young woman, later gives birth to a half-Kirghiz child.

The gloom of the steppe now yields to London, but the Russian story continues in the Western setting. An elderly émigré, a friend of the widowed Maria's, is followed through a day's routine. On this day, he joins an émigré friend at the pub favored by Dickens that provides the story's name. He recounts the family's experience, and the reader learns its aftermath. Maria joyfully accepts the child born of rape, the life force prevailing over the tragedy that had dimmed it. In a final passage, we move from the wakeful émigré in bed in mist-hung London to a simultaneous scene on the steppe. The earth has thawed, the night is clear, geese are flying north — and the three women are "boldly and cheerfully" at work, repairing the dam on a thaw-swollen stream.

"The Old Cheese" is a collage of contrasts: between Maria's

---

[8] Boris Pil'niak, "Staryi syr," in *Angliiskie rasskazy* (Moscow: Krug, 1924), pp. 5–29. The story is dated September 16, 1923. Translations are my own, and parenthetical references are to the 1924 edition. The story has been translated (as "The Cheshire Cheese") by Beatrice Scott in Boris Pilnyak, *The Tale of the Unextinguished Moon and Other Stories* (New York: Washington Square, 1967), pp. 121–36.

girlhood visit to London and her present life; the cultivated Russian settlers and their Asian attackers; the peaceful pub where the story is told and its grisly plot; the family's world and the émigré's. There are two East-West dualities: the internal contrast between Russia's European and Asian parts, and the external contrast of European émigré with Russian survivor.

The former contrast is made sensational: Pilniak's savage nomads seem hardly human. Russia's instability, in this story, stems from the incompatibility of its parts. The country is an unstable mixture of West and East — terms, in this case, standing for the civilized and primitive.

The foreign West of Pilniak's émigré, in contrast, is a calm and protected place, but it seems an unnatural environment. Unlike Bulgakov, Pilniak does not ridicule the Western émigré's position. But the West he creates is also monochromatic — a simple surface on which to place his character. The thoughtful, bookish émigré is drifting, rather like the English fog. The lyrical exaggeration of the fog accentuates his isolation: everything is alone in this London, separated by the fog's opaque walls. Surveyed from Parliament Hill, notes the narrator, London at night resembles a fantastic kingdom on the ocean bottom — to a Russian, it seems like the drowned city Kitezh of Russian myth. The seeming unreality of this foreign place recalls the characters' sense in *Flight* that what surrounds them is illusory. In "The Third Capital" and other works, Pilniak satirizes bourgeois Europe, using the West as a political term; here it is a state of mind.

This émigré is comfortable, his recent images of Russia are terrible — but the pull to return to one's real life nevertheless recurs. In bed he reflects on Russia and on the course of his life, "and the old man realized that nothing would be justified if he did not carry his bones to his own earth" (p. 28). The separate existence he has made for himself is chronically incomplete: the need to recover his whole self can only be satisfied by regaining his native place.

Pilniak's shift from this to the dawning, budding steppe is facile; as in "The Third Capital," Western emptiness is contrasted with a Russian life force that persists despite tragedy. The Russian women have endured horrors, but they vigorously carry on; their lives still have purpose. Their closeness to the land, emphasized in the accounts of their happier time, seems now intensified. They are attuned to nature — working the land, embracing the child, rebuilding the home from which they were routed. Their romanticized attachment to the land is not visibly related to politics or even patriotism. They appear unaware of events beyond the steppe: their trials were personal and their rebuilding is a personal preservation of home, not perceived as part of a national endeavor. This is one important respect in which they differ from the speaker in Akhmatova's poem, who expresses a valuing of country over self. Yet they have stoically borne part of the cost of Russia's upheaval — in this sense they resemble those praised by the poet, those who proceed with Russia into the future regardless of the cost.

The exile in Akhmatova is scorned and pitied; Pilniak shows him sympathetically, and with the same incurable rootlessness. The story's ending resembles Bulgakov's in its expression of the powerful magnetic force of home. In *Flight* Serafima and Golubkov are moved by a desire to return so great that it inhibits a realistic appraisal of their situation. The émigré's pull homeward in "The Old Cheese" is not based on illusion: he knows that his past is irrecoverable. Despite this knowledge, and despite the violent images that represent Russia's present, he feels that only return can make his life complete. The separation from home, whether the replacement is a European home or transit, entails a loss of self. And remaining at home, one is not immune from upheaval: alien hazards to one's wholeness still arise.

7

THE ARTIST, I
Emigration and Metaphor

Viktor Shklovsky, *Zoo, or Letters Not About Love* (1923)

Flight is a fantasy of emigration, dreams shaped in Bulgakov's imagination. Pilniak's story, too, is plotted from image rather than experience. In autobiographical writing on emigration, the line between fact and fiction is not as clearly drawn. Obviously, Soviet literature is not rich in works of this sort: by definition it excludes the writing of émigrés. From the Revolution through the mid-twenties, however, the categorization of writers into "Soviet" and "émigré" was not firmly fixed. Berlin was a major publishing center for Russian literature: writers within Russia often published there to secure international copyright. Also, the Russian writers then living in Europe included some whose emigration proved temporary. The émigré writing of those who returned to literary careers in Russia might legitimately be considered part of Soviet literature. One returnee was Viktor Shklovsky, who in 1922–23 found himself an unwilling exile in Berlin.

Shklovsky had already made a considerable contribution to literary scholarship. His 1914 paper "The Resurrection of the Word" was a ground-breaker in Formalist theory. Between 1914 and 1917 he and other members of the Society for the Study of Poetic Language (Opoiaz) continued their important theoretical work. Then, and in the following years, war and revolution made scholarly work difficult. Shklovsky's life from 1917 to 1922, described in *A Sentimental Journey*

(1923), was a hectic mixture of the two.[1] In early 1922, his previous anti-Bolshevik activities forced him to leave the country. The Cheka had begun arresting Socialist Revolutionary party members; to escape arrest Shklovsky fled to Finland, and soon proceeded to Berlin. *Zoo*, one product of his time in exile, reflects Shklovsky's theoretical ideas in two ways: through its literary commentary and through its form. Emigration was a difficult personal matter for Shklovsky — but as a literary theorist he also took it as a challenge to invent a medium equal to describing it.

The book's full title is *Zoo, or Letters Not About Love: The Third Heloise*.[2] Pinning a genre on *Zoo* is tricky; it has been called "a bizarre epistolary novel," and one could do worse than leave it at that.[3] It is comprised of twenty-nine letters, which have elements of the love letter, of literary theory, and of the personal chronicle. Ruminations about love and not about love are interspersed with portraits of émigré writers and artists. All but three of the letters are exchanged between the novel's "protagonists," Shklovsky and a young Russian émigrée named Alia. Alia was Elsa Triolet, later to become a French novelist. The sister of Lili Brik (wife of the critic Osip Brik and beloved of Mayakovsky), she was indeed in Berlin at the time, and she did write the letters attributed to her — more than ten percent of the book.

Like *A Sentimental Journey*, *Zoo* was regarded as part of the trend toward blurring the line between literary prose and non-fiction. Boris Eikhenbaum cites it as one of a new breed of works that moved away from "invention"; Tynianov considered it "on the border" of what was conventionally termed belles lettres.[4] The author himself, of course, needed no one to make his position clear. In theory and prac-

---

[1] Viktor B. Shklovskii, *Sentimental'noe puteshestvie* (Moscow-Berlin, 1923). See the translation by Richard Sheldon, *A Sentimental Journey. Memoirs, 1917–1927* (Ithaca, N.Y.: Cornell University Press, 1970). Sheldon's introduction describes Shklovsky's early literary activity.

[2] The first edition is *Zoo, ili Pis'ma ne o liubvi: Tret'ia Eloiza* (Berlin: Gelikon, 1923). Richard Sheldon has done a fine annotated translation: *Zoo, or Letters Not About Love* (Ithaca, N.Y.: Cornell University Press, 1971). His introduction and notes contain valuable background material and analysis. Page references in the text are to the Russian edition. Translations are mine, but owe much to Sheldon's.

[3] The phrase is Victor Erlich's; see his "On Being Fair to Viktor Shklovsky or the Act of Hedged Surrender," *Slavic Review* 35, no. 1 (1976): 113.

[4] Boris Eikhenbaum, "V poiskakh zhanra," *Russkii sovremennik*, no. 1 (1924), pp. 230–31; Iurii Tynianov, "Literaturnoe segodnia," *Russkii sovremennik*, no. 1 (1924), pp. 304–5.

tice Shklovsky rejected the division between fiction and non-fiction, believing that generic boundaries could be violated and that the canon of genres was in constant flux. Tynianov analyzed the latter idea in his important essay "On the Literary Fact," where he points to the evolution of the letter (among other genres) from an extraliterary to a literary form.[5] In *Zoo* Shklovsky exploits the letter's possibilities at various points along this spectrum. The correspondence of *Zoo* is a fabric of correspondences and contrasts — between fiction and fact, European and Russian, emigration and home.

That *Zoo* should be placed on a literary border is fitting not only because of its status on the fringes of fiction. The correspondents, though both Russian-born, are figuratively foreign to each other: their letters, though written in Berlin, are a "foreign correspondence," communications across a border. Shklovsky manipulates Alia's image in his letters and in prefaces to hers: he presents her as his opposite, a figure forever alien to him. Identifying himself with the post-revolutionary Russia he has been forced to leave, he sets her up as an émigré whose ties to Russia have weakened. Alia is the assimilated émigré, a Russian turned European; Shklovsky actively plays the alien as intrusive suitor, rebellious exile, and iconoclastic writer.[6] His rejection of the bourgeois European milieu is consistent with his restless and reflexive prose. The epistolary plan and the pieces it links are both grounded in the same contrast of cultures.

The "border-crossing" of the correspondence defines the novel's structure: it moves, on one level, back and forth between poles. Two other types of border-crossing shape it as well. One, which chronologically precedes the book, is the collective journey of Russian Berlin. *Zoo* concerns, in part, the consequences of this move: while the two correspondents are its focal points, the émigré society around them is also important. The exodus westward, in which all participated, is countered in the book by an individual attempt to return. Although Shklovsky denies using a hero or a conventional plot, the three letters outside the correspondence form a skeletal plot that traces his own movement back toward Russia. These three border-crossings — the hero's return, the general emigration, and the correspondence — relate

---

[5]"O literaturnom fakte," *Lef*, no. 2 (6) (1924), pp. 111–13.

[6]Alia's foreignness is made evident as much through Shklovsky's assertions as through her own writing. She does not consistently perform her designated function: her letters (particularly Letter Nineteen, which Shklovsky "crosses out") show her to be more complex than her role as metaphor permits.

respectively to three of the book's genres: autobiography, journalism, and the epistolary novel.

Each of the novel's layers can be linked to one of its three titles. *Zoo* describes the collective emigration; *Letters Not About Love,* though ostensibly referring to the correspondence, can be viewed as the three emplotted letters of Shklovsky's return. The last title, *The Third Heloise,* links *Zoo* to the epistolary novel.[7] Like *A Sentimental Journey,* which also pirates the title of an innovative classic, *Zoo* reflects its debt to the literary tradition by deviating from it.

Isolating the levels clarifies their interrelationship. The role of the zoo in *Zoo* is both literal and figurative. Its literal referent, as Shklovsky points out, is the part of Berlin where the émigré community was concentrated: near the Tiergarten. The word's figurative use capitalizes on this circumstance: the place of residence becomes a metaphor for the émigré condition. The image of the exile as prisoner, important to Akhmatova's "I am not with those who left the land," helps form the mesh of metaphors enclosing Shklovsky's *Zoo.*

The epigraph, Velemir Khlebnikov's poem "Menagerie" (1909), introduces the metaphor of the Berlin zoo, depicting it as a place where alien species are imprisoned and only the natives are free and thriving. The Germans drink beer and bloom with health; the bats "hang suspended, like the heart of a modern Russian." The poem is largely a series of similes describing the animals. Each specimen is released from its cage by the simile and revealed to have unknown dimensions. When Khlebnikov's walrus emerges from the water, "upon his oily weighty body there appears the head of Nietzsche, with its spiky bristles and smooth brow"; at this zoo, "in the tiger's face, with its frame of white beard and the eyes of an elderly Moslem, we pay homage to the first Mohammedan and read the essence of Islam" (p. 13). The zoo is a place of hidden treasures, concludes the poet, "where marvelous potentialities are perishing in the animals, as the Lay of Igor's Host, inserted in a codex, perished in the fire of Moscow" (p. 14).

The problem of confinement in a foreign environment is addressed most explicitly in Letter Six, which relates Shklovsky's impressions of the Berlin zoo. This is one of many points where he indulges in the technique he labeled "baring the device." He describes

---

[7]In the introduction to his translation of *Zoo* (pp. xxv–xxvi) Richard Sheldon discusses Shklovsky's allusion to *La Nouvelle Héloise* and *The Letters of Abelard and Heloise.*

the aquarium only to reject it as irrelevant; the zoo, on the other hand, "could come in handy for parallelisms" (p. 32). (Later he says the same thing of the West as a whole — though Russians have no need of it, it can be useful in drawing parallels.) The chief comparison here is between himself and the ape, "a wretched foreigner" (p. 32). What most strikes him about the ape's condition is its immobility. The animals are not only divested of their native identities: they are also deprived of normal experience.

Russian Berlin, like the zoo, is a rootless enclave where no purposeful change takes place. Images involving energy and stasis are central to the "zoo" reading of the novel. Its plotlessness is inherent in the material: émigré Berlin cannot develop. In one of the last letters, Shklovsky likens émigrés to battery-powered automobiles: their batteries, charged in Russia, are used up in aimless motion until they finally run down. (In a sense this is what happens to Shklovsky's book — it lasts only as long as he can maintain momentum outside Russia.)

The contrast between Russia's dynamism and the emigration's inertia is fully demonstrated in Letter Seventeen. Including himself among the ineffectual émigrés, Shklovsky describes them as refugees who, their flight ended, have become squatters. "Russian Berlin is going nowhere," he writes. "It has no destiny" (p. 68). His personal destiny is at issue as well: he blames the plague of inertia for his failure to win Alia. He speculates that she must be attracted to men more vital than the émigrés, to foreigners with "a mechanical propulsion — the propulsion of an ocean liner, on whose deck it's nice to dance the shimmy" (p. 68). The powerful ship is identified with hypothetical rivals, but its more important association is with post-revolutionary Russia. The liner's engine is like the historical force now at work there. This idea is developed through a sketch of Boris Pasternak which figures prominently in the letter. Pasternak is pictured first in Moscow, sharing in the mood of excitement. He observes to a companion (Lili Brik): "You know, it's as though we're on a ship" (p. 67). With characteristic alacrity, Shklovsky provides a gloss: "This important and happy man, standing among people wearing overcoats and munching sandwiches at the counter in the Press Club . . . was feeling the propulsion of history." Pasternak in Berlin experiences an opposite sensation. His malaise is not caused by the environment's strangeness; rather, its inertia unsettles him. Shklovsky ingenuously comments: "I would say — not because I'm trying to make the letter circular — that it seems to me he feels among us an absence of propulsion" (p. 68). The letter has already noted the vigor of Pasternak's poetry — implying that the émigré condition is incompatible with poetic creativity.[8]

One émigré review of *Zoo* caustically complained that it seemed written for a circle of friends.[9] This point has some merit: in *Zoo* and elsewhere, Shklovsky prominently features himself and his acquaintances. The reviewer's judgment, however, has to be modified with time: most of the "acquaintances" in *Zoo*, if not already famous, were to become major figures in Russian and Western culture. Their presence in the novel largely accounts for its current interest. Shklovsky's sketches of Russians then in Berlin provide insight into their work and into emigration's varied effects. Pasternak is not an émigré but a visitor, and his "loss of propulsion" is thus only temporary. How have others responded to their condition? Marc Chagall, writes Shklovsky, carried his native Vitebsk, his creative homeland, with him to Europe. The art of Ivan Puni has also been unaffected by exile, because of his absorption in his work: "I don't think Puni noticed the revolution and war — he was working hard the whole time" (p. 62). Alexei Remizov, too, appears oblivious to his surroundings: the "Order of Monkeys" he devises is a "zoo" within a "zoo," a self-imposed exile from reality. Those émigrés dependent on a wider world than Remizov's have more difficulty. One is the publisher Zinovii Grzhebin, whose Berlin publishing house issued Russian books aimed at both foreign and Soviet readers. Few of his volumes were reaching the Soviet public. Shklovsky likens Grzhebin's books to prospective immigrants thwarted at the border: "The books come running, one after another; they want to run away to Russia, but are denied entry" (p. 35). Grzhebin is another

---

[8]Shklovsky's descriptive technique here conforms to the method examined in his essay "The Sketch and the Anecdote." Discussing the elements that replace plot in non-fiction, he focuses on devices of comparison: "The feuilletonist's method lies in transposing things to another plane by means other than plot; the feuilletonist compares big things with small, intersecting them at some particular word, or relates an incident which occurred in the West, comparing it with an incident here" ("Ocherk i anecdot," in *O teorii prozy* [Moscow, 1929; rpt. Ann Arbor, Mich.: Ardis, n.d.], p. 249). Both devices are used widely in *Zoo*. All the descriptions in Letter Seventeen — of writing and writers, cars and countries — derive from the opposition between inertia and propulsion; the word *tiaga* ("propulsion") is that "particular word" at which planes cross. The portrait of Pasternak is a simple example of juxtaposing Western and Russian events. As Shklovsky's theorizing predicts, such techniques unify his material.

[9]Mikhail Osorgin, untitled review of *Zoo, Sovremennye zapiski,* no. 17 (1923), pp. 486–87.

kind of foreign correspondent, trying to keep open the lines of communication between Europe and Russia. Émigré writers, of course, were frustrated by the same isolation from a mass audience.

Shklovsky himself strongly felt the separation from Russian literary life. His attachment to Russia, as expressed in the book, is principally to the milieu in which he had been active. He identifies with post-revolutionary Russia's social mores as well as with its literary avant-garde. Those of his generation who stayed through the Revolution, by Shklovsky's account, have no use for bourgeois European or émigré ways. Describing their social uncouthness, he explains undefensively: "We have known no other way of life than that of war and revolution" (p. 47). His nostalgic version of contemporary Russia purposely stresses its distance from Europe.

Shklovsky's first gesture toward returning to the other side of the gap appears in Letter Fourteen, nearly at the novel's center. Along with the first and final letters, it comprises the "letters not about love" that tell the hero's story.[10] These are the only letters sent to Russia, all parts of "foreign correspondences." The first is written by Alia to her sister in Moscow; the other two are Shklovsky's, addressed respectively to his Petersburg friends and to the All-Russian Central Executive Committee. In one of the book's many bits of literary criticism, Shklovsky calls *Zoo* "an attempt to go outside the framework of the ordinary novel" (p. 85). That it is, but it also contains the framework

---

[10]Shklovsky offers a different explanation of the second title, which does not exclude the interpretation I suggest. In the preface, relating *Zoo*'s genesis, Shklovsky describes its components as a network of cause-and-effect interactions. He says he began with the idea of writing a series of sketches about émigré Berlin. His later statement in *Theory of Prose* that "a literary work . . . is not realized by the implementation of its objective" might be recalled here: *Zoo*'s preface illustrates the maxim ("Ornamental'naia proza: Andrei Belyi," in *O teorii prozy*, p. 215). Seeking a unifying principle, Shklovsky decided to cast his sketches as an epistolary novel. The genre is predicated on a reason for communicating — often, in the literary tradition, romantic attachment. But the sketches, ostensibly already written, are about the unromantic subject of Russian Berlin. Therefore Shklovsky invents a correspondent who prohibits her admirer from mentioning love. Since the letters describe the writer's surroundings, he reasons, the correspondent must be defined as a foreigner: "The woman . . . acquired a certain configuration, that of a person from an alien culture, because there's no point in writing descriptive letters to a person of your own culture" (p. 10). By this slick account, the woman's character is the last thing to be determined. The romantic heroine of the epistolary tradition is reduced to a compositional device. (In relegating Alia to this status, Shklovsky is acting not only as author but as unrequited lover: transforming the beloved into a literary tool seems an appropriate form of revenge for a pioneer Formalist.) The pledge to avoid the subject of love is not kept: the title is an ironic description of the correspondence.

of a typical novel. Letter One is expository, introducing the protagonist and his problem; in the middle letter, the intensified problem
motivates him to act; the final letter finds him resolving his dilemma,
ready to quit the scene. While the Alia-Shklovsky correspondence
alternates between poles and the Berlin vignettes are static, this is a
linear plot that moves out of the "zoo" of emigration.[11]

With the preface and epigraph leading the reader down his path,
Shklovsky lets Alia open the body of the book. In Letter One she
describes her current life and presents the initial image of Shklovsky
and of their correspondence. He is not named, but is clearly the persistent admirer who "writes me one or two letters a day." By the middle
of the book, the patient suitor has grown increasingly discontented.
The prefatory note to Letter Fourteen explains: "It is written to Russia; it makes clear that the author is suffering from an idée fixe" (p.
58). That idea is the desire to return to Russia. The letter implies that
Alia is one cause of his frustration and alienation, but her role is
muted. What bothers him even more than her rejection is his estrangement from what is being written and published back home.
Shklovsky swears by his sacred Opoiaz that he would drop everything
if he could return. He begs his fellow writers to help him get permission: "My friends, brothers! How wrong it is that I'm here! Go out in
the street, all of you, out to the Nevsky, and demand that they let me
return" (p. 58). (Realizing that this request for a political demonstration may seem too demanding, he tempers fancy with absurdity, adding: "To avoid any unpleasantness, you might want to ride along the
Nevsky in a tram.")

By the final letter, he has decided on a more direct approach.
Letter Twenty-Nine is in the form of a petition to the Soviet government; it announces his inability to continue living in Berlin and requests authorization to return. His position is forcefully stated: "I am
bound by my entire way of life, by all my habits, to the Russia of
today. I am able to work only for her." He links this feeling specifically
with Soviet Russia: "The revolution transformed me," he writes. "I
cannot breathe without it." Alia, who has moved from her dominant
position in the opening letter to a subordinate role in the middle one,
now disappears completely. Shklovsky denies her existence, partly to
dissociate his desire to return from his disappointment in love. She

---

[11]In "Ocherk i anekdot," in *O teorii prozy*, p. 249, Shklovsky notes that the writer of
non-fiction submits material to a process of "denovelization" (*razromanyvanie*). These
three letters illustrate an opposite process, which one might term "novelization."

reverts to her status in the preface as a literary tool. "Alia is the realization of a metaphor," writes Shklovsky. "I invented a woman and love in order to make a book about misunderstanding, about alien people, about an alien land" (p. 105). This Heloise, namesake of Abelard's beloved and of Rousseau's heroine, dies by a stroke of her expedient lover's pen.

Zoo's ending does what Bulgakov's critics wanted at the end of *Flight:* it states the need to return in terms of a tie to present-day Russia, not to the past. Unlike Bulgakov's characters, Shklovsky is returning without illusions. His realistic understanding of what may await him is made clear at the end of the final letter. The petition's objective and the explanation of Alia begin the letter; it ends with a statement of capitulation ("I raise my arm and surrender") and with an anecdote. Shklovsky recounts the story of an intended Turkish surrender to the Russians that ended in massacre, and asks the authorities not to repeat that pattern. The request to return acknowledges the Bolshevik regime he had fought against; the anecdote expresses his suspicion that it may be impossible to shed his identity as an opponent.

This letter has understandably aroused more comment than any other. Is the petition as a whole capitulatory? How is the anecdote to be understood — is it a repentant plea for mercy or a rebel's jab at the Soviet method of handling opponents?[12] Shklovsky's habitual irony makes the letter difficult to judge, although its tone is predominantly that of retreat rather than aggression. It must not be forgotten that Shklovsky makes of himself a literary persona in Zoo: the lovelorn exile of the book is distinct from its author, and the petition can hardly be Shklovsky's actual application for a visa.[13]

In the context of Zoo, the final letter is aberrant: it makes the book's only distinction between post-revolutionary Russia and the Bolshevik regime. Shklovsky's allegiance to contemporary Russian life

---

[12]Richard Sheldon has argued that the anecdote undercuts the submissive surrender, marking Shklovsky's first use of "the device of ostensible surrender" which he deployed at other points in his career ("Viktor Shklovsky and the Device of Ostensible Surrender," *Slavic Review* 34, no. 1 [1975]: 90–91). See also the above-cited reply by Victor Erlich, "On Being Fair to Viktor Shklovsky or the Act of Hedged Surrender," and Richard Sheldon, "Reply to Victor Erlich," *Slavic Review* 35, no. 1 (1976): 119–21.

[13]Shklovsky's final letter is interesting to consider in the context of other Russian repatriation during the 1920s. A curious sample of the Soviet writing on returning émigrés is an illustrated article in the popular magazine *Ogonek*, which notes that in recent months the Soviet legation in Berlin has been "besieged" with their requests (see "Nazad v Rossiiu," *Ogonek*, July 29, 1923, p. 1).

and culture are repeatedly expressed in *Zoo,* part of its pattern of contrasts; nowhere before the petition, however, does he bring up contemporary politics. Confronting the issue, he wields his words carefully: the Russia he is bound to, he writes, is "the Russia of today" (p. 105). The Bolshevik government is Shklovsky's means of getting there, not his reason for going. While he voices no enthusiasm for the regime, he is conciliatory: he puts his political past behind him, suggesting that the experience of emigration has buried it. Emigration has faded more than his politics: it has also dimmed his energy. *Zoo*'s conclusion should be read in relation to Khlebnikov's poem, where it begins. The menagerie curbs its inmates, as Shklovsky finds himself confined in Berlin. In the petition, he concedes one part of himself to regain the rest. Khlebnikov's "zoo" metaphor and Akhmatova's image of the prisoner seem genuinely his own.

Shklovsky the protagonist rejects the West, while Shklovsky the writer exploits its value. Europe in *Zoo* never strays far from the realm of device. But for Shklovsky the politics of return was a real problem, though tempered with irony in his book. The capitulatory return from the West was not the province of autobiography alone. Yurii Olesha, at a turning point in his career, fictionalized that situation to effect his figurative entry into contemporary Russia. Olesha never left Russia, but his writing of the twenties shows him struggling to come to terms with his presence there. In *A List of Assets,* he tries to cross out of this position into the Russia of the thirties.

8

THE ARTIST, II
Emigration and Melodrama

Iurii Olesha, *A List of Assets* (1931)

The history of artists in emigration is a long one, going back at least to Plato's banishment of the poet from his Republic. Political restrictions on self-expression have often been the cause of expulsion or self-exile. But artists also leave their homelands even when the state does not threaten their right to publish and create. Travel or expatriation can yield social and psychological freedoms that may be curbed at home. Gertrude Stein, a prime example of this sort of expatriation, explains it in a 1936 essay as a necessary consequence of the artist's nature.

The term "artist," with its narrow and broad meanings, is ambiguous; Stein, ever pursuing the precise definition (and ever eschewing conventional punctuation) speaks instead of "every one who makes anything inside themselves that is makes it entirely out of what is in them." For her, it is axiomatic that such people must be free of incursions on their inner lives. Only away from one's native culture, she argues, can one have complete creative freedom: " . . . if you are you in your own civilization you are apt to mix yourself up too much with your civilization but when it is another civilization . . . that stays there where it is you in it have freedom inside yourself." One needs a place one can feel unconnected to, that "is there but it does not happen." The value of a foreign place to an artist lies not in its potential influence but in its indifference; in Stein's memorable formulation: "It was not what France gave you but what it did not take away from you that was important."[1]

Stein notes that it is becoming difficult to find the right sort of "other civilization" in an increasingly homogeneous and interrelated world. But this problem is surmountable. As she shows in discussing literary language, it is possible to develop and preserve an inner creative world in one's native place. What happens, though, in a country where the individual is not free to isolate himself? What becomes of the artist who cannot regard the environment as something "that is there but it does not happen," the artist who is obligated to participate in what is happening? This question is at the heart of Iurii Olesha's *A List of Assets* (1931). The 1930s saw some of the best Soviet writers withdraw from literary life, or at least produce part of their creative work "for the drawer." Olesha began the decade with a work that reveals both his personal development and a historical turning point: the Stalinization of Soviet culture. *A List of Assets* is not a great play; its weaknesses will become clear below. But it is a significant play, because it shows a gifted writer wrangling with the issues of self-fulfillment and social responsibility. The play concerns the need of the artist — and, by extension, of any individual — to develop in his own image, and to regard himself as separate and complete.

In a pre-production article, Olesha called the play's theme "the Europe of the spirit."[2] His object was not to depict Europe, he said, but to deal with an idea. His description of that idea is worth quoting in its entirety:

> In every intellectual, particularly in the intellectual who works in the sphere of art, there lives a certain "idea of Europe." Perhaps this is an attraction to so-called pure art — an attraction which is eliminated with difficulty. Perhaps it is the thought that all should be forgiven talent — the idea of the primacy of the self, an individualistic tendency. Perhaps, because we are now cut off from Europe, this idea mutinies in the soul of the intellectual with particular force, leading the consciousness along the border between despair over the lost primacy of the self and hatred of one's self, of one's "I," which can't humble itself no matter how hard it tries.[3]

---

[1] Gertrude Stein, "An American and France," in *The Story of American Experience in the Old World,* ed. Philip Rahv (Boston: Houghton Mifflin, 1947), pp. 571–78. The phrases quoted are on pp. 571, 572, 576, and 577 respectively.
[2] "Tema intelligenta," *Stroika,* no. 3 (1930), p. 16.
[3] Ibid.

The "idea of Europe" has two definitions here: artistic freedom and individualism. This is clear enough — but the connection between "Europe" the abstraction and "Europe" the place is blurry. In the first part of the passage Europe is a state of mind, a belief; that belief has become intensified in the Russian intellectual, continues Olesha, because Russia is "cut off from Europe." Is "Europe" in this second usage abstract or real? What sort of causal relationship is the writer hypothesizing? Does he mean that it is difficult to espouse beliefs in pure art and in the primacy of the self because Russians have few contacts with Europe? This makes no sense. His statement appears to mean, rather, that artistic and individual freedom have become acute issues because Soviet policy is increasingly antagonistic to them. He means that "we are cut off from the 'idea of Europe'" — an oblique way of saying that the state represses the artist and the individual.

This the writer obviously finds troubling — but by calling his idea "European," he has made it by definition alien to Russia. Europe's dual usage in the article is indicative of its role in the play, which also mixes the abstract Europe with the real thing. Olesha claims that the actual Europe is not his subject; why, then, does most of the work take place there? One might set a play about "the Europe of the spirit" in Moscow or Leningrad; six of Olesha's eight scenes are, however, set in Paris. As the play progresses, it focuses increasingly on the real Europe and less on the idea. This shift of focus is both a retreat from the problem and a sneak attack on it: a retreat because the attention to Europe's problems deflects attention from the idea; an attack because, by reifying the abstract Europe, Olesha makes it easier to destroy.

The most intimate chronicle of Olesha's career[4] considers *A List of Assets* a capitulation to ideological pressure, a major step in Olesha's path toward literary conformity. This is so, but it must be noted that Olesha capitulates the hard way. The play is controversial by virtue of the topic itself. Olesha does muddy definitional waters — but these are dangerous waters he has chosen to enter. The works discussed so far concern emigration's "first wave" — the emigration stemming from revolution and civil war (with Shklovsky a slightly later "surge" of that wave). The departures of Bulgakov's characters

---

[4]A. Belinkov, *Sdacha i gibel' sovetskogo intelligenta: Iurii Olesha* (Madrid: n.p., 1976). Belinkov's insights into Olesha and his milieu are those of a closely involved contemporary. On *A List of Assets* see, especially, pp. 297–410.

and of Shklovsky are circumstantial, motivated by personal safety rather than by a desire to leave Russia. A List of Assets concerns a deliberate departure in a more stable time — a departure motivated not by physical panic but by a kind of mental panic.

Mass emigration belonged to the past, but individual emigration of this sort was topical. In March 1930 Bulgakov wrote to Stalin complaining of banning and censorship and asking to leave the country if he were not to be permitted work in his profession.[5] Evgenii Zamiatin's letter to Stalin requesting permission to go abroad for a year was written in June 1931; he left permanently in November. The actor Mikhail Chekhov (the writer's nephew) had then been abroad for three years with no indication of when he would return. Chekhov was close to Olesha and to Meyerhold (who staged the play); his situation plainly underlay that of Olesha's heroine.[6] An authority on Meyerhold writes that "for many viewers the play was reminiscent of an actual instance of an intellectual's opting for the West."[7]

A quick synopsis shows how Olesha casts the issues. Elena Goncharova, a successful Soviet actress, goes to Paris on a one-month, officially sanctioned trip. In Paris she finds that the tension between emotion and reason that has plagued her since the Revolution is gone. She decides not to return but is dissuaded by Fedotov, a member of a visiting Soviet trade delegation. Her change of heart is remarkably swift, but not complete: while she no longer plans to stay in Europe, she retains some of her doubts. Goncharova has been invited to an international actors' gala; although its sponsor is a reactionary financier, she wants to attend. For that purpose, decrees the plot, she needs a ball gown — and the only gown that attracts her is the extravagant creation of a certain émigré dressmaker. This dressmaker is the mistress of Tatarov, editor of an émigré newspaper; Goncharova's diary, which lists the Soviet regime's crimes and benefits, falls into his hands.

---

[5]Bulgakov's letter is quoted at length by A. Belinkov in Sdacha i gibel' sovetskogo intelligenta (pp. 346–48) to show the gulf between Bulgakov and Olesha at this time. The letter and the ensuing telephone conversation between Bulgakov and Stalin are discussed in Ellendea Proffer's introduction to The Early Plays of Mikhail Bulgakov (Bloomington: Indiana University Press, 1972), pp. xvii–xix.

[6]See Konstantin Rudnitsky, "Meyerhold's Production of Olesha's A List of Assets," trans. Marjorie Hoover, Russian Literature Tri-Quarterly, no. 7 (1974), p. 187. This is an excerpt from Rudnitsky's Rezhisser Meierkhol'd (Moscow, 1969).

[7]Marjorie L. Hoover, Meyerhold: The Art of Conscious Theater (Amherst: University of Massachusetts Press, 1974), p. 210. Hoover links this audience reaction to Mikhail Chekhov's departure in particular.

Tatarov promptly publishes only the "list of crimes," thus exposing her as a traitor. Driven to prove her loyalty, Goncharova tries to murder Tatarov; when this fails, she joins a leftist demonstration of unemployed workers. There an unbalanced young émigré, incited by the police, fires on the communist leader Santillant; Goncharova, shielding Santillant with her body, is killed by the bullet.

Olesha termed the play "a pathetic melodrama"; it has been numbered among several "heroic tragedies" that Meyerhold directed between 1929 and 1933.[8] It might also be regarded as a melodrama grafted onto a drama. The play increasingly develops from a drama about an idea to a melodrama about a place. The tragic strain involves an internal conflict, the heroine at odds with herself. Commitment to the self — "the idea of Europe" — becomes identified with attachment to the actual Europe, and thus with repudiation of Russia. Olesha's metaphoric Europe becomes a concept that can kill.

The Prologue shows the heroine literally as a tragic hero: it takes place after a performance of *Hamlet* in which Goncharova (also the director) plays the title role. The cast's question session with the audience is expository: Goncharova's answers present a sampling of her opinions. On current Soviet plays: "schematic, false, devoid of fantasy, single-minded"; on cultural policy: no good foreign films are shown, and *Hamlet* will probably never be produced again; on the artist's connection to the era: "in an epoch of fast tempos the artist must think slowly."[9] Her answers are repeatedly interrupted by the nervous theater manager; his reaction, evidence of the artist's suppression by authority, makes Goncharova seem both right and rebellious.

A reprise of a scene from *Hamlet* reinforces this impression. At a request from the audience, Goncharova/Hamlet enacts the conversa-

---

[8]Hoover, *Meyerhold: The Art of Conscious Theater,* p. 215.
[9]The edition quoted in the first: Iu. Olesha, *Spisok blagodeianii* (Moscow: Federatsiia, 1931; rpt. Ann Arbor, Mich.: University Microfilms, 1971), pp. 4–5. References in the text are to this edition. My translations draw somewhat on Yuri Olesha, *A List of Assets,* in *Envy and Other Works,* trans. Andrew R. MacAndrew (Garden City, N.Y.: Anchor-Doubleday, 1967), pp. 221–88.
The last phrase quoted ("v epokhe bystrykh tempov khudozhnik dolzhen dumat' medlenno") is printed incorrectly in the first edition, where the final word appears as "nemedlenno." In this context, the incorrect word means "immediately" or "without delay," roughly reversing the intended meaning in a way that sounds absurd: Goncharova tells the audience that "in an epoch of fast tempos the artist must think immediately." Olesha explained the error by joking that the copyreader found the idea so strange that he thought it wrong (see "Rech' na dispute 'Khudozhnik i epokha,'" in Iu. Olesha, *P'esy,* p. 268).

tion with Guildenstern from act 3, scene 2. Making Guildenstern admit that he cannot play the recorder, Hamlet demonstrates his friend's inability to manipulate another's mind: "Why, look you now, how unworthy a thing you make of me! You would play upon me, you would seem to know my stops, you would pluck out the heart of my mystery. . . . 'Sblood, do you think I am easier to be played on than a pipe? Call me what instrument you will, though you can fret me, you cannot play upon me." By highlighting this passage, Olesha is asserting that the inner self is inviolate, and that attempts to penetrate it should be resisted. The scene ends with this affirmation, and with the introduction of another major issue. During the post-performance discussion Goncharova has torn up one of the questions; a final question, tossed onto the stage after the reprise, asks the subject of the discarded one. The question, replies Goncharova unhesitatingly, was whether she would return from her trip abroad; the "honest answer" is that she will. But the matter obviously disturbs her: willing to speak frankly about other controversial issues, she avoids this one. The stage is set for the development of both issues emphasized in the opening: individual freedom and expatriation — the idea of Europe and the departure to Europe.

Hamlet's lines appear ironic in the context of the whole play. For Goncharova is "played upon" by people — she is weaker and more complex than she at first appears. Her susceptibility to manipulation stems in part from a "feminine" weakness written into her character; its more important source, however, is her genuine internal conflict. The prologue shows her distance from the regime; the next scene shows her ambivalence. At home the evening before her departure, she shares with an actress friend her hidden thoughts about Soviet life. They are contained in the two sections of a notebook she calls "the secret of the Russian intelligentsia" (p. 9). One half lists "the crimes of the Revolution" — not petty problems but "crimes against the individual" (p. 10). These are not enumerated, nor are the "benefits of Soviet power," which comprise her other list. Goncharova denies being "counterrevolutionary": the negative list alone does not represent her position. Both lists put together comprise her self — they are "Two halves of one conscience, a confusion which is driving me mad" (p. 10). Her confession prompts the friend to conclude that Goncharova will stay abroad, a suggestion that is firmly denied. Her intention to return soon is repeated in the scene's final line. The issue she hesitated to address in the theater seems clear-cut here, but Goncharova's inner turmoil sustains the suspense.

Doubt of her intentions is also stirred by the scene's treatment of her personal life. Her ambivalence toward Russia's current condition prevents her from feeling connected to it. She cannot oppose it, but neither can she regard it as hers, as home: "I can neither run, nor rebel, nor lie, nor build. . . . Am I really living? I'm flowing . . . flowing" (p. 12). An altercation with neighbors — like Zoshchenko's domestic anecdotes but without the humor — further illustrates her disharmony with her surroundings. Goncharova insists that she will return, yet the scene also shows that what she is leaving behind is not fully her home. She does not suggest that she belongs to Europe any more than to Russia; imagining the trip, however, she calls it "a journey into youth" (p. 9). Away from Russia, Goncharova's feelings are set in relief. In the first Paris scene, she sees the trip as an escape from an unnatural, incomplete life. An earlier version of the scene develops this idea in terms of language, in lines reminiscent of Olesha's earlier writing. The essence of post-revolutionary life is reflected in the structure of its language: one cannot live satisfyingly in Russia, says Goncharova, because "The parts of speech have come undone."[10] The present tense no longer exists, because one is expected to live for the future. This metaphor is touched on in the final version as well: in Europe, says the actress, "I have reacquired verbs of the present tense. I eat, touch, look, walk" (p. 25). She has also found harmony with her surroundings and between the warring sides of her mind. The departure from Russia, Goncharova recognizes, has resulted in a homecoming to self. One thinks of Gertrude Stein's criteria for a place in which to settle and create. Paris has an impact on Goncharova not because it is Paris — not for what it gives — but because it asks nothing.

In a play that begins with *Hamlet,* one might expect the heroine to slip into soliloquy. There is only one soliloquy, but Olesha makes heavy use of dialogue with artificially long, intimate, and orderly outpourings. His play is studded with improbable speeches, such as Goncharova's description of the fulfillment she has found on arriving in Europe. This self-analysis is presented to the friendly but stern Communist Fedotov, whom she has met moments before and whose response is certain to be unsympathetic. His reaction is, in fact, sharp; it remains restrained, however, until the actress declares that she will not return to Russia.

---

[10]Quoted from an excerpt included by Olesha in "Tema intelligenta," p. 16. Two scenes of the first version of the play were published in the journal *30 dnei,* no. 12 (1930), pp. 34–42; a complete version appeared in *Krasnaia nov',* no. 8 (1931). Belinkov discusses the revisions in *Sdacha i gibel',* pp. 323–27.

The angry reply this provokes in Fedotov is a turning point: it is here that the "idea of Europe" and the Europe of 1930 are first interrelated. Fedotov's argument might be reduced thus: It is immoral to place such value on the self — the "Europe of the spirit" is off-limits. Furthermore, the inner harmony Goncharova feels in Europe is illusory, because Europe is about to erupt in class war. Given this situation, to live calmly in Europe is to support the capitalist establishment. One cannot be self-absorbed in Russia, because of one's obligations to socialist construction; one cannot be self-absorbed abroad, because the battle must be fought there as well. Goncharova's fidelity to self is redefined by Fedotov as treason. The "idea of Europe," it appears, can be espoused nowhere; the dangers of embracing it in contemporary Europe unfold as the play continues.

Goncharova has by her own account experienced a decade-long debate between her two internal factions: emotion (the advocate of self) and reason (the advocate of society). The latter has long failed to win, but Fedotov's speech is evidently more persuasive. Goncharova responds with an immediate and succinct assent to his call for allegiance: "Kiss me on the forehead. Officially. In the name of the Embassy" (p. 29).

The play to this point is a prelude to melodrama. The psychological drama has been settled, or its resolution at least begun. Goncharova has accepted Fedotov's reasoning, though she has not yet defended it. The heroine has tempted herself, has fallen, and has been shown the way to redemption. In this drama she is the criminal — guilty of holding her views, of writing them down, of planning to act on them. That would suffice for a whole play; condensed into a few scenes of Olesha's, it prepares the ground for the larger-scale ideological battle to come. Goncharova's internal struggle continues, now waged in distorted form by émigré Tatarov and Soviet Fedotov. From this point, she functions both as the dramatic heroine plagued by doubt and as the virtuous maiden of melodrama.

The classic melodrama of post-revolutionary France, in the model elaborated by Peter Brooks, begins by establishing the identity of virtue: "We see this virtue, momentarily, in a state of taking pleasure in itself, aided by those who recognize and support it." This is precisely what we have in Fedotov's kiss — Goncharova's certification as a true daughter of the Soviet regime. The play's adherence to the melodramatic form continues, the next stage following rapidly on the first. In the classic model, "there swiftly supervenes a threat to virtue, a situation — and most often a person — to cast its very survival into question, obscure its identity, and elicit the process of its fight for recognition."[11] In Olesha's play, about a dozen lines after Goncharova is marked by Fedotov's kiss — enter the villain.

The émigré journalist Tatarov, true to form, wastes no time in announcing what he stands for. From his entrance, he is a thoroughly dastardly villain, the sort at whom an audience could hiss with satisfaction. Flourishing his purpose like a rapier, he announces that he, as the "devil," is ready to engage the "angel" Fedotov in a battle for Goncharova, whom he labels "a righteous soul" (p. 30). In the villain's eyes, as now in those of the reader and audience, Goncharova is an innocent susceptible to corruption, a loyal Soviet citizen who can be lured into the émigré camp. Innocence and its defender prevail in this first encounter: threatened by Fedotov and ridiculed by Goncharova, Tatarov departs. But the first rebuff, in melodrama, is never the last: "The intruder may be driven out temporarily, but only to return triumphant since virtue has not yet established the full proof of its sign."[12] To establish her "sign" — to become invulnerable by identifying fully with Soviet Russia and with collectivism — this is Goncharova's task for the rest of the play.

For Tatarov the actress is not an end but a means: if she remains in Europe, he tells his dressmaker-accomplice, "The famous actress from the land of slaves will call out to the world: don't believe, don't believe in my fame! I received it for agreeing not to think . . . "(p. 38). Goncharova's vulnerability to the West is trivialized by the author. As the plot of melodrama unfolds she appears more frivolous, easier to "fret" and "play upon." (Goncharova's attraction to extravagant finery reminds one of the hilarious Soviet-Western struggle in Ernst Lubitsch's 1939 film *Ninotchka,* in which Greta Garbo plays a Soviet official seduced by Parisian luxury — and by Melvyn Douglas.) The silver dress that serves as Tatarov's bait is a poor symbol of what has really attracted Goncharova to Paris: the harmony of self described in her pre-melodrama speech. Olesha leaves no doubt that he intends it as such a symbol: Tatarov explains that the dress represents "what is forbidden to think about in Russia . . . the desire to live for oneself" (p. 43).

---

[11] Peter Brooks, *The Melodramatic Imagination: Balzac, Henry James, Melodrama, and the Mode of Excess* (New Haven, Conn.: Yale University Press, 1976). Both passages quoted are on p. 29.
[12] Ibid., p. 29.

The émigré's bait works: Goncharova unknowingly signs an IOU for the dress on his newspaper stationery, and carelessly lets him steal her notebook of lists. But the result is not what he predicts: the "righteous soul" converted by Fedotov has lapsed, but only temporarily. Her descent into evil's realm, initiated by Tatarov, continues with her humiliation by another oily Parisian, the director of a music hall — Olesha's stand-in for current European culture. Goncharova's debt forces her to earn some quick money, and she proposes that he hire her to present excerpts from *Hamlet*. Olesha's use of this scene to characterize European culture is as flimsy as his symbolic use of the dress. Goncharova's humiliation in the theater — her second encounter with what passes in the play for Paris — provokes another stage in her conversion process. Having fallen far and fast, she is ready now to internalize the role given to her with Fedotov's kiss. On leaving the theater she delivers the play's single soliloquy, which illustrates this shift.

In tragedy the soliloquy is introspective, revealing the hero's internal conflict. The melodramatic soliloquy expresses a mind certain of itself — it is a "saying of self" rather than an attempt to discover self.[13] Goncharova's post-theater speech is a combination of the two: in it she considers her mind's conflicting tendencies and declares the conflict over. She puts both her internal Satan (the "Europe of the spirit") and its emplotted symbol (the dress) behind her. Now her acceptance of Fedotov's view is based not only on reason but also on experience. The soliloquy's refrain, repeated at the opening, middle, and end, is the line most crucial to the plot: "I want to go home." The third time, it is followed by the curious words that end the speech: "I want to stand in line and cry" (p. 64). This is a telling embrace of one's homeland. Goncharova has already said some standard things about her solidarity with the masses and her foolish attempt to seek personal happiness. The desire to "stand in line and cry" implies her willingness to renounce personal happiness in favor of communal unhappiness. In rejecting Europe and embracing Russia, Goncharova accepts the idea that personal happiness cannot be legitimately pursued by a Soviet citizen in her time. In scene 3 she described Europe as the place where her wholeness was restored; now, having recognized that idea as traitorous, she wants to leave.

This proves more difficult than she expects. The internal battle is

[13] Ibid., p. 38.

won, but the external battle for Goncharova has only reached its climax. Tatarov has published the IOU and her list of Soviet evils: all Paris — including the Soviet embassy — sees her as a traitor and presumes that she has sold the list in exchange for the dress. Ready at last to declare her allegiance to the embassy and to return home, she cannot. Her position is that of melodrama's innocent before the dénouement: "Expulsed from its natural terrain, its identity put into question through deceiving signs, it must wander afflicted until it can find and establish the true signs of proof of its nature."[14]

The code of melodrama has a counterpart in Soviet doctrine. One of Fedotov's colleagues formulates the heroine's "expulsion from her natural terrain" in the play's terms: "A Soviet citizen, once he has gone over to the camp of emigration, places himself beyond the law" (p. 75). As in the classic melodrama, virtue must prove to its judges that it has been wronged. In melodrama this often happens in an actual trial; scene 6 of *A List of Assets*, Goncharova's encounter with Fedotov and his two colleagues, functions as a preliminary trial that leaves the three "judges" far apart. The hard-liner is ready to summon a firing squad; Fedotov, the most sympathetic, is willing to delay judgment. He assures Goncharova that she will be allowed to return and that it can be sorted out when they arrive. His advice: "Let's put it aside until Moscow, and in Moscow we'll discuss it [*obsudim*]. Moscow has forgiven more serious criminals, forgiven outright enemies" (p. 76).

His word for *discuss* — *obsudit'* — is close to the verb *to condemn* — *osudit'*. Goncharova picks up this related word in her emotional response: "I'll be tried? ... But I am my own judge. I condemned myself [*osudila sebia*] long ago." The suggestion of a trial frightens Goncharova into action. (Her fears were well-founded: the sensational Prompartiia [Industrial Party] trial was contemporary with the play's writing, and in bringing a heretic-heroine to justice Olesha was conforming to prevailing policy.)[15] Wanting to prove her innocence by other means, Goncharova steals Fedotov's gun and tries, in the next scene, to kill Tatarov. Thwarted, she finds another battleground in the demonstration of unemployed where the play ends.

The last act in melodrama is typically on a grand scale, "a highly physical 'acting out' of virtue's liberation from the oppressive efforts

---

[14] Ibid., p. 30.
[15] See Belinkov, *Sdacha i gibel'*, pp. 349–61.

of evil."[16] Olesha plays it by the book. (His closing street scene, complete with the double-entendre verses of an onlooker's song, reminds one of Brecht — who also comes to mind because Olesha's Paris is as cardboard as Brecht's Chicago.) In this final scene, Goncharova counters the villain's work by championing Soviet Russia's accomplishments and rallying the crowd. Now her identification with Russia is wholehearted and public, and now her language is that of melodrama — it "implicitly insists that the world can be equal to our most feverish expectations about it."[17] Goncharova lies dying with raving words of repentance and premonitions of European revolution on her lips. But she already knows how severe her judges can be: as if afraid that words alone will not vindicate her, she asks with her dying breath that one of the workers cover her body with a red flag. Pursued by the police, the workers move on without doing so; by her words and actions, however, Goncharova has finally come under the sign of virtue.

She began with a belief in an idea — the primacy of self; she is cut down by the actual Europe that supplants this idea in the play. Olesha began, by his own account, with a metaphor — the attraction to individual and creative freedom that is every artist's "idea of Europe." Ironically, he attempts to upstage this metaphoric Europe by placing a corrupt, evil "idea of Europe" in the spotlight. In the mind of the only artist we see, individual and creative freedom are banished from Russia and from the West. But what of the "every intellectual" in Olesha's article, in whose mind these ideas are "mutinying"? Goncharova addresses this question in the "trial scene" when she says that if she is a criminal "Then all intellectuals are criminals! They should all be shot!" (p. 75). Her "judges" disagree, but her judgment reverberates.

Through Goncharova's words and her experience, Olesha shows the severe consequences of harboring a "Europe of the spirit" in one's head. His warning, cloaked as it is in melodrama, may seem hard to take seriously. The play lacks force, too, because the heroine is so easily manipulated. Olesha does not give her a mind capable of resolving the conflict. Though he engages controversial issues, he resolves them without a satisfying fight.

In *Zoo* Shklovsky lays out his scheme and its central metaphor, "baring" the connection between the Europe from which he was alienated and the "European" whom he could not win. Olesha's defi-

---

[16]Brooks, *The Melodramatic Imagination*, p. 32.
[17]Ibid., p. 40.

nition of his metaphoric Europe comes not in the play itself, but in the earlier article, which few in the audience were likely to have read. His widely-read fiction of the twenties, however, provides additional insight into his use of a real and an abstract Europe. The play marks a change in his literary use of Europe — a point the writer made himself at a forum on "The Artist and the Epoch" in January 1932. Referring to the severe criticisms leveled at his play, Olesha defended it as a necessary stage in his creative development: "If I wrote about Europe, then it was a stage I had thought through, and if I had not written this, I would have been unable to move on to another play about art where I pose the questions: what is art, what is proletarian art. I touch on all the issues which are placed by the epoch on our fragile shoulders because all these issues have been worked out in theory, and we are working them out in practice for the first time."[18]

His remarks suggest that the play enabled him to exorcise an idea. This interpretation makes sense in light of his earlier fiction. The Europe imagined by Kavalerov in *Envy* (1927) is a place of "might have been": to live there is to live in fiction, to have all one's fantasies fulfilled. In Olesha's autobiographical stories about childhood, Europe is also a place of fantasy, but a real and accessible place at the same time. In "I Look into the Past" (1929) his imagination is filled with aviation miracles that were actually happening in Europe; his Europe is not an invented place but a private place. The small boy's visions of fabulous flying machines are presented as the antithesis of the familial world he is obliged to inhabit. In "Human Material" (1929) Europe is also part of the self-enclosed imaginative world that is precious to him. Just as he believes it possible to attain his dreams, the child Olesha feels that the distance to Europe can be easily crossed. The adult writer inhabited by his younger self writes:

> I grab at my own self in myself, grab by the throat that I who suddenly feels like turning around and stretching out his hands to the past.
> That I who thinks that the distance between us and Europe is only a geographic distance.
> That I who thinks that everything that happens is solely his own life, unique and unrepeatable, my all-embracing life, whose end will stop all that exists outside of me.[19]

---

[18]"Rech' na dispute 'Khudozhnik i epokha,'" p. 269.
[19]Iurii Olesha, "Ia smotriu v proshloe," *Izbrannoe* (Moscow: Khudozhestvennaia literatura, 1974), p. 229.

Here, as in *A List of Assets*, the sense of closeness to Europe is linked to an attachment to self. In *A List of Assets*, Olesha approaches the actual Europe for the first time, as if to test his old notion that the distance is just geographic — a distance of miles but not of mentality. Goncharova, having made the journey, finds in Europe her "unique and unrepeatable" self — but she cannot hold on to it, because the real Europe, as Olesha depicts it, does not afford the self the isolation it seeks. Olesha's foray into Europe in this play can be seen as an attempt to exorcise the "idea of Europe" from his own imagination. Only by convincing himself that the artist must subordinate self to social interest, he implies in the above-quoted 1932 speech, could he continue to write. In affirming the artist's subordinate position, he casts off the autonomy that Stein — stating the view of many artists through the centuries — deems indispensable to creative accomplishment. Stein takes one extreme, contending that one must become an expatriate in order to achieve complete inner freedom. In *A List of Assets*, Olesha tries to show that expatriation is not the solution — and that anyway there is no problem. He makes the "Europe of the spirit" as foreign to the Russian as the real Europe, and as fatal.

Among the ideas convicted in *A List of Assets* is the notion that emigration can remove one from the conflicts that prevail at home. Departure from Soviet Russia, like internal emigration into one's private world, is shown to be an inescapably political act.[20] In its emphasis on the ideological implications of emigration, this play differs from the works of the twenties analyzed above. Olesha is the most explicit in showing that one's personal identity cannot be considered

---

[20]Viewing emigration as such is not a Soviet innovation. In 1855, for example, Herzen wrote from his duty-imposed European exile that the Russian tendency to view émigrés as traitors stems from the Russian devaluation of the individual:

> Man must respect liberty in himself, and he must esteem it in himself no less than in his neighbour, than in the entire nation. . . . If you call my withdrawal an escape . . . , this will mean that you yourselves are not wholly free. . . . Even in the worst periods of European history, we encounter some respect for the individual, some recognition of independence. . . . This respect not merely for material but also for moral force, this unquestioning recognition of the individual — is one of the great human principles in European life.

In contrast to Russia, Herzen continues, "In Europe a man who lives abroad has never been considered a criminal, nor one who emigrates to America a traitor." A. I. Gertsen, *S togo berega*, in *Sobranie sochinenii*, 30 vols. (Moscow: Akademiia Nauk SSSR, 1954–65), VI, 14–15. Translation is from Alexander Herzen, *From the Other Shore and The Russian People and Socialism*, intro. Isaiah Berlin (New York: George Braziller, 1956), pp. 12–13.

apart from the nation's identity. Bulgakov focuses on characters for whom personal categories transcend political ones: *Flight* was banned partly on those grounds. The politics of revolution and emigration is also muted in Pilniak's story, where the decision to stay or depart is a private concern. In Bulgakov and Pilniak, the drive to return is motivated by personal satisfaction. This is true in Shklovsky's *Zoo* as well. He introduces the political dimension of emigration in the ending — the petition to return — as a pragmatic measure: he must state his allegiance in order to get permission to return.

These works all end on the brink of return (or, in the case of Pilniak's story, in contemplation of its impossibility). In *Flight* and *Zoo*, those characters who intend to return are attached to a self that can exist only at home. They had left post-revolutionary Russia for reasons of safety — self-preservation, let us call it; their return is self-preservation in a psychological sense. Olesha's heroine is different: her intended return is an act of self-sacrifice, figurative and literal. In resolving to reverse her single crossing, she recovers country but forfeits self.

Each writer devises the kind of West that suits the other components of his creation. Bulgakov's would-be returnees are indifferent to Europe: it is not a variable in their decision making, because they do not want a life in exile. By caricaturing the émigré-turned-Parisian, Bulgakov is not condemning Europe, but rather showing the falsification of self that life in emigration can entail. Shklovsky molds Europe to fit the parallelisms he needs for his *Zoo*. Only in *A List of Assets* is Europe a positive force that attracts a protagonist to emigrate. A distinctly negative Europe — a place that can outweigh the "idea of Europe" that drew his heroine abroad — is essential to Olesha's purpose. This play is characteristic of the thirties not just because it pits European corruption against Russian accomplishments and aims. That contrast, as we saw in Part 1, was used in Soviet literature from the beginning (and in earlier Russian writing). *A List of Assets* conveys the mood of its time in that Soviet Russia is now extremely rigid in its definition of the individual's relationship to country.

Russia or Europe, home or exile — it was a brutal choice, whether made early or late. One can calmly enough toy with weighing Europe against Russia (as though some colossal, blindfolded deity straddled the border, holding scales of judgment). But to experience the choice was to play for keeps. Those who reversed their single crossing were the exception.

Exceptional, too, particularly after the early twenties, were the travelers — those who visited the West without having to define themselves and their destination. Travel, though, naturally generates such definitions, because one makes sense of new experience by comparing it with what one knows. Travelers — especially if they are writers — are addicted to collecting the comparisons. As the cliché has it, travel is broadening: the more ground you cover, the more that mysteriously infinite space inside your head expands. Writers are used to translating exterior space into words and images — that is, converting perception into description. Mandelstam described the process well when he wrote of how "that traveler, the eye, presents his ambassadorial credentials to the consciousness"[21] (a diplomatic ritual that begs to be called a rite of passage). In the following chapters, we see what Mandelstam and other writer-travelers saw, as they journeyed away and back.

[21]Osip Mandel'shtam, "Puteshestvie v Armeniiu," in *Sobranie sochinenii,* ed. G. P. Struve and B. A. Filipoff, 3 vols. (New York: Inter-Language Literary Associates, 1964–71), II, 199.

PART THREE

THERE AND BACK:
RUSSIAN TRAVELERS AND THE WEST

Western writers who visited Russia during the twenties and thirties came to see a new country, to match Soviet reality against burgeoning legends of the first workers' state. Wells, Dreiser, Shaw, Gide — the list of the curious is lengthy, and their impressions comprise an absorbing chapter in intellectual history. Less attention has been paid to the flow of traffic in the opposite direction. Russian émigrés crossed the border only once, losing what they left behind. Emigration, however, was not the only path to the West. Travel — actual, fictional, and abstract — continued to link the West to Russia.

Despite post-revolutionary constraints on foreign travel, a number of Soviet writers visited the West during this period, and some published accounts of their experiences. The venerable Russian genre of the European journey continued to develop. As non-fiction travel accounts evolved, so also did related forms — imagined journeys, fictional journeys, travel to a figurative West of the writer's own definition. The following chapters present four literary approaches to traversing the border.

The most straightforward sort of travel is summarized by Mayakovsky's title for his 1930 collection of travel poetry: *There and Back*.[1] The cover design captures this kind of travel even better than the antonyms. Aleksandr Rodchenko's cover, a stark geometric composition in gray, white, and red, has two parallel arrows pointing in

---

[1] V. Maiakovskii, *Tuda i obratno* (Moscow: Federatsiia, 1930).

opposite directions. These routes of departure and return are linked by a giant Russian "and." The single Cyrillic letter that constitutes this word is a backwards N, which in Rodchenko's hands is unmistakably a zigzag road. Mayakovsky and other writers who took and chronicled that road are the period's most visible literary travelers. Not all their writing is as superficial as the simple back-and-forth scenario suggests. Reading it, one sees not only geographic changes of scene, but also a change of eras. Writers were conscious of seeing the West from a different perspective than had earlier travelers. Their prose and poetry show an awareness that their personal experiences abroad were related to the new identity of their country.

The pattern of departure-sojourn-homecoming, loosely followed in non-fiction, bends to even more variations in other genres. In the hybrid picaresque of Ilya Ehrenburg's *Julio Jurenito*, the meanings of "away" and "home" lose precision. The roving narrator (the author's alter ego) combines the roles of traveler and émigré. Rodchenko's east-west arrows reverse direction in this book: the hero's route begins and ends in Europe, after a long excursion into revolutionary Russia. Bound to no place by national consciousness, he is unbound by the law of inertia that Laurence Sterne deems a plague on the would-be traveler. "It must have been observed by many a peripatetic philosopher," muses Sterne, "That nature has set up by her own unquestionable authority certain boundaries and fences to circumscribe the discontent of man: she has effected her purpose in the quietest and easiest manner by laying him under almost insuperable obligations to work out his ease, and to sustain his sufferings at home."[2] Ehrenburg's picaro eludes nature's authority by calling no place home, remaining an unaligned traveler.

Chance and conniving readily propel the picaresque traveler from place to place. The backdrop advances, like a revolving canvas of painted scenery, as one situation slides into another. Outside fiction, one's surroundings are harder to transform. The scenery's crank often resists turning — and each frame of the canvas may repeat the same scene. When circumstances are static, the machinery of imagination is set in motion. This is the case in Isaac Babel's "Italian Sunshine," where fantasy tempts a dreamer over reality's barriers. Sterne, ever ready to catalogue life's mysteries, proposes in *A Sentimental Journey* that only three factors can induce one to overcome nature's decree of

---

[2]Laurence Sterne, *A Sentimental Journey Through France and Italy* (Harmondsworth, England: Penguin, 1967), p. 33.

immobility: "Infirmity of body, Imbecility of mind, or Inevitable necessity."[3] In Babel's story the means of propulsion is intense psychological necessity, which suffices only to change the scenery of the mind.

European travel remains for Babel's dreamer an obsessive abstraction: he is lured by that westward-pointing arrow, but cannot follow it. Another sort of restraint is at issue in Mandelstam's "Journey to Armenia," which deviates more subtly from the straight path of those border-crossing arrows. This account, as its title indicates, is not literally about European travel. My final chapter explains why Mandelstam resolved not to revisit Europe, and the sense in which his essay involves Europe as well as Armenia. Mandelstam's work — like all the works discussed here — also illuminates the position of the Russian at home. In the late twenties, Olesha had lamented that Europe now seemed separated from Russia by more than geography.[4] Accounts of actual journeys during the twenties and thirties demonstrate that the trip there and back could still be made. "Journey to Armenia" suggests, obliquely but powerfully, that in a more profound way Russia's western border has been closed.

---

[3] Sterne, p. 34.
[4] Iurii Olesha, "Ia smotriu v proshloe," *Izbrannoe* (Moscow: Khudozhestvennaia literatura, 1974), p. 229.

9
THE UNALIGNED TRAVELER

Ilya Ehrenburg, *Julio Jurenito* (1922)

Among Soviet writers of his generation who wrote about the West, Ilya Ehrenburg may have been the best-traveled and the most prolific. From the mid-twenties until World War II, he spent much time in Europe as a correspondent; in those years and after, Europe was a focal point of his life and work. His reportage and fiction involving the West were generally compatible with official Soviet views. Ehrenburg's first novel, *Julio Jurenito*, widely considered his best, is the work of a more irreverent pen. It is the novel of a traveler — of a young man trying to characterize his time and, in the manner of a traveler, attracted to those scenes that promise some clues. The spectacle of Europe and Russia as they coped with world war and two revolutions provided him with prime territory.

Ehrenburg first lived in Europe from 1909 to 1917, having left Russia to evade prosecution for revolutionary activity. When news of the February Revolution reached Paris, he went home in time to see another revolution. In 1921, with official sanction, he returned to Europe. A sketch of Ehrenburg in early-twenties Berlin is among the portraits of émigrés and passers-through in *Zoo*. Shklovsky bluntly points out how unusual Ehrenburg's status was as a Soviet citizen in Europe who could travel back and forth. "Nature has endowed Ehrenburg generously," Shklovsky observes; "he has a passport."[1]

---

[1]Viktor Shklovskii, *Zoo, ili Pis'ma ne o liubvi: Tret'ia Eloiza* (Berlin: Gelikon, 1923), p. 94.

Julio Jurenito is partly autobiographical, but the relation between Ehrenburg's life and writings will not be pursued here. The "unaligned traveler" of my title is the novel's narrator, a sometime poet and habitué of Paris cafes named Ilya Ehrenburg. (He is henceforth termed "Ehrenburg +" to distinguish him from the author.) This roving skeptic shares the foreground with Jurenito, an iconoclast who early in the novel attracts seven disciples: an assortment of Europeans, an American, an African, and the Russian-Jewish narrator. The book is ostensibly a *vita* of "the Teacher" and "Great Provocateur" by the disciple Ehrenburg +, and it exhibits some of the conventions of a saint's life.[2] But basically it is a picaresque novel in which Ehrenburg + and Jurenito are two variants of the picaro type — Jurenito, "the skilled manipulator," and Ehrenburg +, "the man of many adversities."[3] It spans the years from 1913 to 1921, and its occasionally farcical chapters fall into two parts. The first and longer section takes place mostly in Western Europe up to 1917; then the Teacher and his followers proceed to Russia, where they remain until 1921. In the final chapter, Ehrenburg + and the others (now without their dead master) make their way back to the West.

The novel's border-crossings (which plainly correspond to those of the author) are worth considering in some detail. The first — the arrival in Russia — shows how two revolutions look to foreigners and natives who are quite unprepared for what they find. The reader discovers, along with them, that in the process of "progressing," Russia is being spun upside down. When the travelers leave, it is largely to regain their equilibrium.

Andrei Bely, returning to Moscow in 1923 after two years abroad, described finding himself "in a surging, creating, somewhat insane and motley turmoil, feeling that this turmoil is the creative laboratory of future forms, perhaps as yet unknown to the world."[4] Bely's entrance into the crazy liveliness of Russia recalls the same transition in *Julio Jurenito*: an "insane and motley turmoil" is precisely what Jurenito and his disciples enter. They perpetrate and fall

---

[2] Veniamin Kaverin tells of a mid-twenties lecture he delivered on *Julio Jurenito's* resemblance to hagiography, and of the ensuing lively debate on its genre. See V. Kaverin, *Sobesednik* (Moscow: Sovetskii pisatel', 1973), pp. 24–27.

[3] The terms are Robert Alter's, in *Rogue's Progress: Studies in the Picaresque Novel* (Cambridge, Mass.: Harvard University Press, 1964), p. 72. *Julio Jurenito's* similarity to the archetypal picaresque novel, *Lazarillo de Tormes,* is detailed by Erika Ujvary-Maier in *Studien zum Frühwerk Il'ja Èrenburgs: Der Roman "Chulio Churenito"* (Zurich: Juris Druck, 1970), p. 79–96.

[4] Andrei Belyi, "Evropa i Rossiia," *Zvezda,* no. 3 (1924), p. 70.

victim to outlandish schemes in Europe, and Ehrenburg satirizes all quarters of Western society. But Europe, for all its absurdity, does not match the condition of Russia in revolution. Europe's old order may be straining its limits; Russian society's norms have already collapsed.

The shattering of forms was a literary as well as a social issue at this time, and *Julio Jurenito* is of particular interest because it involves both. It was enormously popular, and was enthusiastically appraised by such varied readers as Evgenii Zamiatin and Bukharin (who supplied a preface). A sampling of contemporary reactions reveals the range of literary concerns in the early twenties. The Formalist Yurii Tynianov criticizes Ehrenburg's failure to devise a new novelistic form and thus point Russian prose in a badly needed new direction; in terms of form, he writes, *Julio Jurenito*'s episodic plot is "the line of least resistance."[5] Zamiatin, while also critical of the novel's construction, finds it "very significant and (in Russian literature) original." He particularly admires the author's sharp irony, calling it a "European weapon" that Russian writers too seldom wield. And he praises him for directing that irony at all available targets, using the term that for Zamiatin marked a real artist: "He is, of course, a genuine heretic (and therefore — a revolutionary) of genuine proportions. A genuine heretic has the same property as dynamite: the explosion (creative) takes the line of *most* resistance."[6] Refusing to call anything sacred, Ehrenburg has resisted the pull of any ideology that might give him a fixed perspective.

Pro-Bolshevik critics faulted Ehrenburg for his lack of a fixed (and proper) perspective, but some were more astute than others. The formal and ideological properties of *Julio Jurenito* were perceptively interrelated by Shaginian. Ehrenburg's episodic form and skeptical stance, she points out, are both to be expected in a "period of liquidation," when the familiar world has been leveled. His loosely structured form is well-suited to the dynamite he ignites. Shaginian does object to the author's "moral relativism," but she rightly places his novel in the context of the satires of antiquity, which also ranged widely and irreverently over a culture in transition.[7]

---

[5] Iu. Van-Vezen [Iurii Tynianov], "200,000 metrov Il'i Erenburga," *Zhizn' iskusstva*, no. 4 (1924), p. 13.

[6] Evg. Zamiatin, "Erenburg," *Rossiia*, no. 8 (1923), p. 28.

[7] Marietta Shaginian, "Il'ia Erenburg: *Xulio Xurenito*," in *Literaturnyi dnevnik: Stat'i 1921–1923 gg.*, 2nd ed. (Moscow-Petersburg: Krug, 1923), pp. 143–50. First published as "Roman Il'i Erenburga" in "Literaturnaia nedelia," supplement to *Petrogradskaia Pravda*, no. 128 (1922). Il'ia Gruzdev, a young critic who belonged to the Serapion group, saw Ehrenburg's novel as a valuable experiment that successfully dealt

The genre she refers to is Menippean satire, mastered by Lucian and Petronius; *Julio Jurenito* conforms to it in many respects. The menippea is among those genres that the literary theorist Mikhail Bakhtin terms "carnivalized literature." His ideas about carnival and "carnivalization" are useful in analyzing how Ehrenburg handles his travelers' crossing from Europe to Russia and back.

Bakhtin argues that the features of the carnival celebration, which played an important role in antiquity and in Europe through the Renaissance, transformed literary culture, breaking down linguistic barriers and disrupting hierarchies. Carnival accounts for the generic heterogeneity of the menippea, "an astounding combination of what would seem to be absolutely diverse and incompatible elements: philosophical dialog, adventure and fantasy, underworld naturalism, utopia, etc." These elements were "bound into the organic whole of the genre," asserts Bakhtin, by "carnival and the carnival attitude toward the world." After the late seventeenth century, carnival largely ceases to be an immediate source of literary development. Carnivalization becomes a literary tradition, continuing to erode barriers between genres, and between ideologies.[8]

The European and Russian sections of *Julio Jurenito* are both carnivalized in the literary sense: philosophical argument, satire, and parody intermingle with the comic, the extraordinary, and the outrageous. What distinguishes them is expressed by the title of the second chapter set in Russia: "Everything Upside Down." The phrase comes from Jurenito's French disciple, M. Delet, who is brought to hysterics by 1918 Moscow. "Oh my dear Ehrenburg," he exclaims in distress, "the most terrible thing has happened to your country, it has turned upside down."[9] In the European chapters, Ehrenburg satirizes the

with the traditional novel's dissolution. His comments are quoted in A. G. [?], "Diskussii o sovremennoi literature," *Russkii sovremennik*, no. 2 (1924), p. 274.

[8]Mikhail Bakhtin, *Problems of Dostoevsky's Poetics,* trans. R. W. Rotsel (Ann Arbor, Mich.: Ardis, 1973), pp. 110–11. Bakhtin's theory and Ehrenburg's novel are discussed at greater length in my "Revolution as Carnival: Il'ja Ėrenburg's *Xulio Xurenito*," *Russian Language Journal* 34, no. 117 (1980): 127–33.

[9]*Neobychainye pokhozhdeniia Xulio Xurenito i ego uchenikov* (Moscow-Berlin: Gelikon, 1922), p. 247. Further references in the text are to this edition. The novel's page-long title, which begins *The Extraordinary Adventures of Julio Jurenito and His Disciples . . . ,*" catalogues the protagonists and some of the locales and topics. (Since the title character's name is transliterated into Russian from the Spanish, references to it in the Latin alphabet generally use the original spelling.) My translations incorporate parts of Ilya Ehrenbourg, *The Extraordinary Adventures of Julio Jurenito and His Disciples,* trans. Usick Vanzler (New York: Covici-Friede, 1930).

rigidity of Europe's social structure and values; in Russia, he satirizes the country's anomie. In the wake of revolution, people of all types are thrown together, adopting new roles and behavior. Russia, as Ehrenburg portrays it, is experiencing a communal inversion of behavior, a feature of the carnival mentality stressed by Bakhtin. "The carnivalistic life," writes the theorist, " . . . is to a degree 'life turned inside out,' 'life the wrong way 'round.' "[10] In Ehrenburg's "upside-down" Russia, the social effects of revolution resemble those of carnival (with obvious qualifications). And the literary impact of revolution on Ehrenburg and other writers is also comparable to the literary role of carnival in an earlier era.

One critic hostile to *Julio Jurenito* ridiculed its depiction of Russia by writing that "the whole revolution looks to Ehrenburg like some 'Karl Marx Cabaret.' "[11] What he intended as derision is actually a good description, particularly of the first scene set in Russia. Arriving in Petrograd, Jurenito and his disciples attend a mass meeting held at midnight in a circus arena. One speaker after another presents his or her version of the revolution's meaning. (The variety of their "acts" prompts the frustrated chairman to request that they "stick to the subject of the meeting, 'The Revolution and the Universe.' ") In Jurenito's speech, he marvels at the Russians' extraordinary delirium. "This isn't living you're doing here," he proclaims, "but raving." His frame of reference is the Europe he has just left; crazy as it may be, it is no match for this. The contrast between Russia and the West is made explicit as Jurenito tells the crowd: "I salute your insanity, your crack-brained whoops, your meaningless resolutions, and this circus arena in which you are piously and in absolute seriousness turning somersaults before a flabbergasted Europe!" (p. 235). The circus arena becomes a metaphor for the international scene — an arena in which a staid Europe watches an uninhibited, unhinged Russia "turn revolutions."

Ehrenburg's Russia differs from his Europe stylistically as well as socially. Because Soviet society is in a formative stage, it is less suited to standard satirical images. In the other countries visited, each disciple fits into an established hierarchy; they are all caricatures of national and social types. M. Delet is a self-indulgent Parisian, the American Mr. Cool a millionaire entrepreneur, Schmidt an ascetic

---

[10]Bakhtin, *Dostoevsky's Poetics*, p. 101.
[11]Ia. Braun, "Mefistofel' ili tsyplenok? (Tvorchestvo Il'i Erenburga)," *Sibirskie ogni*, no. 3 (1923), p. 167.

German chauvinist turned internationalist. Ehrenburg later said that he brought these characters to Russia in order to show how very far from Europe it then was: "I fantasized: what would a good French bourgeois or a Roman *lazzarone* do, finding himself in revolutionary Russia?"[12] Some of his foreigners experience reversals of status: Mr. Cool is thrown in jail, while the downtrodden African receives a high post in the Commissariat of Foreign Affairs. As in the carnival, one finds "a *jolly relativity* of every system and order."[13] Some role reversals also occur in Europe, but they entail a shift from one place in a hierarchy to another. In Russia old hierarchies have been dissolved. The case of Ercole, the happy-go-lucky Italian, illustrates the difference.

At home Ercole escapes the wartime army by masquerading as a priest, and makes a meteoric rise from tramp to Papal aide. Arriving in Russia and learning that one must earn one's ration ticket, he considers resuming his calling. He is quickly advised that religion is a field to be avoided, and finds an easy job with a Commission to Preserve Art Treasures. His duties are to go from street to street and pose as one or another ancient Roman statue. The distance between Ercole and a marble god is as great as that separating him from a priest. But in Rome he rises from one end of the social spectrum to the other, while in Moscow he is not usurping a position of status. A transient human statue fits nowhere in a social system: it is an unprecedented category. Ercole's Russian transformation is a more innovative literary device — and it reflects a society that proclaimed "the last shall be first," but in which changes of status were far more complex.

What Bely called Russia's "creative laboratory of future forms" changes Jurenito as well. His earlier exploits were aimed at hastening the destruction of Western civilization. During the world war, Jurenito researches better methods of killing, defending it as an extreme but necessary means of cleansing society. He is indifferent to what sort of world will follow. As a provincial commissar in Russia, however, his advocacy of destruction is combined for a time with a utopian concern for ends. As he becomes increasingly aware of the Soviet state's hypocrisy, Jurenito's utopianism wanes. His disillusionment is due not only to his fundamental nihilism, but also to what might be termed Russia's "de-carnivalization."

---

[12] Il'ia Erenburg, *Liudi, gody, zhizn'*, in *Sobranie sochinenii*, 9 vols. (Moscow: Khudozhestvennaia literatura, 1962–67), VIII, 297.

[13] Bakhtin, *Dostoevsky's Poetics*, p. 102.

In the spring of 1921, returning to Moscow from the provinces, Jurenito and his companions find that a resumption of pre-revolutionary forms (otherwise known as the New Economic Policy) is underway. The foreign capitalists are elevated from the bottom to the top of the social scale. Ehrenburg satirizes the Soviet regime's pragmatic reconciliation with bourgeois governments by having Cool and Delet courted as representatives of Western trade.[14] In other respects, too, the era of "delirium" was yielding to a more ordered existence. As Jurenito puts it, "people no longer walk on their heads here. They walk on ordinary, though very emaciated, legs" (p. 323). Ercole's services as a human statue are no longer required, and he is outraged to find Russia seeming more like Europe. "How everything changes overnight," he complains. "Some comptroller came around and offered me, Ercole Bambucci, a job! What sort of a job do you suppose? Shooting firecrackers? Hanging banners? Nothing of the sort. 'Productive labor!'... What's the use of Soviets in that case? How is this any different from Germany?" (p. 323). Jurenito agrees that Soviet Russia no longer represents an alternative to Europe, but for reasons of greater significance. He argues that the differences are only superficial, that neither society is genuinely pursuing its ideals. Fed up with promoting causes and with negating them, the "Great Provocateur" stages his own murder, leaving his disciples to sort things out for themselves.

To the harassed and hungry Ehrenburg +, the contrast between Europe and Russia still seems very great. Russia may be more stable than it was, but Europe is still far more predictable — and far more comfortable. Ehrenburg + unabashedly admits that he is longing for Europe's material comforts, but he adds (overtly rationalizing) that he is also attracted to Europe because he needs to concentrate. The first disciple has resolved to record his beloved Teacher's story, and he finds it impossible to write in Moscow. Not only is he handicapped by endless meetings and by shortages of food and paper: he also lacks the necessary peace of mind. In his words, "the atmosphere of history in

---

[14]Ehrenburg's description of Mr. Cool's dealings with Soviet officials resembles H. G. Wells's account of an American financier named Vanderlip whom he encountered on his 1919 visit; see his *Russia in the Shadows* (New York: George H. Doran, 1921), pp. 150–51. There is no reason to suppose that Ehrenburg borrowed this detail from Wells. Wells is mentioned, however, in connection with Jurenito's meeting with the "important communist," who is certainly Lenin. This encounter is primarily a parody of the "Grand Inquisitor" section of *The Brothers Karamazov*, but it also parodies the interview with Lenin that Wells reports in *Russia in the Shadows*.

the making was hardly favorable to the quiet labors of the chronicler" (pp. 335–36). The book's fictional author heads back to Europe because it is a place where one can live without being encroached upon, and a place where one can write.

The other disciples share his desire to leave "the purgatory of revolution" for "that cozy hell or, if this definition seems ill-advised, that unaired paradise" (p. 336). As these epithets suggest, the return to Europe is described with a heavy dose of the irony used throughout. But Ehrenburg is not entirely ironic when he describes the westward journey as "a single unbroken demonstration of the triumph of peace, order, prudence, and civilization" (p. 338). The West's injustices and absurdities, amply illustrated in the earlier chapters, are still present, and Ehrenburg continues to satirize them. After revolutionary Russia, however, the narrator is content to settle in among them. Once in Europe, his initial euphoria fades, and he slips back into skepticism. Civilization may seem more firmly established in the West than in Russia, but Ehrenburg + retains what Bukharin tolerantly called his "nihilistic 'hooliganism.' "[15] That phrase nicely characterizes the verbal finale, a multilingual farewell to the reader that concludes with a resounding, onomatopoetic crash.

Julio Jurenito is regarded in Soviet literary history as the forerunner of Soviet satires on the West. This need not be disputed, but it should be added that this novel, like many artistic progenitors, is atypical of the works that followed. Most Soviet writing that surveys the West implicitly or explicitly contrasts it with an idealized Russia. *Julio Jurenito,* as we have seen, does not. Not surprisingly, it is still criticized on those grounds. A Soviet scholar writes that Ehrenburg's treatment of Russia is inconsistent with the movement of the novel, since the reader expects that the chapters satirizing the West will be followed by an affirmative picture of Russia.[16] But one finds contradiction only if one assumes, with the scholar, that in a Soviet work the return from the West to Russia is by definition positive. In *Julio Jurenito* the crossing into "upside-down" Russia is not valorized: neither the return of Ehrenburg + to Russia nor his departure for Europe is based on principle. Russia may be chaotic and Europe may serve as a haven — but Ehrenburg +, always the traveler, does not fully identify himself with either place.

[15]N. Bukharin, "Predislovie," in Il'ia Erenburg, *Neobychainye pokhozhdeniia Xulio Xurenito i ego uchenikov,* 3rd ed. (Moscow-Leningrad: Gosizdat, 1927), p. 5.

[16]S. A. Malakhov in *Istoriia russkogo sovetskogo romana,* ed. L. G. Ershov et al. (Moscow-Leningrad: Nauka, 1965), I, 71.

His stance on leaving Russia recalls Dostoevsky's mocking description of Russian travel to Europe: "We Russians love the West; we love it, and when the going gets rough, westward we go."[17] Dostoevsky accuses his compatriots of going abroad because they are too lazy to do anything constructive in Russia. Ehrenburg +, free of nationalism, would see no need to defend himself against such a charge. His detachment is due neither to anti-Soviet sentiment nor to his identity as a Jew; while the author brings up the "Wandering Jew" image, he makes little of it. The hero's nihilism is attributable to the state of the twentieth-century world, which he finds an altogether problematic enterprise. Ehrenburg's traveler is unusual among fictional travelers of the twenties — and among Soviet writer-travelers themselves — in seeing both Europe and Russia as an outsider.

---

[17]F. M. Dostoevskii, *Zimnie zametki o letnikh vpechatleniiakh,* in *Polnoe sobranie sochinenii,* 30 vols. (Leningrad: Nauka, 1972–), V, 62.

10

EUROPE IMAGINED
The Lure of the Foreign

Isaac Babel, "Italian Sunshine" (1924)

Dostoevsky wrote disparagingly of Russians in Europe that they were seeking "a pleasant refuge," evading the demands of what he considered a meaningful and useful life. "We do not like difficulties," he moralizes in the account of his own European journey; "we are not accustomed to advancing a step at a time; we prefer flying to the goal in a single leap."[1] Since that is impossible, he implies, intention degenerates into inaction. The fictional Ehrenburg in *Julio Jurenito* does consider Europe a refuge from the difficulties of revolutionary Russia — but in doing so he is not betraying his goals for Russia, for he has none. In Isaac Babel's "Italian Sunshine," part of his story-cycle *Red Cavalry,* the desire to escape Russia's problems is linked with the desire to engage them — and to solve one of them "in a single leap."

Babel creates his character's obsession in the intense, compressed style that makes *Red Cavalry* a high point in twentieth-century prose. Victor Terras has written that "The Babelian short story at its best seems to realize that poetic balance between thought and image, line and color, movement and structure in a way which is characteristic of great lyric poetry."[2] "Italian Sunshine" is one of the best, and the

---

[1]F. M. Dostoevskii, *Zimnie zametki o letnikh vpechatleniiakh,* in *Polnoe sobranie sochinenii,* 30 vols. (Leningrad: Nauka, 1972–), V. The passages quoted are on pp. 63 and 62, respectively.

[2]Victor Terras, "Line and Color: The Structure of I. Babel's Short Stories in *Red Cavalry,*" *Studies in Short Fiction,* no. 3 (1966), p. 156. An excellent brief discussion of "Italian Sunshine" is in Martin B. Klotz, "Poetry of the Present: Isaak Babel's Red Cavalry," *Slavic and East European Journal* 18, no. 2 (1974): 166–67.

oppositions it balances are among those found in the greatest poetic works: light and dark, action and contemplation, power and impotence, the imagined and the real.

The contrast between abstraction and reality has been raised repeatedly in these chapters: all the works surveyed involve the distinction between the "made-up" Europe and the "real" Europe on which Tynianov rightly insisted.[3] The West imagined by writers and their characters is a distorted image of the actual place. Distortions differ in degree but they are always present, an immutable feature of the relation between object and image. "Italian Sunshine" is fascinating because it creates an image of Europe that combines two images: one peaceful and timeless, the other violent and contemporary. They have in common a polarity to the Russia surrounding the dreamer. "Italy" represents in the dreamer's mind a distant, exotic place; the respite and glory it promises are as far away as he can imagine from the Civil War front.

In *Flight,* as we have seen, Bulgakov shows the Civil War from the perspective of those who opposed the Revolution; *Red Cavalry* is set among Bolshevik troops and the civilians they control. The works are similar in their use of visual and psychological shading: both writers powerfully capture the stresses and uncertainties of the time. Both explore, too, the power of imagination to provide respite from pain. Respite is repeatedly sought in *Red Cavalry* by the narrator, Liutov. The cycle is based on Babel's experience as a journalist attached to General Budenny's cavalry in the Polish campaign of 1920. Liutov, the author's fictional counterpart, is an outsider in this milieu — an inexperienced intellectual among hotheaded Cossacks, merciless officers, and simple victims. It is often pointed out that the contrast between Liutov's qualities and those of the soldiers around him is the book's dominant opposition. But Babel's use of contrast goes beyond the painting of distinct opposites. One strength of his writing is the way he penetrates characters and images that appear to be of one piece.

Sidorov, who yearns for "the sun of Italy" (a possible translation of the title), is such a character. He seems wholly different from Liutov, and in most respects is: he appears to be a *chekist,* or secret police agent, the archetypal "insider" of the Civil War period. Babel's study of the inner Sidorov, however, reveals him to be another of *Red Cavalry*'s dreamers. In "Italian Sunshine," Liutov the dreamer

---

[3]Iurii Tynianov, "O slonenke," *Peterburg,* no. 1 (1922), p. 20.

encounters Sidorov the dreamer, in a surreptitious venture into the territory of a stranger's imagination. Their silent confrontation forms one strand of the brief story's drama.

On the evening of the story's action, Liutov has found warmth near the stove of a civilian kitchen redolent of fir twigs. That same tranquil corner is the setting of the preceding story. There Liutov had been stirred by his encounter with Pan Apolek, the magical, story-spinning artist. By beginning "Italian Sunshine" in that setting, Babel continues the mood of "impracticable dreams" in which "Pan Apolek" concluded. As Liutov walks home through the town's moonlit ruins, his mind goes on transforming the surrounding reality to fantasy. He dreads seeing Sidorov, billeted with him in the house of the grieving woman whose murdered father haunts *Red Cavalry*'s opening. To his relief, Sidorov is intently writing, and Liutov can be alone with his dreams. Late at night, Sidorov is called to headquarters. Liutov does not resist the impulse to add Sidorov's mind to his store of imaginative nourishment. He reads part of the letter left on the table, too timid to look for the first page.

Liutov says of Sidorov, when first describing him, that he "brought down upon me nightly the hairy paw of his melancholy."[4] Through his letter Sidorov affects him far more powerfully, not simply dampening his spirits, but tearing into bits "the pink cotton of my imagination" (p. 47). Compared to Sidorov's, his own dreams seem childlike and innocuous. That comment is all we are told of Liutov's reaction to the letter; the rest of the story elicits the reader's own.

The letter is written to a woman named Victoria, who seems responsible in part for Sidorov's frustrations: he refers to her as "bride who will never be wife" (p. 48). His discontent is more generalized than this, however: the letter details his anger with everything around him. The Civil War is being waged stupidly, and the Bolsheviks' political tacticians are no better than their military ones. His proposal for "a plan of real work" (p. 47) has been rebuffed at the Kremlin, and has won him only orders to the cavalry army at the front. An old

---

[4] I. Babel', "Solntse Italii," *Izbrannoe* (Moscow: Khudozhestvennaia literatura, 1966), p. 46. References in the text are to this edition. My translation draws on Isaac Babel, *The Collected Stories,* ed. and trans. Walter Morison (New York: World, 1960). The story was first published, as "Sidorov," in *Krasnaia nov',* no. 3 (1924). In the first edition of *Red Cavalry (Konarmiia)* (Moscow: Gosizdat, 1926), it appears with the title subsequently used.

wound prevents him from riding, however, and therefore from fighting. Sidorov is desperate to leave this place, where he can only be impotent. His plea is blunt: "Save me, Victoria. This governmental wisdom is driving me crazy, I'm drunk from boredom" (p. 47). His plan for escape is the outline of his fantasy.

Sidorov's plan is to be sent to Italy; Victoria, he hopes, has the influence to arrange for permission. He is already preparing for the trip, he tells her, by seriously studying the language. And yet linguistic skill seems irrelevant to his stated objective: to assassinate the Italian king, whose popularity and accommodation with "tame Socialists" (p. 48) are delaying a revolution that is ready to begin. He cautions Victoria to conceal his idea from the authorities, who would certainly oppose it. Let them be told that he's ill and depressed, that he has earned the trip, that he wants "Italian sunshine and bananas." Demonstrating his absorption in his destination, he emphasizes: "[Tell them it's] to get well again — and *basta*" (p. 48). In the last lines Liutov reads, Sidorov's reasoning gives way to longing, and his deeper feelings emerge: "Italy has gotten into my heart like an obsession. The thought of that country I have never seen is as sweet to me as a woman's name, as your name, Victoria..." (p. 48, ellipsis in original).

The violent act and the vision of Italian sunshine are polar but inseparable parts of Sidorov's dream. The desire for warmth and comfort is not a "cover" for his revolutionary plan; nor does he devise the plan to rationalize his longing to escape. Sidorov plots the assassination for the thrill of acting dramatically and alone, of single-handedly speeding world revolution. His vision of an exotic, sensuous place fulfills the other side of his desire to be free of constraints, and to be emotionally satisfied.

Finishing the letter, one understands how well Liutov's description of Sidorov as a "pining murderer" (p. 47) captures the man. Emotional words link Italy with Victoria, but Sidorov's behavior indicates that his pining cannot be satisfied by a woman. He returns before dawn; Liutov, unable to sleep, watches as he settles again at the table. The narrator had already seen some of the material of Sidorov's dreaming: an Italian textbook, a picture of the Forum, and a map of Rome covered with crosses and dots. (The map itself hints of Sidorov's dualism: are the spots marked for sightseeing or sabotage?) Now the methodical dreamer turns to two other props, each feeding one part of his fantasy. Liutov's vantage point cannot be improved upon:

Stooping, he sat down at the table and opened an album of Rome. The magnificent gilt-edged book stood before his olive expressionless face. Over his rounded back gleamed the jagged ruins of the Capitol and the Colosseum, illuminated by the sunset. A photograph of the royal family was inserted right there, between the large glossy pages. The scrap of paper torn from a calendar pictured the amiable puny king Victor Emmanuel with his black-haired wife, his heir Prince Umberto, and a whole brood of princesses. [p. 49]

Babel's juxtaposition of a letter with a photograph powerfully concludes his story "A Letter," placed shortly before this in the collection. In "Italian Sunshine," two pictures also condense the oppositions carefully built up from the story's opening lines. The vista, unreal in its gilt-edged frame and mellow in the evening light; the prosaic closeup of a family that is unknowingly posing as a target. These seeming opposites form a figurative double-exposure that is a likeness of Sidorov's dream. Italy promises timelessness and repose — and also the chance to instantaneously move history.[5]

One is reminded of Olesha's heroine in *A List of Assets,* who identifies Europe with individual freedom. The use of Europe in "Italian Sunshine," however, is quite different. Olesha is exploring a contemporary political issue: the nature of the Soviet and Western systems. It is essential to the play that Europe be the heroine's destination. Sidorov's plan to start an Italian revolution does relate to a topical problem — the Soviet need for successful revolutions in Europe. Here, as in Olesha, the protagonist regards Europe as a place where one can act independently. But Italy — the most exotic part of Europe to a Russian, and one with many associations in Russian poetry — functions in the story primarily as an opposite to "here," not as a part of the West. Its polarity to the setting and to the protagonist are more important than its Europeanness.[6] It is incongruous that Sidorov, the murderous Cheka agent, should gaze so fixedly at symbols of Europe's past, and should dream so helplessly of light and warmth.

---

[5]The final image of Sidorov furthers the idea of his duality. In the dark, gloomy room Liutov observes "the lifeless face of Sidorov, an inanimate mask, hanging above the yellow flame of the candle" (p. 49). Sidorov, lit by what might be a conspirator's or a dreamer's candle, is linked with both the light and the darkness.

[6]Vladimir Lidin wrote several stories in the twenties about yearnings for foreign respite in which the dreamer's destination was significant not in itself, but in its polarity to Russia. See, for example, V. G. Lidin, "Ispaniia," *Ogonek,* no. 35 (1923), pp. 4–5, and "Koroleva brazil'skaia," in *Myshinye budni* (Moscow-Berlin: Gelikon, 1923), pp. 27–39.

One must bear in mind, evaluating the literary uses of the West, that "Europe," "America," and their parts can stand for the antonym of an individual's definition of 'Russia," and that they thus have an infinite number of meanings. Babel's story describes a plan for a journey to Italy, but it tells more about a figurative sort of travel: the power of the imagination to transport an individual from one place, and from one state of mind, to another. It also demonstrates the power of Babel's talent for transporting the reader into his artistic world.

"Italian Sunshine" lies near the "imagined" pole of Tynianov's two Europes; the accounts of actual Western travels in the next chapter move us toward the other extreme. *Toward* the real West, but not quite there. A place one observes is still imagined — a set of images gathered by the individual traveler, who transports it into the medium of language.

I I

WRITERS ABROAD
The Role of Soviet Traveler

Russian literature is rich in accounts of European journeys. The life and landmarks of Europe have been described by generations of Russian travelers, including most major writers since the eighteenth century. By the turn of the twentieth, the situation of the Russian in Europe was rife with clichés. The literary repertoire contained many permutations of traveler types, from admirers to sharp-tongued satirists. It may well have seemed to the prospective writer-traveler that every move in what Hugh McLean calls "the tourist's game of comparing cultures" had been made.[1]

Writing of Nikolai Leskov's 1875 trip to Europe, McLean comments that "for an educated Russian in the nineteenth century this game was hard to win." Western Europe was so obviously ahead in so many respects that the Russian traveler was hard pressed to make a case for Russia's superiority: "The Russian could only resort to intangibles: national character, the nation's 'youth' (whatever that might mean), its pristine vigor." What McLean calls "intangibles" were given a definite shape by the Revolution. The nation in its new form was now literally young. Russia's status as the first socialist state was a visible index not only of its potential, but also of its achievement. Technologically, Russia might still lag behind the West; ideologically it could claim to have advanced beyond it.

---

[1]Hugh McLean, *Nikolai Leskov, The Man and His Art* (Cambridge, Mass.: Harvard University Press, 1977), p. 318. The quotations that follow are on the same page.

Most writers traveling abroad after the Revolution were thus conscious of playing a different role than had their predecessors. The traditions of pre-revolutionary travel writing influenced Soviet writers: traces of such forerunners as Fonvizin, Karamzin, Dostoevsky, Saltykov-Shchedrin, and Gorky surface in their works.[2] But while inventing new moves in the Russian tourist's game of comparing cultures, they were also starting a fresh game. The role of "the Russian abroad" now belonged to the past; "the Soviet citizen abroad" was a role awaiting interpreters.

The traveler often feels a tension between his or her individual identity and the unavoidable position of national type and spokesperson. Because travel was strictly controlled in Soviet Russia, particularly after the mid-twenties, Soviet citizens abroad were much more likely than pre-revolutionary writers to play the role of national representative. Writers did, however, make personal trips as well as official ones; Babel and Pasternak were among those who visited relatives in Europe in the early twenties. Others also pursued personal business, many passing through Berlin and consulting with Russian publishers there. The literary record is only partial, of course: not all writers recorded or published their experiences. The variety of published travel writing, however, is broad. It includes sketches such as Sergei Esenin's "The Iron Mirgorod" (1923), fictionalized trips like Mikhail Slonimsky's "Westerners" (1928), essays and letters, journeys in prose and poetry.[3] The diversity of approaches points the scholar in as many directions. In this chapter, I follow one path — writers' conceptions of

---

[2]References are to Denis Fonvizin, *Letters from the Second and Third Journey Abroad* (1777–78, 1784–85); Nikolai Karamzin, *Letters of a Russian Traveler* (1791–92 and 1794–95, complete edition 1801); Fedor Dostoevskii, *Winter Notes on Summer Impressions* (1863); Mikhail Saltykov-Shchedrin, *Abroad* (1881); Maksim Gor'kii, *City of the Yellow Devil* (1906).

[3]Sergei Esenin, "Zheleznyi Mirgorod," in *Sobranie sochinenii*, 5 vols. (Moscow: Khudozhestvennaia literatura, 1962), IV, 257–68; Mikhail Slonimskii, "Zapadniki," in *Sochineniia*, 4 vols. (Moscow-Leningrad: Zemlia i fabrika, 1928–29), II, 5–54. Also of interest is Vsevolod Ivanov, *Chudesnye pokhozhdeniia portnogo Ivana Fokina* (Leningrad: Gosizdat, 1925). Ivanov's satirical picaresque was written before he had traveled abroad. He humorously suggests that he has chosen to write about a European journey because he is tired of writing in the detailed way in which one feels obliged to write about Russia (p. 42). Ivanov's fictional journey is an example of a writer's desire for respite from Russian subject-matter.

Among the other contemporary travel accounts by professional writers are Vera Inber's 1928 *Amerika v Parizhe*, in *Sobranie sochinenii*, 4 vols. (Moscow: Khudozhestvennaia literatura, 1965), III, 5–128; Ol'ga Forsh, *Pod kupolom* (Leningrad: Priboi, 1929); and Boris Pil'niak, *O'kei: Amerikanskii roman* (Moscow: Federatsiia, 1933).

the new role of Soviet traveler — and turn down two of its branches. We consider first the non-fiction travelogues of several prose writers, and then selected poems by Mayakovsky. His travel-linked poetry, which arises from seven foreign trips between 1922 and 1929, shows the complexity of the traveler's role.

A look at the travelogues brings out several facets of the traveler's image. The awareness of representing a new country was not imposed on travelers by Soviet constraints alone. Roles were also shaped by Western assumptions about the Soviet regime. As citizens of a place about which much was imagined, but little known, Soviet travelers were observed with particular curiosity abroad. The spirit of this curiosity varied widely according to milieu: leftists were adoring, while those antipathetic to the Soviet experiment were suspicious at best. In *Now in the West* (1924), Nikolai Nikitin summarizes a widespread attitude of the early twenties, when many European governments did not even recognize the Soviet state: "All of us — those people from Soviet Russia, eccentric, dangerous and mad — all were cooks of that kettle which Europe feared, where revolution was being made."[4] Nikitin's comment suggests that the traveler's identity was in part based on nationality and imposed by observers. This typologized role, as I have suggested, was likely to diverge from the individual way in which each traveler saw himself.

One's control over the written journey, it should be remembered, is vastly greater than over the lived journey. On paper, each returning traveler can maintain complete control over his image. The writer-traveler designs the role he wants to play — a design that may be completed even before setting out from home. Nikitin's literary approach to the role of traveler illustrates the writer's guiding hand. He describes his book's origins and genre in a foreword reminiscent of Shklovsky's in *Zoo*. While not dwelling on structure and device, Nikitin resembles Shklovsky in stressing his contrived and personal use of a non-fiction form. The book itself has both documentary and fictional elements: it is largely reportage, but includes letters and a few short stories. Nikitin pointedly distinguishes it from journalism, terming it "a novel of a person who left Russia and found himself in other circumstances." Yet he also avoids a fictional extreme, joking that his travel companion Pilniak has gone too far. No one should believe what

---

[4] Nikolai Nikitin, *Seichas na Zapade: Berlin–Rur–London* (Leningrad-Moscow: Petrograd, 1924), p. 46.

Pilniak prints about this trip, he warns: Nikitin has seen his notes and attests to the discrepancy between experience and depiction. The distinction between experience and its literary use has been emphasized in the chapter on Shklovsky, that most self-conscious of formal manipulators. *Now in the West* is not as stylistically clever as *Zoo*; like any ostensibly non-fiction travelogue, however, it is shaped by the author's artistic conception of the traveler as narrator and protagonist of a story.

The gap between experience and depiction is one place to pause in a search for the writer-traveler; the gap between experience and expectation is another. On the road, all travelers learn that preconceptions and intentions are vulnerable to reality. Vignettes of expectations overturned recur in travelogues of the twenties. Given the vivid presence of Europe in Russian thought and literature, the expectations of these travelers were likely to be firm. Those who had previously been in Europe brought with them memories as well. For seasoned travelers, as for everyone going abroad, Russia's post-revolutionary condition was an added piece of mental baggage. The status of Soviet Russia as a country in flux, a homeland with a new identity, made writers particularly sensitive to how they saw the West.

One experienced traveler was Andrei Sobol, who had lived in Europe from 1909 to 1915 as a political émigré. In 1926 he published *Through Foreign Parts*, a group of essays about a recent journey. Sobol (known for his pre-revolutionary prose and for fiction concerning post-1917 transition pains) has an eye for moments of foiled expectations. The book opens on an overcrowded westbound train; the author's first encounter is with a Russian woman who excitedly anticipates that when they cross the European border everything will suddenly become orderly and comfortable. She runs out on her first "European" platform to breathe the "cultured air," only to find three Latvian soldiers in the midst of a raging brawl. Sobol satirizes the long outmoded supposition that Europe will be a model of decorum and advancement; approaching Berlin, however, he lapses into the same posture. While convinced of Soviet Russia's ideological progressiveness, Sobol is also aware of its current chaotic state. Russians arriving in Berlin, he writes, used to feel that they had left Asiatic chaos and dirt for Western order. Now, with Moscow in far greater disarray than before the Revolution, how could he escape the same feeling? Setting off around Berlin, this Soviet traveler admits to experiencing the old trepidation of the "barbaric" Russian. But his reversion to the clichéd role does not last long. Expectation and observation take over, as Sobol finds his ideological preference for Soviet Russia supported by Berlin's own troubled condition. The decadent and unstable Berlin of the twenties, he decides, is not to be envied such unique attractions as its "political menu," which "offers a new item daily, just as in the finest restaurants."[5] Soviet travelers, certainly, were not alone in making such evaluations of post-war Europe, with its many economic and political difficulties. Especially in Germany, it was easy to find confirmation of the view that Europe, too, needed revolution.

Writers' preconceptions, experience, and literary design all intermingle in the traveler one meets in print. Facts can be hard to isolate. Sobol, for one, does not aim at documentary scope or detail. He takes his time with miscellaneous impressions — the comic punctiliousness of a Cook's Tour, the atmosphere of an evening sirocco in Sorrento. The writer of *Through Foreign Parts* seems a particularly unfocused traveler by comparison with Boris Kushner, whose title heralds his precision: *103 Days in the West, 1924–1926*. In his sweep through ten countries Kushner plays the pragmatic, didactic traveler, concerned primarily with what his country can learn from the West. Among literary reportage of the period, this is the most thorough treatment of European technology. Kushner wants to transform Russian attitudes as well as Soviet industry: one of his aims is to dispel the "haze of romanticism" still covering Europe.[6] But that does not make his picture of Europe uniformly somber. Capitalism might be exploitative and decaying; Western technology, however, merited admiration and study. Kushner's dogmatic stance is summarized by his own terse comparison between the West and Soviet Russia: "A technological culture that outstrips ours by many decades. A social culture that lags behind ours by a whole era." The book abounds in such formulaic statements, and it reflects the Soviet drive to industrialize and to demonstrate the superiority of socialism. The style is notable for more than its rhetoric. *103 Days in the West* is a good sample of the sort of documentary writing ("literature of fact") espoused in the late twenties by such writers and theorists as Nikolai

---

[5] Andrei Sobol', *Po chuzhim kraiam* (Moscow: Ogonek, 1926), p. 24.

[6] Boris Kushner, *103 dnia na Zapade, 1924–1926 gg.*, 2nd ed. (Moscow-Leningrad: ZIF, 1930), p. 25. Subsequent quotations are on pp. 6 and 270, respectively. The first edition was published in 1928. Parts of the book had previously appeared in *Krasnaia nov'*, *Novyi lef*, *Novy mir*, and *Zvezda* between 1925 and 1927.

Chuzhak, Sergei Tretiakov, Osip Brik, and Shklovsky.[7] Kushner is explicitly engaged in forging a new breed of foreign observer. What we need, he argues, are techniques of description capable of conveying the rapid, unceasing motion of the present. Literary technology must advance at the rate of machine technology. Writers today cannot settle for what Kushner calls the "old-time traveler's" easy-going method. He half-seriously comments that formerly writers faced with the task of describing a city would spend a whole chapter in lively dialogue with a hotel proprietress about the slow arrival of their fried eggs. No such artful dodging will satisfy the dedicated factographer. In Kushner's rendition, the role of Soviet writer abroad is that of a keen-eyed gatherer of useful data. For a traveler who thus defines his role, Europe is a means to a Soviet end.

Mayakovsky also dramatically illustrated the Soviet traveler's reaction to Western technology. His penchant for making the abstract literal shows up in his earliest poem inspired by foreign travel, "Paris (Chats with the Eiffel Tower)" (1923). A friendly, cajoling poet tries to convince the symbol of European progress to come to Russia, where it will be more valued and put to better use. The poem's silliness works: it captures the Soviet traveler's desire to acquire technology, and his conviction that in Soviet society it will play a nobler role than under capitalism. "Broadway" (1926) also combines admiration of Western technology with an assertion of Soviet achievement. Overwhelmed by New York's skyscrapers and glitter, the poet loses his composure; he begins to sound like the narrator of "150,000,000" in the technological wonderland of mythical Chicago. At the end of the poem, though, he defines his place amidst all these buildings that reach to the moon:

[7]Shklovsky found Kushner's reportage exemplary, calling it "a textbook of how to see." See V. Shklovskii, "*103 dnia na Zapade* B. Kushnera," *Novyi lef*, no. 11–12 (1927), pp. 71–72. Reprinted with other articles on documentary prose in *Literatura fakta*, ed. N. F. Chuzhak (1929; rpt. Munich: Wilhelm Fink, 1972), p. 250. Another article of interest, praising the factographic writing of Kushner and of Sergei Tret'iakov, is V. Pertsov, "Noveishaia proza," *Novy lef*, no. 12 (1928), pp. 15–21.

Tynianov's papers evidently include a satirical "dream" about a *Lef* editorial meeting at which Mayakovsky and others try to indoctrinate him in the value of writing reportage. He and another timid, dubious outsider finally screw up the courage to ask how they're supposed to write travelogues if they can't afford to buy a ticket. (Mayakovsky sternly advises them that one can sit at home and write about Paris.) The humorous sketch is quoted (apparently complete) in V. Kaverin, *Sobesednik* (Moscow: Sovetskii pisatel', 1973), pp. 136–39. Tynianov makes some interesting comments on writing about the West from a distance under his pseudonym Iu. Van-Vezen ("Zapiski o zapadnoi literature," *Knizhnyi ugol*, no. 7 [1921], pp. 31–36).

"Soviets / have their own pride: / at the bourgeois / we look from on high."[8] Mayakovsky expresses the same ideological supremacy in "Verses on the Soviet Passport," which concludes his collection *There and Back*. Insulted by the nasty reaction to his papers on a European train, the poet angrily displays his badge of citizenship, inviting the world to envy his status. The West may be "higher" in some respects; the Soviet traveler, however, looks up to no one, because he is ahead of everyone in history.

Conclusions of this sort punctuate most Soviet travel impressions. "Broadway" illustrates the frequently fine line in Soviet travel writing between the traveler as individual observer and as pronouncer of certainties. Writers slip from the first person singular into the first person plural, obscuring the distinction between them. Observations are often formulaic, packaged in standard sets of contrasts: the exploiters and exploited of the West; Western problems and Soviet promise; capitalism's arbitrariness and the Soviets' rational purpose. It can be difficult to judge when a writer is repeating standard views and when he is speaking for himself. One cannot assume, because a writer may espouse an official position, that he is being hypocritical: he may well have come to that position by his own route. Sometimes, however, one can see a line between the "individual" and "national" perspectives in a given work, and separate the writer from the "Soviet citizen abroad" he is playing. Having sketched some contours of the writer-traveler, let us look more closely at this feature. Mayakovsky's poetry offers good examples of the tension that can exist between the single and collective voice.

This tension is particularly evident in works involving depar-

---

[8]Vladimir Maiakovskii, "Brodvei," in *Polnoe sobranie sochinenii*, 13 vols. (Moscow: Khudozhestvennaia literatura, 1955–61), VII, 57. Other poems mentioned in this paragraph are "Parizh (Razgovorchiki s Eifelovoi bashnei)," in *Polnoe*, IV, 75–78 and "Stikhi o sovetskom pasporte," in *Polnoe*, X, 68–71. There are, it should be said, some significant differences between travel commentary on Europe and on America. America was less known, more exotic territory. Aleksandr Rodchenko's impressions of his stay in Paris while working on the Soviet pavilion for the 1925 International Exposition of Fine Arts are interesting in this regard. "I should really go see America," he writes, "not this old-womanish Paris. . . . In terms of artistic taste, Paris is the provinces" ("Rodchenko v Parizhe: Iz pisem domoi," *Novyi lef*, no. 2 [1927], pp. 15–16). Mayakovsky's article "Parizhskie provintsii," as the title indicates, makes a similar point. The Russo-European tables have turned: Soviet Russia is culturally as well as ideologically avant-garde (*Polnoe*, IV, 254–56). On Rodchenko and others involved in the 1925 Exposition see S. Frederick Starr's stimulating *Melnikov: Solo Architect in a Mass Society* (Princeton, N.J.: Princeton University Press, 1978), which has much of value on Soviet and European design of this period.

tures and returns, transitions between the West and Russia. Points of crossing are of heightened intensity, and can spark introspection in the most jaded of travelers. In "Homeward!" the contrast between the West and home is bound up with Mayakovsky's identity as a writer. Within the poem, written at sea en route from America in 1925, he begins to shed the role of Soviet writer abroad and to contemplate the role he will take up at home.

The first part of "Homeward!" describes the returning traveler's unsettled state — a mood exacerbated by the carousing on the deck above. He has felt useless abroad: the role of traveler has pushed aside his role as writer, and he feels his talent rusted and wasted. The senseless foreign environment yields in his thoughts to the ordered, rational society where he is headed. His desire to reclaim the roles of native and of writer is so strong that it is propelled into hyperbole. In a series of demands so extreme that they border on irony, he declares his wish to become indispensable to his country. Let him be regulated by commissars, set a quota of verses, regarded as a vital part of Soviet production. These lines reflect Mayakovsky's long-standing ambivalence about the writer's relation to the state; they also reflect the desire of the depressed returning writer to be fully integrated into his native country. The list of demands that he be central to the country's well-being accelerates, ending on a note of certainty that he will be. But the original closing lines, excised by the poet, present the possibility that the returning traveler will have to remain a traveler:

> I want my country to understand me.
> But if I'm not understood / what of it.
> I shall pass through my native land / to one side
> as a slanting rain passes by.[9]

The poet has learned while abroad how unsatisfying the role of writer-traveler can be; he now anticipates exchanging it for that of native. But the role of "Soviet writer at home," the closing suggests, may also prove difficult to play. Traveling in the West has both inten-

---

[9]Maiakovskii, "Domoi," in *Polnoe*, VII, 92–95. The variant ending is on p. 489. Edward J. Brown analyzes the poem in his thorough and sensitive *Mayakovsky: A Poet in the Revolution* (Princeton, N.J.: Princeton University Press, 1973), pp. 297–302. The lines quoted are in his translation, p. 301. An important analysis of the impact of Mayakovsky's early travels on him and on the LEF circle is Robert C. Williams's chapter on the poet in his *Artists in Revolution* (Bloomington: Indiana University Press, 1977); see especially pp. 148–49.

sified his tie to home and renewed his anxiety over how satisfactorily the elements of poet and country can combine. Mayakovsky does not propose an alternative to his "native land" — there is no place where he could be better understood. The only alternative, if poet and country prove incompatible, appears to be homelessness.

"Homeward!" shows the writer trying to merge his individual and national selves. Two selves of this sort can also be identified in other poetry of border crossing. *The Shadow of a Friend* (1936), Nikolai Tikhonov's cycle about his European travels, provides a contrasting example from the following decade. In Tikhonov the poet's two roles are separable, but coexist without conflict. Tikhonov had been widely regarded as a promising poet in the early twenties; he was influenced by Gumilev and the Acmeists, and later by Khlebnikov and Pasternak. By the early thirties, he had become an official of writers' organizations and an establishment figure. In this travel cycle, a dichotomy between the individual and collective is evident starting with the title poem. Konstantin Batiushkov's 1814 poem of the same name, to which Tikhonov implicitly alludes, is an elegy for a close friend; here, however, the "friend" is the masses of European workers struggling against capitalism and fascism. The best parts of *The Shadow of a Friend* are those passages in which Tikhonov turns from ideology and travelogue to contemplate the creative process. One such passage concludes the title poem. Like Batiushkov's elegy, it is set at night on shipboard. At the end of a long reverie, the narrator watches the sea birds sweeping in and out of the waves, and likens their flight to the writing of poetry. The endeavor of the poet merges with the scene he observes. The final lines carry Tikhonov's metaphor, better than the translation can convey: "We cut into the wave / Of verse / With a despairing wing / And with a mocking cry / and with an intimate cry."[10]

Here the poet is a lonely seeker, throwing himself into the uncertain process of finding the words that express his unique self. A polar voice, in which the poet turns his observations into certainties, characterizes a number of the poems which follow. Tikhonov's stance of supra-individual traveler is illustrated by the closing poem. Called "Gas Mask," it is a melodramatic warning to Europe about the war that hangs over it. This is a postscript to the journey: the previous

---

[10]Nikolai Tikhonov, "Ten' druga," in *Izbrannye proizvedeniia,* 2 vols. (Moscow-Leningrad: Khudozhestvennaia literatura, 1951), I, 132.

poem, "Return," describes Tikhonov's homecoming to Leningrad. Having returned home, he looks back on a misguided Europe from a place where "reason has not died out." The writer is speaking not as an individual but as one who belongs to that realm of reason, as a spokesman for what he calls "the land of lands." The poem's rhetoric (and that of much of Tikhonov's cycle) is typical of travel writing of the thirties, which focused on fascism's rise.

Mandelstam's "Journey to Armenia" does not fit this pattern; it also breaks the mold of the "European journey" by assuming a different definition of Europe. In "Homeward!" Mayakovsky, the most complex creator of the role of Soviet traveler in the twenties, raised an issue explored by Mandelstam in the most original travel work of the thirties. "Journey to Armenia," like "Homeward!", is written by a traveler who ends by questioning how one can now play the role of native.

12

NARROWED BORDERS

Osip Mandelstam, "Journey to Armenia" (1933)

Mandelstam's widow has written that he could have been among the writers who traveled to Europe during the twenties. Bukharin, who intervened on their behalf in many matters, had given him a supporting letter, as had the editor-critic Aleksandr Voronsky. The poet had been abroad in his youth: after finishing St. Petersburg's Tenishev School in 1907, he spent about a year in Paris, and in 1909–10 he studied at Heidelberg. Both trips included brief visits to Italy. His Italian travels, according to Nadezhda Mandelstam, left him frustrated, feeling that he had never really been there. He regarded the Mediterranean as the center of culture and of history; his ties to European culture were personal and deep. Why then, she asks, did he not pursue the possibility of a return journey? This is her answer:

> In my younger days I did not always fully understand the connection between M.'s actions and what he wrote. . . . I have now found the reason for his renunciation of a second journey to Europe in his article on Chaadayev, where he writes that Chaadayev, having visited the West, "the historical world," nevertheless returned to Russia. The fact that he found his way home again was very much to his credit in M.'s eyes. With the same naive and stubborn consistency because of which he refused to have a watch, he thought of Chaadayev's return to Russia and himself decided to renounce the chance of revisiting Europe.[1]

---

[1]Nadezhda Mandelstam, *Hope Against Hope*, trans. Max Hayward (New York: Atheneum, 1970), p. 252. The poet's ideas about "the historical world" arise in numer-

Nadezhda Mandelstam's explanation itself raises further questions: how did Mandelstam interpret the philosopher's return a century before, and how did it relate to him? My discussion of the 1915 Chaadaev essay (see Part 1) presents his position. Mandelstam assumed Russia's cultural unity with Europe, and felt Russia to be linked with the West by a common view of the individual's primacy. The poet interpreted Chaadaev's return from his European travels as an affirmation of Russia: it affirmed Russia's unique national identity, and at the same time affirmed Russia's connection to the foundations of European thought. In committing himself to Russia, Chaadaev was not cutting himself off from the West, but demonstrating that for the Russian who understands their close relationship, no border exists.

But why should his example have made Mandelstam resolve not to leave Russia for a visit to the West? Only a journey was at issue, not permanent departure. Nadezhda Mandelstam has said that he feared he would not be permitted to return home,[2] but the above excerpt from her memoirs points toward theoretical rather than practical considerations. Apparently Mandelstam felt that to have sought permission for a European trip would have implied his belief that Russia had lost its historical identity, that it had been deflected from its own heritage and from what it shared with Europe. One could no longer travel abroad as easily as in Mandelstam's youth; the border between Russia and the West was now a more formidable barrier. Approval had to be sought from authorities who believed in Soviet Russia's separateness from capitalist Western Europe. And one now needed a purpose for foreign travel — a reason that could be interpreted as an acknowledgement that Europe did, in fact, represent something Russia lacked. For Mandelstam to have gone to Europe, then, would have been in a sense the same as for Chaadaev to have remained in Europe. Tortured logic, perhaps, but the memoirist's comments about her husband's "naive and stubbon consistency" support it. "Some things in his writing had the force of vows for him," she writes. "Such was . . . the renunciation of Europe in the article about Chaadayev. This article was written in his early youth, but his view of the world

---

ous parts of the two volumes of his widow's memoirs; see for example *Hope Against Hope*, pp. 247–52, and *Hope Abandoned*, trans. Max Hayward (New York: Atheneum, 1974), pp. 468–70 and 489–95. On Mandelstam's time abroad see Clarence Brown's evocative *Mandelstam* (Cambridge: Cambridge University Press, 1973), pp. 32–46. Other relevant material can be found in the burgeoning critical literature on Mandelstam.

[2]The comment was made in conversation with the author, September 1980.

had already formed, and he was true to the vows he took then until his death."[3]

Mandelstam's "renunciation of Europe" did not extend to those areas within the Soviet Union which he regarded as part of Western culture. These were the Crimea and Armenia, linked by the Black Sea and by history to the Mediterranean. Nadezhda Mandelstam writes that he viewed them "as outposts . . . of Christianity, of the Hellenistic and Judaic world."[4] He felt a particular affinity for Armenia, with its ancient links to Biblical times and to Greece and Rome, and long desired to go there. Going to Armenia, while it did not entail crossing the Soviet border, also required permission — and this was not easy for a suspect writer to obtain. Finally, with Bukharin's help, the journey was arranged, and the Mandelstams visited Armenia from May to November of 1930. Since the mid-twenties, he had written little poetry: those were very difficult years. The trip brought that period of silence to an end.[5] It left a mark on his prose as well as on his poetry: the following summer he wrote his last published work, a highly unconventional travelogue entitled, conventionally enough, "Journey to Armenia."

Writers were on the move across the Soviet Union during the thirties, dispatched to the various republics to report on agricultural and industrial progress. Reportage and fiction based on such travels account for a substantial proportion of the decade's literary output. (One example is Valentin Kataev's novel *Time, Forward!*, discussed in Part 4.) Much of this writing focuses on the yielding of the old social and economic order to the Soviet system. The title of "Journey to Armenia" suggests that it belongs to this genre; the work itself, therefore, appeared to flaunt the genre's conventions. Here were no blast furnaces or mass agricultural projects: the author paid far more attention to Armenia's ancient cultural resources than to its present development. He also devoted much space to his own thoughts, and to ideas that seemingly bore no relation to his subject. Had the eight brief essays comprising "Journey to Armenia" been published separately or under a different title, they might have provoked less furor than they did.[6]

---

[3]*Hope Against Hope*, p. 252.

[4]*Hope Abandoned*, p. 491.

[5]Nadezhda Mandelstam writes in *Hope Against Hope* that "the journey to Armenia restored the gift of poetry to M., and a new period of his life began" (p. 180).

[6]On the attacks on Mandelstam for "Journey to Armenia," and on the effort to have him repudiate it, see Nadezhda Mandelstam, *Hope Abandoned*, pp. 418–22.

While "Journey to Armenia" is wholly different from the works describing Soviet society's transformation, it does have to do with how society was being reordered — with what Mandelstam in an earlier essay called "social architecture."[7] It deals more explicitly with individual development, focusing on how individuals perceive and order the world around them. "Journey to Armenia" is largely about the individual's relationship to the outer world. The seemingly disparate observations on Armenia and on much else can be reduced to a few common denominators. They concern what might be called personal systems of seeing, insights or patterns that one can acquire from several sources: from culture, from language, from nature, from other people.

One expects the writer of a travel account to observe his surroundings with care; Mandelstam's preoccupation with sight is intense. It is clear from the opening paragraph that he believes observation to be an active art which rewards dedication. "On the island of Sevan," he begins, "which is distinguished by two most worthy architectural monuments of the seventh century, . . . I spent a month . . . schooling myself to the contemplation of the two or three dozen tombs scattered as if they were a flowerbed amidst the monastery dormitories, which repairs have made young again."[8] The relics of Armenia's history fascinate him, as this excerpt indicates: he is drawn to them for what they tell of the past and for what they can teach about seeing and understanding the present. Even an eye accustomed to close observation, he suggests, cannot absorb things fully at first sight. He makes this point when he writes, of another product of Armenia's Christian heritage: "The teeth of your vision crumble and break when you look for the first time at Armenian churches" (p. 207). His descriptions of objects viewed in his memory while in Armenia are equally expressive. The passages on French Impressionist painting contain an extensive and vivid account of how to see. Preparing to look at the Impressionists, writes Mandelstam, "I stretched my

---

[7]Mandel'shtam, "Gumanizm i sovremennost'," in *Sobranie sochinenii*, ed. G. P. Struve and B. A. Filipoff, 3 vols. (New York: Inter-Language Literary Associates, 1964–71), II, 394–96.

[8]Mandel'shtam, "Puteshestvie v Armeniiu," in *Sobranie sochinenii*, II, 175. Parenthetical references in the text are to this edition. My translations rely on two fine versions: those of Sidney Monas, in his edition of Osip Mandelstam, *Selected Essays* (Austin: University of Texas Press, 1977), and Clarence Brown, in *Quarterly Review of Literature* 18, no. 3–4 (1972): 261–97. "Journey to Armenia" was first published in *Zvezda*, no. 5 (1933), pp. 103–25.

vision and sank my eye into the wide goblet of the sea, so that every mote and tear should come out of it" (p. 196). Among the passages most reminiscent of Goethe's *Italian Journey* (a work with important similarities to Mandelstam's) are those concerning perception.

Contemplating cultural artifacts is one way of expanding the limits of one's vision. Language, the most fundamental part of the cultural heritage, is another of Mandelstam's preoccupations in this work. Through language the individual continually interacts with the past and creates the future. Mandelstam worked at learning Armenian during his stay, and a number of passages express his admiration for the language and his excitement in exploring its structure and sounds. Like any beautifully crafted piece of writing, "Journey to Armenia" arouses fascination with how language works and what it can be made to do.

Parts of the work concern the great naturalists, who through observation developed new systems of ordering the world and new languages to describe them. One learns, as in reading Mandelstam's poetry, how a single object can yield insights into how the world is put together. The naturalists manipulated observations on a large scale. Mandelstam refers to a system such as those they devised as "a method of creative cognition and a worthy means of life-probing" (p. 201). This definition applies to all the kinds of observation that make up "Journey to Armenia."

One lives fully by probing the patterns of culture and nature, and also through interacting with others engaged in the same process. Among the most vivid portions of "Journey to Armenia" are the vignettes of people — from strangers encountered during his stay to Lamarck and Linnaeus (who are sketched with intimacy and affection). The warmest words describe the biologist B. S. Kuzin, with whom he established a close friendship in Armenia. Mandelstam's character portraits and his comments on friendship convey the satisfaction of simple connections with individuals, and the value of each human contact.

The eight sections of "Journey to Armenia" comprise an inventory of how one can broaden and deepen one's world. Mandelstam infectiously conveys his pleasure in using his senses: he writes at one point of "the impatience with which I live and change my skin" (p. 183). The work's final pages are particularly poignant, because the reader, along with the poet, is suddenly plunged into the opposite condition: a state of confinement, of once ripe senses decayed. The body of "Journey to Armenia" is about the expansion of borders; it ends with a stark glimpse of the narrowing of borders, and of the ultimate confinement, death.

The ending was prohibited by the censorship when the work was passed for publication; the editor who decided to print the complete manuscript lost his job as a result.[9] The offending passage is brief. Its abrupt interruption of the narrative and terse style signal its importance. It consists of a numbered series of seventeen statements, ranging in length from a few words to a few lines. They tell the story of King Arshak, imprisoned in a fortress by the conquering King Shapukh. The first eight statements describe the prisoner and his thoughts:

1. The body of Arshak is unwashed and his beard has run wild.

2. The fingernails of the king are broken, and wood lice crawl over his face.

3. His ears have grown stupid from silence, but once they listened to Greek music.

4. His tongue is scabby from jailer's food, but there was a time when it pressed grapes against the roof of his mouth and was adroit as the tip of a flutist's tongue.

5. The seed of Arshak has withered in his scrotum and his voice is as thin as the bleating of a sheep.

6. King Shapukh — thinks Arshak — has got the better of me, and, worse than that, he has taken my air for himself.

7. The Assyrian grips my heart.

8. He is commander of my hair and my fingernails. He grows me my beard and swallows my spit, so accustomed has he grown to the thought that I am here in the fortress of Aniush. [p. 213]

Arshak is a man accustomed to deriving pleasure from his senses, from the same joys the reader has come in the course of the work to more fully appreciate. He has lost not only his kingdom and the world beyond his cell, but even the domain of his own body. The miniature chronicle continues, telling of a former official of Arshak's time who has cunningly gained Shapukh's favor, thereby earning a reward for his loyalty. The reward he requests is the story's final item: "17. Give me a pass to the fortress of Aniush. I would like Arshak to spend one

---

[9]On the editor, Cesar Volpe, and this episode, see *Hope Against Hope*, p. 139, and *Hope Abandoned*, p. 410.

additional day full of hearing, taste, and smell, as it was before, when he amused himself at the hunt and busied himself with the planting of trees" (p. 214). Presumably, after this final day of exposure to what he has lost, Arshak will again be confined, his memory of life painfully keen.

The modern reader is informed by a note that Arshak was king of Armenia in the fourth century; the Assyrian Shapukh overran the area and attempted to convert it from Christianity. Mandelstam adds no explanations; the story is included in "Journey to Armenia" not for what it tells about Armenian history but for what it tells about Mandelstam and about Soviet development.[10] Arshak is a figurative ruler — the individual ruling the self, free to experience the world through whatever "worthy means of life-probing" attract him. The passage suggests that the individual has been dispossessed of his realm. Travel works traditionally end with a return home; this one ends with the traveler's fear that "home" — the self that is one's real native land — has been invaded. The narrative resumes briefly after the Arshak story, and the concluding words echo all the preceding passages about experience. As the exhilarated and exhausted writer drifts to sleep after a long day ascending a mountain on horseback, his body is still awake with the sense of the road. The final line expresses the desire to go on exploring: "Last thought: have to ride around some ridge. . . ." The words are hopeful; in the wake of the Arshak episode, however, they seem to describe not limitless experience, but the final day of reprieve.

That reprieve for Mandelstam was the trip to the Caucasus. "Journey to Armenia" describes his visit to part of the domain with which he identified, Mediterranean culture. It is for him a journey to Europe, in his broad and personal definition of that term. It is also a celebration of the individual — and in this sense, too, for Mandelstam, it is a journey to Europe, the home of humanism.

Ten years earlier, in an essay entitled "Humanism and the Present," Mandelstam had described the reordering of society in terms that amplify one's understanding of "Journey to Armenia."[11] He

---

[10]In the Matenadaran, the state library in Erevan, I was drawn to an ancient manuscript on exhibit that tells a legend of King Arshak and King Shapukh locked in a battle of wits over who is to be sovereign. Lettered above the story is a reminder of the fine line between legend and experience: "In legends . . . in figurative form historical truth lies hidden."

[11]Mandel'shtam, "Gumanizm i sovremennost' "; the first two passages quoted are on p. 394, the last on p. 396.

writes of his apprehensions about the "monumentality of form of the oncoming social architecture," wondering whether it will celebrate or subjugate the individual. He and his contemporaries live in the future's shadow "with fear and perplexity, not knowing whether it is the wing of oncoming night or the shadow of our native city that we are about to enter." What Mandelstam regards as "native" is that place where the individual is an end rather than a means, that place where one can rule one's inner "native city." The essay suggests that in this transitional time, there is no such place: "the gold coinage of the European humanistic heritage" has gone out of circulation. Mandelstam anticipates a time when it will again become common currency. During the decade after 1923, this time seemed increasingly remote. In "Journey to Armenia," we find that the Soviet system has made the area within its borders figuratively foreign to the individuals who inhabit it.

Other works discussed in the preceding chapters touch on how the traveler's experience abroad can influence his perception of home. Ehrenburg finds Russia "upside-down" in comparison with Europe; Nikitin and other travelers write of their excitement on returning to a place where so much was in motion; in his poem "They and We," Mayakovsky describes the returning traveler's difficulty in readjusting his vision;[12] Tikhonov, having seen Europe, declares Russia "the land of lands." The ending of "Journey to Armenia" also functions as an assessment of the Soviet system. In "Chaadaev" the young Mandelstam had placed individual freedom at the center of Russian national and personal identity. The contrast between most of "Journey to Armenia" and the concluding Arshak section seems to show the present distance between the Western and Russian traditions, on one side, and Soviet territory, on the other.

Describing the "Journey" in a letter, Mandelstam wrote of the deep necessity of traveling widely. "The greatest reward for an artist," he continued, "is to awaken to the worlds of those who think and feel differently from himself."[13] What Sterne had called the "Inevitable necessity" of getting outside one's environment is expressed in most literary treatments of travel, and those discussed here are no exception. The needs pursued by these westward travelers vary greatly, as do the destinations they envision and find. Babel's craver of sunlit

---

[12]Maiakovskii, "Oni i my," in *Polnoe*, X, 44. This 1929 poem describes how backward Moscow looks after Paris; it concludes with the poet's recognition that he must shed his "foreigner's" perspective and look at Russia's present in light of its future.

[13]Mandel'shtam, "[Iz pis'ma], 1931–32," in *Sobranie sochinenii*, III, 169.

Italy is also a schemer who plots to replace its peace with revolution. "Italian Sunshine" merges the abstract obsession with the concrete one, creating a dramatic set of contrasts between violence and serenity. Ehrenburg's unabashed cynic requires the latter, and to find it heads back to his sensually vivid, hyperbolized Europe. He withdraws from the current upheaval, relegating action to his adventurous eye. Ehrenburg spares nothing his satire, including his own need to witness the era from a safe distance. The role of observer is also self-consciously played by such writers of European reportage as Kushner, Nikitin, and Sobol. Despite the diversity of their approaches, they have in common an eagerness for perspective on their country and times. Their desire for distance from home coexists with a desire to know contemporary Europe and to understand a wider piece of the present.

Mandelstam is very much aware of the present era, but the West he needs is a timeless and borderless one. "Journey to Armenia" concerns travel to a novel environment and the acquisition of experience; at the same time, it concerns the feared loss of the self thus being developed. The schematization of culture proposed by Lotman and Uspensky is helpful in viewing this work, and this entire section, in a broader context. They note that every culture has a need for "structural variety" — varied spheres of existence, including special realms within the culture (the monastery, gypsy life) and ventures outside it. This structural variety must be balanced with structural unity if a culture is to be cohesive. In order to achieve cohesion, each culture comes to develop a model of itself which, when "imposed onto the reality of this or that culture . . . exerts a powerful regulating influence, preordaining the construction of culture, introducing order, and eliminating contradiction."[14] What is eliminated, in other words, is considered extraneous and alien. The problem of distinguishing internal from external, native from foreign, is a subtle and vital matter. The traveler, with distinctly different places set before him in sequence, finds it easy to judge. At home and over time, as Part 4 shows, it may be harder to recognize what the limits of one's culture ideally and actually encompass, and what they exclude.

---

[14]Yu. M Lotman and B. A. Uspensky, "On the Semiotic Mechanism of Culture," trans. George Mihaychuk, *New Literary History* 9, no. 2 (Winter 1978): 227. The article first appeared in *Trudy po znakovym sistemam* 5 (Tartu, Estonia, 1971).

PART FOUR
THE FOREIGN PRESENCE

Before the thirteenth century, many foreigners visited Russia from Europe and Byzantium; those contacts were curtailed by the Mongol conquest, accountable for so much in Russia's history. A renewed opening to the West began during the reign of Ivan III (1462–1505). After that time, it was accepted that Russia's development would be linked to its interchange with the West (though the nature of that interchange, then as now, was controversial). By the early seventeenth century European travelers and residents were so prevalent in Muscovy, writes the historian S. F. Platonov, that "they had become familiar to every Russian."[1] Their influence on technology and on thought

---

[1] S. F. Platonov, *Moscow and the West,* trans. and ed. Joseph L. Wieczynski (Hattiesburg, Miss.: Academic International, 1972), p. 50. The original's first edition is *Moskva i Zapad v XVI–XVII vekakh* (Leningrad: Seiatel', 1925). Regarding early contacts with the West, see also Donald W. Treadgold, *The West in Russia and China,* 2 vols. (Cambridge: Cambridge University Press, 1973), I, *Russia: 1472–1917,* especially pp. 1–23. Another valuable source, which stresses the importance of the Russia-West issue, is James H. Billington, *The Icon and the Axe* (New York: Vintage-Random House, 1970). He writes (p. 78): "The conflicts that convulsed Russia throughout the seventeenth century were part of an awkward, compulsive search for identity in an essentially European world."

Of particular literary interest is Aleksei Veselovskii, *Zapadnoe vliianie v novoi russkoi literature,* 5th ed. (Moscow: n.p., 1916). Veselovsky relates the ancient consciousness of foreign lands to the early interchange between Russia and the West. He writes that the Russian legends and saint's lives abound in references to the mysterious

was substantial. Platonov, focusing on their psychological and cultural impact, describes seventeenth-century Muscovy in terms that apply, *mutatis mutandis,* to every later era:

> The foreigner who had come for service, the "German" merchant, the foreign technician who was an "expert" in one or another line of work . . . , the Polish or Czech sectarian who felt it possible to base faith upon reason — all these types flashed before the eyes of the Muscovites, startled their imagination, awakened their reflection and disturbed their consciences with problems of life, the soul and faith.[2]

This characterization of the foreigner's historical role is relevant to the literary function of the foreigner as well. Intrusions from the outer world upset a society's equilibrium: even if the society rejects them, it changes in the process of doing so. In literature, as in life, outsiders cause internal realignments. When sharply contrasting elements are used in any art form, they define the whole into which they are introduced. Analyzing foreign elements in literary works can be more complex than one might assume. Outsiders are not always of a different nationality: the alienated and exceptional populate literature so heavily that they appear to be in the majority. The problem may be thought simpler if one looks only at actual foreigners, but it is not. While passports unambiguously certify the identities of foreign visitors, the label of a fictional foreigner cannot be scanned with such assurance.[3] Nationality may be insignificant, or it may not mean what its surface implies. The foreigners considered below are not all literally Western, and their status as "native" or "foreign" is not uniformly easy to discern. Each work involves a foreign presence which, in the historian's words, startles the imagination, awakens reflection, and disturbs the conscience — sometimes of observers within the fiction, and always of the reader, whom the author draws inside it.

Foreigners may be conspicuous catalysts of change, but cultures

---

coming of strangers from a misty, remote realm. Such foreigners were at first received with trepidation, their homelands imagined with apprehension. The lands that so captured the Russian imagination, in Veselovsky's view, were those to the West. As the centuries passed they appeared less threatening — without, however, losing their mystery (p. 33).

[2]S. F. Platonov, *Moscow and the West,* p. 61.

[3]One example of the sort of scholarly study that does "read labels" rather than considering the foreign character's function is Valentin Kiparsky, *English and American Characters in Russian Fiction* (Berlin: Osteuropa-Institut an der Freien Universität Berlin, 1964).

also generate their own doubt and enlightenment. No culture is entirely uniform, nor does absolute unity prevail between individuals and the system of which they are a part. From the vantage point of each individual, features of his or her country may appear figuratively foreign — alien to the individual's concept of its nature. One might even see a defining feature of a society (its dominant values or political structure, for example) as a figuratively foreign presence — foreign in that it excludes or damages what one deems fundamental. What I refer to as a "foreign presence," then, can be a literally foreign individual or idea, or something internal that is figuratively alien. These may be interrelated in a given work, and the actual stranger may not be the most alien feature. In Platonov's "The Epifan Locks," for example, a foreigner's alienation shows that the policies he implements and the tsar he serves are alien as well. In all the fiction to be discussed, foreign characters serve to highlight the shifting components of Russia and to probe what is, or is not, now alien.

The use of foreigners in early Soviet literature presents a particularly interesting problem. Society was disrupted; certainties were becoming heresies or doubts. The structure of the new society had been decreed: in discarding its former identity, Russia had adopted what Lotman calls "a new system of self-description."[4] But society's components did not promptly range themselves along the diagrammed lines. The process of transforming the pre-revolutionary system into a more homogeneous one meant that some of its elements would have to be eliminated and other, "Soviet" parts introduced. The definitions of "native" and "foreign" were thus in flux: as we see in Konstantin Fedin's *Cities and Years*, natives could find themselves turned foreigner, and vice versa.

In order to satisfactorily describe an evolving "system" (the political and semiotic terms coincide) one must look simultaneously within and outside it. As a system changes, it rejects present elements and absorbs new ones. Lotman terms this an interchange between the "extrasystematic" and the "systematic" (that recognized as belonging to the system). "One of the chief sources of the dynamism of semiotic structures," he writes, "is the constant process of drawing extrasystematic elements into the realm of the system and of expelling systematic elements into the area of non-system."[5] Foreign characters can

---

[4] Ju. M. Lotman, "The Dynamic Model of a Semiotic System," trans. Ann Shukman, *Semiotica* 21, no. 3–4 (1977): 200.

[5] Ibid., p. 196.

dramatize this process — by carrying alien ideas or by challenging native ones. Or, as in Platonov and Fedin, they can be integrated into the system and become identified with its essential traits, thus ceasing to be entirely foreign.

A Biblical metaphor conveys how a hitherto peripheral feature can become fundamental. Psalm 118 rejoices: "The stone which the builders rejected has become the chief cornerstone." In the psalm this refers to the Jewish people's emergence from oppression; in New Testament usage the cornerstone is Christ, destroyed by the system of his time but become the foundation of a new one. The metaphor (cited by Lotman) operates in the reverse as well: cornerstones on which a structure rests can be slipped out and replaced by ones of a different design. This is the case in *The Master and Margarita*. As Scripture implies, recognizing something as integral or external is all a matter of perspective — a function of what sort of structure one aims to build.

The literary structures occupying the following chapters are quite diverse: these author-builders, to follow the metaphor a bit farther, work from idiosyncratic blueprints. They have in common the presence of a foreign figure who can be termed a "specialist" in some area useful to Russia. These are the typological descendants of the foreign visitors of centuries past. Stylistically, the works trace an irregular curve across the twenties and thirties, illustrating a range of techniques: modernist plot-scrambling (Fedin); the camera-eye documentary novel (Kataev);[6] historical fiction (Platonov); merging of the fantastic and realistic, the philosophical and satirical (Bulgakov — who warrants still more adjectives). They also engage public issues of various phases of national development. Veniamin Kaverin's surrealistic sketch fools around with Soviet Russia's initial form, while fooling around with its own form. The experimentalism of the early twenties is also reflected in *Cities and Years* (though in some ways the work points back to the nineteenth century). Fedin's psychological adventure novel shows the intensity of the revolution's aftermath.

Platonov is always hard to characterize. His potent framing of contemporary issues and his poignant language set him apart. "The Epifan Locks" is not typical of late-twenties prose: its connection to

---

[6]Edward J. Brown notes Kataev's effective use of cinematic techniques in his foreword to *Time, Forward!* trans. Charles Malamuth (1933; rpt. Bloomington: Indiana University Press, 1976).

the era is too oblique for that, and its implications too bleak. By contrast, Kataev's *Time, Forward!* (which has the status of a classic) derives so completely from the period that it is subtitled "*A Chronicle.*" Following the practice of many writers during the first five-year plan, Kataev spent several months at the industrial plant about which he writes; his observations are the basis for this fictionalized account of one day in its operation.

No novel of the thirties is less similar to such five-year-plan fiction than *The Master and Margarita.* This is the best of those novels written "for the drawer" (in the Russian phrase) during the Stalinist period. As did other works of the twenties and thirties that waited decades for a reader, *The Master and Margarita* changed literary history with its appearance. Its interweaving of foreign presences is subtle and powerful. The thirties were documented in such novels as Kataev's; Bulgakov's novel, which leaps the boundaries of socialist realism, presents a far denser picture of the Soviet system and of the realm outside.

13

DEFINING THE NATIVE

Konstantin Fedin, *Cities and Years* (1924)

The qualifications for citizenship are variously determined in different societies. Generally a state requires the individual to demonstrate his or her integration into its culture — through birth, residence, or acceptance of the dominant ideology. The Soviet state in its early years broke with many conventions of government, improvising new institutions. The establishment of nationality was among them. Seeing themselves as the vanguard of an international proletarian movement, the Bolsheviks (in theory at least) rejected nationalism. They enacted their belief in the supremacy of class divisions over national ones by revising the meaning of citizenship. If class alignment moved individuals and molded history, then one could be a Soviet citizen regardless of one's national origin if one aligned oneself with the interests of the proletariat. The Soviets "repudiated the traditional concept of 'foreigner' and the legal concept of 'citizenship' and recognized as citizens of the Soviet republic prisoners of war or other 'nationals' of foreign countries who accepted Bolshevism, or . . . were 'ideologically close to the Soviet regime.'"[1]

In practice this did not mean much. It belongs to the raft of regulations proclaimed in the state's utopian infancy and either neglected or contradicted as time went on. The new definition of citizen-

[1]Xenia Joukoff Eudin and Harold H. Fisher, *Soviet Russia and the West 1920–1927: A Documentary Survey* (Stanford, Calif.: Stanford University Press, 1957), p. xxxii.

ship is notable because it implies its opposite: that a native who is "ideologically far" from the regime forfeits his right to citizenship. The issue of who and what can be considered "native" and "alien" figures in one of the important novels of the twenties, Konstantin Fedin's *Cities and Years*. The dual processes of the foreign becoming native and the native growing estranged are the main structural features of Fedin's complex plot.

The publication of *Cities and Years* in 1924 was a significant literary event. Short genres had predominated in the preceding years of revolution and war — poetry, the journalistic sketch, the short story. The trend toward short forms was widely attributed to the era's upheaval, and was also seen as evidence of Soviet literature's immaturity. Fedin's first novel marked an end to this period: reviewers hailed it as a sign of "the revival of the sort of novel that is rich in varied contemporary material and soldered with a strong plot."[2] D. S. Mirsky, in emigration, called *Cities and Years* the most interesting work written since the Revolution.[3]

Discussion focused on both its literary merit and its portrayal of the times. Two aspects of the novel aroused particular interest: the plot's rearranged chronology and the portrayal of character. If Fedin's innovative form grouped him with the modernists, his approach to character branded him a reactionary. The latter raised a venerable issue in Russian literary history: the use of a foreign protagonist who is more decisive and ideologically progressive than his Russian counterpart. In helping to revive the novel, Fedin also revived the nineteenth-century debate about the role of Western protagonists in Russian fiction.

This issue concerned those Marxist critics who believed in literature's obligation to portray the Revolution and Soviet state-building efforts in positive terms. They raised the objection made sixty-five years before to Turgenev's novel *On the Eve:* why must the author look abroad for his men of action? In 1860 the radical critic Dobroliubov had argued that Turgenev could have fostered the

[2]Nik. Belen'kii, untitled review of *Goroda i gody, Krasnaia nov'*, no. 1 (1925), p. 271. A similar point is made in another interesting contemporary discussion: A. Lezhnev, untitled review of *Goroda i gody, Pechat' i revoliutsiia*, no. 2 (1925), p. 271. On the discussion about genre in the early twenties, and on the novel's reception, see Robert A. Maguire's extremely useful *Red Virgin Soil: Soviet Literature in the 1920's* (Princeton, N.J.: Princeton University Press, 1968), pp. 276–79.

[3]Kn. D. Sviatopolk-Mirskii, untitled review of *Goroda i gody, Sovremennye zapiski*, no. 24 (1925), p. 433.

emergence of a Russian revolutionary type by creating a literary prototype. With literary history in mind, a 1925 reviewer fulminated that given the countless triumphant revolutionaries now in Russia, it was preposterous that Fedin should "travel to Germany for his 'strong' people."[4] Was the tradition of Turgenev and Goncharov (in whose *Oblomov* the half-German Stolz tries to rouse the title character from lethargy) really so irresistible?

Literary tradition does figure in Fedin's use of a weak Russian hero: the young writer acknowledged to his mentor Gorky that he had succumbed to tradition despite the present "heroic epoch."[5] "So what?" one may ask. What difference does it make to *Cities and Years* that the active, pro-Bolshevik Kurt should be a foreigner and the passive, confused Andrei a Russian? Had Fedin given Kurt's role to a Russian, how would it have changed the novel? One might justifiably argue that Fedin is showing his indifference to national labels and promoting internationalism. The destructive nationalism of World War I is lampooned in the novel, and socialist internationalism is made to seem the alternative. Kurt's foreignness does imply that nationality is an anachronistic category: one effect of his foreignness, late in the novel, is to demonstrate its own inconsequence. But the more significant implication of Kurt's foreignness is this: that what Kurt represents is figuratively foreign to Russia. By making Kurt foreign, Fedin dramatizes the redefinition of what is native. The novel's pairing of an alienated native with an assimilated foreigner illustrates the magnitude of Russia's change. It also suggests that some aspects of what had previously been accepted as native might now be defined as alien.

Cities and Years is set in Germany between 1914 and 1920 and in Russia from 1918 to 1922; it shows the violent transition to a new era in both places. Kurt and Andrei were close friends before the war in Germany, where Andrei had gone to study. Both enter Russia toward the war's end — Kurt as a prisoner of war and Andrei (caught in Germany by the war, as was Fedin himself) with repatriated Russian

---

[4]"Ne-kritik," "Roman lishnego cheloveka," *Zvezda*, no. 1 (7) (1925), p. 299. Also of interest is the later comment of the American critic Joseph Kunitz that "in the past the Russian writer had to invent an efficient foreigner . . . to offset native indolence; now it is the Russian Communist who supplies the active prototype." See his "Men and Women in Soviet Literature," in Joseph Freeman et al., *Voices of October* (New York: Vanguard, 1930), p. 86.

[5]Konstantin Fedin, letter to Maksim Gorky, December 7, 1924, in Fedin's memoir *Gor'kii sredi nas* (Moscow: Molodaia gvardiia, 1967), p. 219.

prisoners. Kurt arrives as a foreigner, Andrei as a native. In the ensuing four years their roles are reversed: the German becomes a dedicated communist, thoroughly assimilated into Soviet life, while the Russian grows increasingly estranged from it. The foreign Kurt emerges as the novel's quintessential native.

His assumption to the role is rapid: he immediately embraces the country's goals and gains a position of responsibility. But the final step in what could be termed Kurt's "naturalization" comes only at the end, as a result of the novel's climactic (but off-stage) event: his murder of Andrei. The novel's reordered chronology gives it two endings: the chronological (or "story") conclusion and the "plot" conclusion on the last page. Both endings focus on the murder. In the novel's last sentence, the narrator foreshadows the murder and appears to approve it. In the chronologically final scene, Kurt is called before an investigative committee; the authorities sanction his action and invite him into their ranks. By killing Andrei, Kurt completes the Russian's long decline into homelessness, and replaces him as the novel's chief native protagonist.

One's view of this process depends on how one interprets the murder. Kurt explains to the committee that he killed Andrei because the Russian was guilty of the most heinous crime a native can commit — treason. Andrei had arranged the escape of a German war prisoner wanted as an anti-Bolshevik agitator (the Margrave von zur Muhlen-Schönau, who embodies the crumbling European aristocracy). Andrei releases him for the sorts of reasons that contemporary critics called "bourgeois": partly to return a favor, and largely to contact his beloved in Germany. Love moves him more strongly than any other force. Three years later, deeply depressed, Andrei turns to Kurt for help. He confesses part of the story; Kurt guesses the rest. Later Kurt explains to the committee: "No doubt remained: from personal motives he had saved the life of our enemy and betrayed the cause which we all serve. As a man he became odious to me, as a friend . . . loathsome. I killed him."[6] Kurt represents his act as the natural reaction of a committed communist. But the careful reader is given reason to suspect that Kurt is roused by personal motives of his own. He has a private hatred for the margrave, and Andrei serves him

---

[6]Konstantin Fedin, *Goroda i gody* (Moscow: Sovetskii pisatel', 1967), pp. 12–13. Parenthetical references in the text are to this edition. The translation used is that of Michael Scammell in Konstantin Fedin, *Cities and Years* (New York: Dell, 1962).

as a proxy target. He conceals this from the authorities, who not surprisingly approve his political explanation.[7]

One need not read the book with an anti-Bolshevik bias to regard Kurt's actions as suspect. Readers of various stripes have questioned whether he is entitled to the designation of exemplary Soviet comrade.[8] Yet this foreigner, who represents not only the strict valuing of ends over means but also deception, is welcomed into the elite. This seems an ominous sign of how Soviet citizenship is now established. Although Kurt acts alone, those in power, who endorse him, are also responsible. The question of whether Kurt's qualities are alien to Russia also applies, by extension, to them.

The shift in roles between Kurt and Andrei, regardless of how one validates the actions of each, is a clear example of the model of change described above. It demonstrates the interchange between a society's "outer" and "inner" realms. In the last scene before his death, Andrei speaks of his futile effort to get "into the circle" of what is happening; by removing him, Kurt gains admission into what we call "the inner circle." The native withdraws from the circle's periphery; the foreigner gains its center.

What is Russia losing in Andrei? He is, as Fedin indicates, an heir of the Russian literary tradition's "superfluous man." His alienation is attributable to his indecisive, introspective character: he might well have been estranged from any regime. But there is one substantial difference between Andrei's fate and that of other weak Russian heroes: he is violently ejected from society, with official sanction. Fedin may be un-Soviet in using a foreign Bolshevik; he is quite Soviet in suggesting that society will no longer tolerate a hesitating hero.

---

[7] In the novel's last sentence, the narrator refers indirectly to the murder as the correct behavior of "a comrade, a friend, and an artist." Kurt, a painter, does not mention his profession to the committee, but it is the key to understanding his motivation. The margrave had been Kurt's despotic patron — he had bought all his paintings and kept them from public view. Those paintings play an important role in the plot. They are responsible for the margrave's favor to Andrei in Germany, and they indirectly figure in Andrei's death. Kurt strikes out against Andrei at least in part because Andrei has enabled the margrave to return to his castle and resume control over the paintings.

[8] See, for example, S. Vrzhosek, "Tvorchestvo Konst. Fedina," *Zvezda*, no. 2 (1927), pp. 134–38. Another study critical of Kurt's characterization is Miroslav Zahrádka's *O khudozhestvennom stile romanov Konstantina Fedina* (Prague: Gosudarstvennoe Pedagogicheskoe Izd., 1962), pp. 8–9. Valuable recent articles on the novel have been written by Elizabeth Klosty Beaujour: "Some Problems of Construction in Fedin's *Cities and Years*," *Slavic and East European Journal* 16, no. 1 (1972): 1–18, and "The Uses of Witches in Fedin and Bulgakov," *Slavic Review* 33, no. 4 (1974): 695–707.

The "foreign presence" of Kurt, then, has psychological, historical, and political significance. It heightens, by contrast, the alienation
of the Russian protagonist; it dramatizes the beginning of a new
period; it implies that the Soviet establishment's values are alien. All
this would be so regardless of the foreigner's nationality. That he is
German adds other implications. Germany was regarded as the Western country closest to revolution; a German revolution was the one
most hoped for by the Bolsheviks. Kurt does represent the communist
ideal of erasing the boundary between Russia and Europe and joining
them in a stateless proletarian community. But given the novel's structure, he is more closely identified with the Soviet state than with
internationalism. In his single-mindedness and rationalism, Kurt conforms to the German stereotype; contrasting him to Andrei, however,
is not simply a reworking of the "active European/passive Russian"
literary cliché. While Fedin was criticized for perpetuating the cliché,
the novel actually shows it to be outdated. Russia is being
redefined — not becoming "Western" (a term without importance in
the novel), but changing into a new form of itself. The new Russia,
with adherence to ideology a requisite of citizenship, has a troubling
foreign presence at its center.

14
PROGRESS AND THE WEST

Veniamin Kaverin, "Engineer Shvarts" (1923)
Andrei Platonov, "The Epifan Locks" (1927)
Valentin Kataev, *Time, Forward!* (1932)

A country speeding self-consciously toward the future often looks to the past in setting and evaluating its course. The West, particularly after the time of Peter the Great, had been instrumental in Russia's development; Peter's resolve to "hack a window through to Europe" (as Pushkin put it in "The Bronze Horseman") increased Russia's absorption of Western technology and ideas. His reign (1682–1725) saw a large influx of foreign experts, brought to help implement Russia's plan to become a modern power. The tsar himself was widely perceived as a foreigner who was tearing Russia from its native roots.[1] The question of whether massive change directed from above is an alien process often involves the figure of Peter. He is a convenient symbol of a Russian state that adopts foreign ways in the name of progress.

Each work discussed in this chapter concerns a plan for Russian progress; each uses the past, and the West's role in Russia's past, to deal with the present. Peter the Great surfaces in the two short stories. Kaverin conjures up his image to hint playfully at a parallel between Peter's reorganization of Russia and that of the Soviets. In "The Epi-

---

[1] There is a fascinating discussion in semiotic terms of the popular rejection of Peter as a foreigner in B. A. Uspenskii, "Historia sub Specie Semioticae," in *Semiotics and Structuralism: Readings from the Soviet Union,* ed. Henryk Baran (White Plains, N.Y.: International Arts and Sciences Press, 1974), pp. 64–75.

fan Locks," set in Peter's reign, Platonov implies a more profound similarity between historical and contemporary change. Kataev's *Time, Forward!*, as the title implies, shows Russia rapidly moving away from the past. It also demonstrates that Russia is outgrowing the need for a Western presence.

◆ ◆ ◆

The unconventional form of *Cities and Years* reveals the influence on Fedin of the Serapion Brothers, a literary circle he joined in 1921. Fedin was a literary conservative compared to most of the others. Veniamin Kaverin, the youngest Serapion, was among the most experimental, and among the most convinced of art's autonomy from reality and from politics. His early writing, full of fantastic situations and characters, was inspired in part by the stories of E. T. A. Hoffmann. Nearly all the stories in his first collection, *Masters and Apprentices* (1923), parody Hoffmann and take place in a semblance of medieval Germany. Describing the collection to Gorky (mentor to many), Kaverin explained that two stories were set in Russia. But he insisted that this did not contradict his belief that one could write contemporary prose without regard for contemporary circumstances. His use of Russia, he said, was purely in the interests of literary experimentation, "because it's interesting to devise fantastic things with Russian material."[2]

Only one of the "Russian" stories is contemporary with the time of writing: a slight but intriguing fantasy called "Engineer Shvarts." It is intriguing because it employs a phantom foreigner who exemplifies a historical phase. The story justifies Kaverin's assertion that in using Russian material he is not becoming any more conventional. But he does conform to most fiction of the period in one respect: "Engineer Shvarts" involves the Revolution. Kaverin announces his adherence to this convention in a characteristically playful way, using the technique the Formalists termed "baring the device." The admission comes about midway through the story: "I don't know who this engineer Shvarts is or whether there ever existed an engineer named Shvarts. But I write about him anyway, because after all it's necessary to write

---

[2]Veniamin Kaverin, letter to Maksim Gorky, September 24, 1922, in *Literaturnoe nasledstvo*, 92 vols. (Moscow: Akademiia Nauk SSSR, 1931–80), LXX, 171.

about the revolution."[3] His irony would have been clear to contemporary readers, who knew that those who really believed in the necessity of writing about revolution did so more directly than Kaverin.

Shvarts is among the most bizarre examples of a type one meets on occasion in fiction of the twenties and thirties — the Western specialist. The foreign engineers of socialist realist fiction are all variations on a few models. This foreign expert is not even real: he is a creation of the protagonist Korchaga's imagination. The degree of his foreignness is also questionable. Shvarts appears to embody a native, not a foreign phenomenon.

The year is 1922; the scene is "Petersburg" (as the city continued to be called by many). The symmetrical design of the city, that "unnatural," "fantastic" city at the center of so much Russian fiction, is important here as well. Korchaga's perception is conditioned by two factors: his obsession with geometry, and the grid of Petersburg on which he walks. The geometry of the city and the student's sleeplessness after nights laboring over graphs and equations provide the motivation for the appearance of a strange foreigner named Ludwig Shvarts. Kaverin's use of geometry as a device for describing setting, character, and the nature of the state recalls the technique of Zamiatin (who lectured to the Serapions). Shvarts is a hallucination, too contrived to be very sinister, but he represents a mentality of the sort frighteningly portrayed in Zamiatin's anti-utopia We.

Kaverin teases the reader with the title character's identity throughout the story, and has him fading in and out of view. We are finally indulged with some exposition in the eighth of the story's ten sections — a letter written home by Shvarts to "the land of Geometrists." Shvarts, it appears, had been dispatched by his government at the time of the Revolution to help Russia fulfill its goals. The nature of these goals is indicated by Shvarts's account of his phenomenal success: "Under my influence," he writes, "they even began to think geometrically" (p. 65). But recent changes have brought confusion and chaos back again. Shvarts had virtually succeeded in making everyone two-dimensional; now they were regaining the third dimension. Soci-

[3]V. Kaverin, "Inzhener Shvarts," in *Mastera i podmaster'ia. Rasskazy* (Moscow and Petersburg: Krug, 1923; rpt. Ann Arbor, Mich.: University Microfilms, 1966), p. 63. An interesting perspective on the story, which coincides with some of my observations, is in Hongor Oulanoff, *The Prose Fiction of Veniamin Kaverin* (Cambridge, Mass.: Slavica, 1976), pp. 31–33.

ety was deviating from other precepts as well: "The streets, which until recently were faithfully fulfilling the tasks of linear existence, are again filled with people, whose traffic spoils the purity of the perspective" (p. 65). Shvarts himself is under suspicion, and decides that the time has come to depart.

What is Kaverin up to? Shvarts, who arrived on the scene with the Revolution, represents its initial stage: he embodies the state's dogmatic blueprint for reorganizing Russia. The "sudden changes" disrupting progress seem to refer to the New Economic Policy, which marred ideological purism by allowing a partial return to capitalism. The recovered third dimension — *tolshchina,* meaning both geometric thickness and human stoutness — alludes to the eased conditions during NEP. After the privations of War Communism, life resumed at least some of its habitual patterns. People were getting fatter, and life was getting looser. Russia was straying from its plotted course — a course which, as Kaverin sketches it, had left no room for human deviation. All this is suffused with whimsy, but it does bear on actual circumstances. It also makes sense in terms of Lotman's model of change. Shvarts is the system's new "self-description" incarnate; when a revised plan is adopted, he recedes into nonexistence.

The foreigner's identification with a plan for transforming Russia is reinforced by the appearance of the city's founder. Peter the Great, one of the chief architects of modern Russia, maintains at least an implicit presence in much of the fiction set in his capital. His function here is to lay another allusion on Shvarts's already laden shoulders. The tsar smiles into his whiskers with satisfaction as he looks at the city's regular lines. The Russians learned it all from foreigners, he tells Korchaga; he had been right in predicting how beneficial foreign ways would prove. Peter's cameo role suggests that Shvarts is the current version of the European technicians imported to modernize Russia.

But despite his German name (which links the story to the others in the collection), does Shvarts bring anything "Western" to Russia? This may be a play on the Western origins of Bolshevik ideology, with "Shvartsism" retreating from Russia just as Marxism yields to NEP. Shvarts did not make the Revolution, however; nor did he set its goals. He is pursuing the aims set by Russia's leaders (leaders who could be judged "alien," but only figuratively). The planned state represented by Kaverin's foreigner is "Western" only in the sense that rationality and order are associated with the "Western" aspect of the Russian character. This foreign expert's homeland is the Soviet state.

Kaverin is more concerned with contrivance than with conclusiveness; his own literary plan is not too sturdy. But his story is provocative: it suggests that the unswerving, arbitrary aspect of the Revolution is alien, and that more natural, native tendencies are now resurfacing. In its experimentalism and whimsical approach to ideology, the story reflects literary reality of the early twenties, when publishing was less restrictive. Kaverin's game of "fantastic devising" also reflects the political reality of that period, with a mirror of his own invention.

◆　◆　◆

In Kaverin the mechanism of change appears simple — a flash of the pen, a wink of the eye, and phases of history come and go. In *The Hurdy-Gurdy,* Platonov lampoons this notion of fundamental change. The play shows the gulf between societal design and reality. Platonov's long story "The Epifan Locks" also concerns the problems of implementing a vision of national transformation. As does Kaverin's, this story approaches the present obliquely. The added dimension here is not fantasy but history.

The story is based on a historical episode involving an English engineer named John Perry (renamed Bertrand Perry by Platonov). In 1698 Peter had invited him to work on the tsar's master plan to link Russia's waterways, thus enhancing the country's power and creating a route from Europe to the East. We know that Platonov came across documents relating to the episode while supervising a land-reclamation project in Tambov. We also know that his work there was difficult and disillusioning; he referred to the Tambov period as "my exile."[4] There are plainly parallels between the author's experience and his protagonist's. But the story's relevance to the twenties would

---

[4]Quoted from the archive of the writer's widow, M. A. Platonova, in Anthony Olcott, "Andrej Platonov: The Citizen-Artist" (diss., Stanford University, 1976), p. 35. Also cited from the archive is the information that Platonov's superiors in Tambov threatened him with imprisonment or death when his project deteriorated; this further suggests his closeness to the character of Perry. On Platonov's use of the historical records see T. A. Nikonova, "Kommentarii k povesti A. Platonova 'Epifanskie shliuzy'," in *Tvorchestvo A. Platonova,* ed. A. M. Abramov et al. (Voronezh: Izd. Voronezhskogo Universiteta, 1970), pp. 204–10.

be evident regardless of the biographical connection. "The Epifan Locks" is about Peter's time, about Platonov's time, and about a timeless issue: the human cost of change imposed from above.

The figure of Perry has several dimensions. He is an extension of Peter's will, in that he pursues the tsar's plan and mirrors his ruthlessness. A Russian protagonist could also have served Platonov's purpose, but the engineer's foreignness increases the story's impact. Perry's literal estrangement from Russia emphasizes the distance between those in power and the environment. As in Fedin and Kaverin, the use of a foreigner implies that ideas at the roots of the Russian state are figuratively alien. The actual foreignness of the engineers imported by Peter is significant as well: their failure is due partly to a Frenchman's miscalculation. But the greater, more tragic error is that of the Russian tsar. The foreigners' blindness reflects Peter's disregard of the social and natural forces that are Russia's real native rulers. Peter challenges their dominion, and unleashes all the force he can to master them. The populace and nature itself reject the canal, as an organism rejects a foreign body. The peasants refuse to work and flee to their fields; the land is dry and the spring rains never come. No force can fill the canal, but vengeance can be had on the people. Despotism, not unsuitable European technology, is the crucial foreign presence in the story.

Perry is first the agent of despotism and then its victim. Determined to succeed, he orders thousands from their homes and to their deaths. The Russians are not alone in finding the work unsupportable: foreign technicians also slip away, heading homeward. Perry punishes rebellious foreigners and natives alike, with power derived from Peter. The source of Perry's authority is emphasized: Peter grants him a general's rank, and Perry signs one repressive order with the tsar's name. This mass suffering is troubling, but distant, to the reader. At the end, when Perry himself is put to death at Peter's command, the horror of the story's violence is made revoltingly vivid. He is slowly tortured by a sadistic Kremlin executioner. The unnaturalness of his death echoes the unnaturalness of his mission in Epifan; however much we empathize with the engineer's fate, we see that his punishment fits his crime.[5]

Perry is foreign, then, in the sense that Peter is foreign: removed from reality, and determined to rule it whatever the cost. But the

---

[5]Olcott also makes this point (p. 143).

Englishman is not just a henchman following orders: that would have made the story less deep than it is. Platonov explores his foreignness on a psychological level as well as on a political one. As a foreigner, Perry has in intensified form certain traits characteristic of Platonov's characters: alienation, apprehension, speechlessness. Russia is for him a place of wildness, of the unknown. Its challenge lures him from afar. "He had become fascinated with Peter while still in Newcastle," relates the narrator, "and wanted to become his collaborator in the civilization of that wild and mysterious country."[6] Reality confirms his expectations only in part. Russia is indeed untamed, and the enormity of its breadth and beauty is thrilling. But it will not easily yield its secrets.

Setting off from Petersburg into the interior, Perry is awed by the land's wealth and by its latent power. The few pages describing the journey to Epifan are among the story's most important and moving, though the plot moves not at all. Here we first understand the odds against the project's success and realize the boldness of Perry's (and Peter's) dream of "civilizing" Russia. Platonov implies that Peter does not sufficiently comprehend the might of the forces that resist his will. In the course of the journey, Perry begins to acquire such comprehension directly, through his senses. Platonov beautifully orchestrates the foreigner's perceptions of the passing landscape. His feelings are complex, as the land itself is complex. Mystery inspires two reactions — attraction and fear; massiveness can be perceived as grandeur, or as threat. Among the story's key words are those deriving from the word "fear" (strakh). The individual is vulnerable, however strong his will: fear is inherent in the environment. Moving toward the country's center, Perry is stunned by the "frightening height of the sky above the continent, a height impossible above the sea and above the narrow British island" (p. 29). As the project sinks into disaster, fear penetrates his stoic exterior. He resists it by losing feeling, by becoming indifferent to his fate. Nature's potential terror and the terror of Perry's circumstances flare up again in the execution scene, with a harsh brightness.

"The Epifan Locks" is a masterful study of the psychology of foreignness — of the "spiritual foreign land" that so many of

---

[6]Andrei Platonov, "Epifanskie shliuzy," *Velichie prostykh serdets,* ed. M. A. Platonova (Moscow: Moskovskii rabochii, 1976), p. 24. Parenthetical references in the text are to this edition. Translation is mine; there is also a translation by Marion Jordan in Andrei Platonov, *Collected Works* (Ann Arbor, Mich.: Ardis, 1978), pp. 223–56.

Platonov's characters inhabit.[7] The psychological and political strands of the story are intertwined. Perry is distant from Russia both psychologically, as a foreigner, and institutionally, as implementer of an unpopular, repressive policy. Because he does not understand his environment, his attempts to control it are frustrated, and he begins to violate it in desperation. The tsar is depicted as one to whom despotism comes naturally; Perry's inhumanity is a consequence of his effort to control what cannot be controlled.

A policy that thrusts human and natural existence from their accustomed patterns, suggests Platonov, breeds violence. Progress is desirable: the story does not imply that change is inherently destructive. The ruler's dream for Russia is daring and inspiring. But for Peter, as for all rulers, the destiny of the nation overshadows the brief and vulnerable lifespan of the individual. Platonov later commented directly on the inevitable collision between historical time and human time in an article with the typically Soviet title of "Pushkin, Our Comrade." He writes in the concluding section: "Pushkin, of course, clearly understood that to remove the fetters from history and at the same time to liberate the freedom-loving soul of man was not a simple matter."[8] Ends, in other words, demand means. In the name of worthy national ends, alien methods are often employed. In the mid-twenties, as Platonov the engineer-writer struggled to achieve his country's ends through morally defensible means, he appears to have experienced this contradiction. His major fiction after "The Epifan Locks" is devoted to exploring it.[9]

The foreignness of Platonov's tsar and of his Englishman is the foreignness of anyone who moves history at the expense of the present. The planners of the Soviet future had aims as grandiose as any the world had seen, and they were in a history-making hurry. The enormous scale of the Soviet effort to construct a new society and

---

[7]The phrase in Russian is *dushevnaia chuzhbina*. Quoted from Platonov's "Prois-khozhdenie mastera" (a section of the novel *Chevengur*) by Vladimir Vasil'ev in "Pre-krasnaia sushchnost' cheloveka," introduction to *Velichie prostykh serdets*, p. 9.

[8]A. Platonov, "Pushkin — nash tovarishch," in *Razmyshleniia chitatelia. Stat'i* (Moscow: Sovetskii pisatel', 1970), p. 35. First published in *Literaturnyi kritik*, no. 1 (1937). The centenary of Pushkin's death in 1937 prompted many articles with similar titles. Platonov's comments on "The Bronze Horseman" in this article are of particular relevance to "The Epifan Locks."

[9]Olcott sees the year 1927 as a turning point for Platonov: "Platonov seems in Tambov to have become as disillusioned with social engineering as he had with mechanical engineering, and to have concentrated his art upon the chaos wrought by social change" (p. 120).

economy had consequences of commensurate scope. "The Epifan Locks" shows how one region and one builder were destroyed by the process of forced change. Platonov's own time held many such examples. As the twenties gave way to the thirties, the gap between rulers and ruled widened, a politically created no man's land between two alien realms.

The foreign identity of the protagonist is motivated by Platonov's subject. Does it matter that he is a European foreigner, rather than some other sort? Given the story's setting, of course, he could not be anything else: it was the West to which Peter had turned for the keys to Russia's future. Perry fails, though, not because he is Western, but because he is alien to the place he tries to change. Perry does not represent Europe: he is part of Russia's drive to catch up with Europe. The West as it appears in the story is a personal, rather than political, realm. England is simply "home," a place of comfort and calm in contrast to the uncertain land where Perry ventures, knowing it may cost his life. Europe functions in the story as a psychic homeland — that place of innocence and equilibrium which so often exists only in a person's memory. A Soviet scholar has proposed that Perry's tragedy is that of the West — "the tragedy of the narrowness of the private, individual consciousness, albeit noble, but confined by an arithmetic reason."[10] Platonov can treat his Westerner with some degree of sympathy, the scholar argues, only because he was writing before the full horror of fascism had become apparent. This faulty interpretation illustrates how susceptible literary uses of the West are to being stuffed into prefabricated pigeonholes of meaning. "The Epifan Locks" has nothing to do with the West of the 1920s; it has a great deal to do with the Soviet Union of the 1920s. The mentality of Russia's planners and builders, not that of the "Western consciousness," is Platonov's concern. The tragedy explored in the story is not the West's but Russia's. The Western protagonist is a tool of its artistic expression.

◆ ◆ ◆

The Western characters in Fedin, Kaverin, and Platonov are ostensibly external to Russia, but they are used primarily to explore aspects of Russia's development rather than of the West's. Fedin also

---

[10]L. A. Anninskii, "Zapad i vostok v tvorchestve Andreia Platonova," *Narody Azii i Afriki*, no. 4 (1967), p. 104.

devotes attention to the contemporary West, as does Kataev in *Time, Forward!* The two American characters in this classic five-year-plan novel represent twentieth-century capitalism at an impasse. Kataev satirizes his foreigners and through them shows the West's economic and spiritual crisis — the standard Soviet treatment. They are memorable caricatures: the pathetic engineer Bixby, broken by the Depression, and Roupe, the pompous millionaire tourist, mired in malaise. These types play supporting roles: they are only one manifestation of the West in the novel. *Time, Forward!* also addresses Russia's historical relationship to the West, disproving the old assumption that Russia needs the West in order to progress. Now Russia is figuratively becoming its own "West" — developing the industrial capacity and national image that will enable it to surpass the West of modern capitalism.

The chief ingredients of Soviet success as seen in *Time, Forward!* are economic achievement and a new national identity. They are interdependent: a confident, goal-oriented mentality is both a condition and a result of progress. The novel's structure reflects the importance of both. Its plot follows an event that hardly seems compelling: an attempt to set a record for mixing concrete. But Kataev, a skilled and lively writer, injects as much suspense as the subject will bear. The opening chapter sparks, and the final chapter satisfies, the reader's curiosity about whether our boys in the brigade can break the previous Soviet record. These chapters form what might be called the novel's "outer frame." The second and penultimate chapters (there are sixty-nine altogether) constitute an "inner frame" that buttresses the plot, placing it in historical perspective. (The second chapter is actually chapter 3: Kataev flirts with narrative innovation by placing chapter 1 just before the end.) The concrete-mixing plot demonstrates Russia's ability to reshape itself; the inner frame carries the significance.

Chapters 3 and 68 take as their text a 1931 speech of Stalin's. The first five-year plan was then in its fourth year, and more dramatic results were required. Official Soviet rhetoric is full of exhortatory passages like the one quoted; this speech was the exhortation of the moment, and Kataev showcases it. Stalin asserts Russia's ability to meet the 1931 quota and affirms the necessity of doing so. He paints Russia's past in shrieking colors, presenting it as a debacle that economic might can erase. Part of the excerpt quoted by Kataev catalogues Russia's history of humiliations, listing all the conquer-

ors — from "Mongol khans" to "English and French capitalists" — who
have taken advantage of its backwardness.[11] Kataev repeats parts of
the speech in both chapters, and punctuates them with an exhortation
of his own. The novel's setting is the massive industrial complex at
Magnitogorsk, in the Urals — the conventional dividing line between
the European and Asian continents. Chapter 3 takes place on a train
proceeding eastward across the Urals; in chapter 68 the train heads
back toward European Russia. The post marking the boundary between Asia and Europe serves Kataev as a symbol of an outmoded
definition of Russia. "Asia" in Kataev's usage means stasis — it represents those qualities which Russia must eliminate in order to move
forward. Russia may still be geographically part-European and part-
Asian, but it will no longer be "the East" in any other sense. The
author's pronouncement, juxtaposed as it is with the leader's, carries
the force of official policy:

> Flickering across the windows from left to right, swirls the obelisk:
> "Europe — Asia." It is bleached and peeling. . . . A senseless post. Now
> it is behind us. Does that mean we are in Asia? Curious. We are moving
> toward the East at a terrific speed and we carry the revolution with us.
> Never again shall we be Asia. [p. 139]

Repeating the refrain at the end, he is even more emphatic:

> A senseless post . . .
> I demand that it be taken down!
> Never again shall we be Asia.
> Never, never, never! [pp. 423-24, ellipsis in original]

If not Asia — what, then? Clearly Russia is not becoming more
"Western" in the sense that Europe and the United States are Western.
That way, as the novel shows, lies ruin. Russia is "westernizing" in the
sense that it is eliminating its backwardness, expelling "Eastern"
complacency from its identity. The Soviet Union is on its way toward
surpassing the West (meaning the capitalist world). Advancement is

---

[11]Valentin Kataev, *Vremia, vpered!* in *Sobranie sochinenii,* 9 vols. (Moscow:
Khudozhestvennaia literatura, 1968-72), III, 139. Parenthetical references in the text
are to this edition. My translation relies in part on that of Charles Malamuth cited
above. The speech quoted was delivered by Stalin on February 4, 1931 to the first
All-Union Conference of Leading Personnel of Socialist Industry. A translation is included in J. V. Stalin, *Works,* 13 vols. (Moscow: Foreign Languages Publishing House,
1952-55), XIII, 31-34.

now identified with Westernness only figuratively. The machinery with which the brigade breaks the record is Western — but the men achieve their astounding production rate by revising the foreign instructions. In the sense that Russia is headed toward remarkable industrial accomplishment, it is becoming more "Western" than the West itself. The Americans in the novel are alien, but so obviously so that their role is minor. The more important foreign presence in *Time, Forward!* is the "Asian" component of Russia's identity.

Time, Forward! is considered one of the best of the "production" or "industrial" novels of the thirties. It may be unique in this genre in one respect: its dénouement is datelined "Paris." Kataev's misplaced chapter 1 is an authorial letter from abroad — the final form in which the West appears in the novel. Here we see not the crumbling capitalist West but its impressive revolutionary past. What Kataev notes about Paris is the care with which it has preserved the history of its revolution. The novel rejects the West as a model for Russia's future, but Kataev sees the French approach to the past as an example to Soviet artists who are engaged in chronicling their revolution. The Soviets are "too young" to have acquired a sense of history, he writes; they must therefore work at creating one by recording each state through which they pass. *Time, Forward!* is obviously intended as a contribution toward this goal.

Russia's plan in Kataev's novel is articulated by the country's leader, but it appears to require no coercion. Progress demands sweat, but it is the sweat of self-motivated exertion. Platonov's perspective is far less sanguine. "The Epifan Locks" was written before the full-speed-ahead push of the five-year plans, but the story is nonetheless relevant to the period described in *Time, Forward!* Transforming a nation, for Platonov, entails careful balancing of natural and human forces that are not readily disturbed. The process is more complex than eager shock-brigading on a nationwide scale. Change may entail the introduction of alien elements into a society — a point Fedin, Kaverin, and Platonov use foreign characters to make. Their foreigners are alien in similar senses: Kurt because he is unbending and deceiving, Shvarts because he is inhumanly rational, Perry because he is repressive and uncomprehending. These three are connected to the methods of the state, and their foreignness is therefore not easily done away with. By contrast, the Western characters of *Time, Forward!* are innocuous, because they represent a literally foreign West whose principles Russia rejects. Kataev's crippled Westerners help confirm that

Russia's path is emphatically natural and native. His rhetoric, and Stalin's, promises that Russia's only alien element — its Asian backwardness — will soon be in the past. In the other works, however, the meanings of "native" and "foreign" become blurry, ambiguous: the foreign does not stay neatly outside the border. Native and foreign, especially in Platonov and Fedin, are terms for which "Russian" and "Western" are not consistent synonyms.

15

VIOLATING RUSSIA'S BORDERS

Mikhail Bulgakov, *The Master and Margarita* (1928–40)

The idea that history began anew in 1917 is an unremarkable bit of rhetoric: any society self-consciously entering a new era proclaims a fresh beginning. In *Time, Forward!* Kataev pronounces the Soviet people "too young" to have acquired a sense of history, as though the Soviet era were unconnected to the Russian past. Such assertions are seldom intended or interpreted literally. They inevitably distort reality, sometimes dangerously so. The interaction between former and future stages is unceasing (though often evident only with time). In the process of putting aside the past, parts of it that should remain are likely to be swept away, redefined as external to the current system. Lévi-Strauss defines a culture as "a fragment of humanity which . . . presents significant discontinuities in relation to the rest of humanity."[1] Straightforward enough — but not as simple as it may appear. How are these demarcation lines established? A culture has natural borders, gradually worn into the collective mind over time. Each successive political system and each successive political policy might be pictured as laying its own grid on top of it. These new lines may lie outside the culture's boundaries, thus allowing it to maintain its integrity and continue to develop; or they may cross into it, narrowing it and omitting parts of the culture that to some inhabitants, at least, are vital.

---

[1]Claude Lévi-Strauss, *Structural Anthropology*, trans. Claire Jacobson and Brooke Frundfest-Schoepf (New York: Basic Books, 1963), p. 295.

The works surveyed in the previous two chapters show Russia in the variously confusing, exhilarating, or wrenching process of drawing new boundaries. In *The Master and Margarita*, Soviet society appears rigidified: its boundaries are only growing narrower, eliminating more and more from the realm of the acceptable. Bulgakov is concerned with the values excluded from the system — with traditions of thought and behavior that should be at its core. Russia's natural borders are violated by the regime: it excludes principles essential to Russia's humanity. In order to demonstrate the culture's present narrowness, Bulgakov "violates" its borders in a literary sense, by thrusting two "foreign" elements into the Moscow of the 1930s. The society satirized in the novel can be schematized as a circle containing several smaller, intersecting circles: the theater world, the mental clinic, the literary establishment, and the other microcosms of Bulgakov's Moscow. Surrounding this large circle, and concentric with it, is a far larger one, which encompasses what is excluded from the system. From this "extrasystematic" realm come the devices that penetrate the closed system: the story of Pilate and Jesus, and the supernatural dimension of Woland. If the system thinks it has become insulated from judgment, exults Bulgakov's muse, it is in for a shock.

This now renowned novel, which lay unpublished for a quarter-century after the author's death, has so many riches that no brief treatment can mine them all. The scholar who said that after reading it one has the sensation of having lived through a festival put it well: one becomes engrossed in each segment, and on emerging one looks back at a brilliant whole.[2]

The figure of Woland dominates the work; it is sometimes thought of as "that novel in which the Devil comes to Moscow." On a structural level, this punishing and redeeming Devil plays the role of a foreign specialist who brings with him the skills and insight of his foreign world. Beside him, other literary examples of the type pale in comparison. All the foreign figures previously discussed can be viewed as alien to Russia in some specific sense; this one represents an alien

---

[2]V. Lakshin, "Roman Bulgakova *Master i Margarita*," *Novyi mir*, no. 6 (1968), p. 285. An abridged translation (by Carol Palmer) of this excellent article appears in *Twentieth-Century Russian Literary Criticism*, ed. Victor Erlich (New Haven, Conn.: Yale University Press, 1975), pp. 247–83. There has been a proliferation of commentary on the novel. A fine introductory essay is Ellendea Proffer, "The Master and Margarita," in *Major Soviet Writers*, ed. Edward J. Brown (New York: Oxford University Press, 1973), pp. 388–411.

realm of a much broader sort. As the novel unfolds, we increasingly see that Woland transcends not only borders but time and matter.

Woland is (among other things) a parody of the foreigner imported in the name of progress. He and his henchmen do not come to serve the aims of the state. One of the novel's many echoes of Goethe's *Faust* is the epigraph — Mephistopheles' self-introduction as a part of that force "which wills forever evil and works forever good" (lines 1335–36). "Progress," like "good" and "evil," is a relative term: one's judgment of Woland depends on where one stands. The reader who is averse to what he destroys, and who values what he saves, sees that he "wills evil" and "works good" with keen discretion.

Literary devils commonly adopt the guise of a stranger. Goethe's enters as a traveling scholar; Woland presents himself as a foreign professor (of black magic). Before he explains this, the uneasy editor and poet whom he accosts stab at clues to his identity. Each of them mentally runs through a range of possible nationalities, and the chapter contains a slew of synonyms for the word "foreigner." This visitor cannot be tucked into any of their categories. From the beginning, they have no doubt of Woland's absolute foreignness to the world of Moscow (or of his uncanny familiarity with it). Nor does the reader doubt the profound impact he will have on it. Woland loses no time in unpacking his foreign wares — his control over mere matter, his power to challenge the established order, and the story of Pontius Pilate and Jesus (called "Yeshua") that he begins at the end of chapter 1.

This story, spread through the novel in four parts, seems at first as alien to Moscow as Woland himself. Its foreignness has several aspects. The most evident is spatial and temporal distance — the setting in ancient Jerusalem; it is also stylistically distinct from the Moscow chapters. This study of a ruler gripped by the insights of a daring philosopher and moved to repent for having condemned him is, however, closely connected to the novel's Moscow level. Its relevance (implied by its very inclusion in the novel) emerges gradually. It becomes apparent with each installment of the Jerusalem story that the issues it raises are hidden in Moscow. They are conspicuous by their absence. The exercise of political and moral power, the problems of conscience, of justice, of cowardice — these are important to Bulgakov's Moscow, but he develops them more explicitly in the Jerusalem setting.

What impact does this use of a separate context have? One effect is to provoke the question of how distant from the present this story actually is. The reader (who may be as stimulated after the first episode as Woland's Muscovite listeners) is induced to work out the story's significance. The issues must be pondered more deeply than might be the case if they arose only in the contemporary setting. Certainly the reworking of this fundamental episode of Christianity — with its central place in Russian culture and in Western civilization as a whole — gives the issues power and breadth. The biblical subject aside, the use of a separate context, whether one so loaded or not, has another effect. It suggests that this story could not be given a Soviet setting — that in the contemporary world of Moscow one cannot find a high official who is susceptible to a power higher than the state, who can be made to doubt his own authority, who is tormented by his conscience. Nor, we are prompted to think, can one find the belief in human goodness, the honesty, the healing presence of so penetrating a preacher. Given the system of which Bulgakov was writing, his use of external figures is a device essential to his purpose. The system allows inside itself nothing capable of successfully challenging it. "The foreign" is, therefore, needed to expose the native. First-century Jerusalem and Woland's supernatural must puncture the border of the Soviet present.

Within the Jerusalem level, foreignness of a sort demonstrated in Fedin, Kaverin, and Platonov plays a role. Pontius Pilate and the Roman government he represents are a foreign presence in Jerusalem. It is emphasized that he detests the city in which he must serve, detests the populace crowding its streets. The cities of Jerusalem and Moscow are linked in the novel; thus one is led to find the Soviet state figuratively alien, and antipathetic to those under its control.

The Pilate-Yeshua story cannot be examined without discussing its status as a novel within the novel, and without turning to the character who is its author. The constraints on contemporary existence may be many, but this is, after all, a novel written in a Moscow basement apartment. Its creator is a Muscovite who, eschewing the now debased title of "writer," calls himself a "master." (By one of those unfortunate quirks of translation, the English word, in addition to conveying the Russian meaning of "expert artisan," adds the misleading connotations of ownership and domination.) The Master's writing is not an isolated element of the book. At the end his manuscript merges with the larger novel, and we come to see that the whole book, not just the novel within it, is the work of the Master — and that his identity is tied to Bulgakov's. Within the system, then, it *is* possible to generate an independent, heretical work of art. But to do so requires an exceptional individual and exceptional circumstances. The Master can partially transcend his environment through chance — a winning lottery ticket that allows him to work for himself — and through the loving dedication of Margarita. But while he can thrive for long enough to write the novel, the system drives him to destroy it — to burn it in a fit of despair (as Bulgakov himself did with part of *The Master and Margarita*). Not only could the manuscript not survive in that environment: its author could not either. Broken by the assault of the critics — and by his brief imprisonment, due to an informant who wants his apartment — the Master withdraws to a mental clinic. A figure fundamental to Bulgakov's system of values finds himself unable to exist within society. Recall the "cornerstone" metaphor. The individual who raises challenging issues is pressured out of society, its present cornerstone — its power structure and dominant values — rejecting what he represents.

The Master is returned to his love, and the novel restored to life, by Woland. His intervention is also needed to bring the manuscript to Bulgakov's reader. (Its first part is told by the intruder Woland; the next is dreamed by Bezdomny after meeting Woland and the Master; the rest is read by Margarita from the pages Woland has reconstituted from ashes.) When the lovers find themselves again in the beloved basement, the Master is skeptical about the forces that have brought them there. Encouraged by Margarita, he acknowledges that no earthly force could be responsible — that such "ravaged" people as they could expect salvation only from the supernatural. The word "supernatural" in Russian is *potustoronnii;* etymologically it refers to something from "the other side." Only an alien from the "outer circle" surrounding the system can overcome the system's power. But Bulgakov's supernatural crew do not substantially change the system: they simply wreak a little havoc and attack a few objectionable targets. There is no question of destroying Moscow's foundations. The system stands, and the hero and heroine survive it only by departing their earthly lives and being spirited away to the "eternal refuge" made possible by Woland and Yeshua.

By training, the Master is a historian and translator. He tells Ivan when they meet in the asylum that he knows five languages: English, French, German, Latin, Greek, and a little Italian. He is connected to the intellectual heritage Russia shares with Europe — and that heritage is obviously important to Bulgakov. The author's use of the Bible and of Goethe are indications of his tie to the cultural past and of his belief in the absence of cultural walls. The home to which Woland directs the two lovers at the end is another. In Woland's description it seems a soft-toned scene from an old book, a setting of no specific time or place. "Oh, thrice romantic master," he persuades, "wouldn't you like to stroll with your love under newly blossoming cherry trees in the daytime, and listen to Schubert in the evening? Won't you enjoy writing by candlelight with a goose quill? Don't you want, like Faust, to sit over a retort in the hope that you'll succeed in fashioning a new homunculus?" Margarita says of their future home as they approach it: "I know that in the evening people will come to see you, people you care for, who interest you, who will not upset you."[3] While this wholly untroubled haven is an idyllic realm, the eternal home embodies eternal values achievable on earth: the freedom to strive in one's own way, to live in harmony among one's friends. These values are absent from the society depicted in the novel — made "discontinuous" with it, to use Lévi-Strauss's term. The system's boundaries have been falsely drawn: too much that is human is on the other side.

What is involved here is partly a loss of contact with the moral and intellectual heritage of the past. Not of the national past alone, but of the open-bordered past that holds Western civilization's experience. (Hence the Master's training in history and languages, and the fact that Ivan, his partly comprehending disciple, becomes a professor of history and philosophy.) The contemporary West is out of sight, peripheral to Bulgakov's concerns in this novel. When Moscow becomes inhospitable terrain for the Master and Margarita, their only exit point is an intangible border that lies "up," not westward. One of the issues implicit in the novel is how Russia can be native space again, a place in which individuals can thrive. Barring that, there is no satisfactory way of living — except through the sort of transcendence which Bulgakov (with evident pleasure) creates for his protagonists.[4]

Recalling the titles and graphic representations of previous sec-

---

[3]Mikhail Bulgakov, *Master i Margarita,* in *Romany* (Moscow: Khudozhestvennaia literatura, 1973), pp. 798–99. My translation relies partly on that of Michael Glenny (New York: Signet–New American Library, 1967).

[4]The phrase "vertical transcendence," suggested to me by Sidney Monas, describes the hero's path well. It might be noted that in *Dr. Zhivago* (another influential novel by a member of the same generation) the West is not a desired haven either (though perhaps a possible one in Zhivago's case). But Zhivago also needs a realm beyond the difficult life his own has turned out to be. Pasternak, like Bulgakov, creates for his writer a transcendent realm — the Master's an immortality that enables him to go on creating, and Zhivago's the immortality of his art.

tions (moving forward, westward, back and forth), one at first might think of Part 4's scheme as an east-pointed arrow extending into Russia, an arrow importing some external phenomenon. As will now be evident, the "foreign" origin of that "import" may be only figurative — a notion the above design does not convey. An additional design is needed to more fully schematize the foreign presences discussed here. Imagine an arrow entirely inside one country — a line no longer arrow-straight but capable of encircling segments of thought or matter, reshaping them, and becoming an internal boundary. Changing configurations within society are certainly not by definition destructive, but they can be. Policies of national development in Platonov's story bar the populace from its way of life, and the foreign implementer of policy is violently caught between the two. The native in *Cities and Years* who can find no place for himself is barred from existence — eliminated by a foreigner who is linked to the state. In *The Master and Margarita,* the codes of an alien state claim to outweigh spiritual codes; institutions block challenges, perceived or real, to their own legitimacy and power. The novel's supernatural intruders perform supermanlike bending and traversing of barriers. Internal boundaries, as well as international ones, are the stuff of literary border crossings.

AFTERWORD
The First Decades and Beyond

In 1922 a new journal joined the post–Civil War literary revival: a promising but short-lived review called *The Contemporary West* (*Sovremennyi Zapad*). Its editors were Evgenii Zamiatin, Kornei Chukovsky, and A. N. Tikhonov; their purpose, as stated in the inaugural issue, was "to give the Russian reader as full and strictly objective a picture as possible of the intellectual and artistic life of contemporary Europe."[1] The six numbers published before the journal's demise in 1924 included articles on the European cultural scene by Russian émigrés, translations of such current sensations as Pirandello, Cocteau, and Proust, and illustrated pieces on Dada, Expressionism, and Picasso. But the journal was not exclusively a bastion of modernism. A surprising contributor opened the first issue: Rudyard Kipling, with his "The Ballad of East and West" (1889). The poem is best known for its refrain, which begins: "Oh, East is East, and West is West, and never the twain shall meet. . . ."[2]

What did the sophisticated editors have in mind, one wonders, in featuring Kipling's colonialist ballad so prominently? Their intent may well have been humorous: the use of Kipling seems a joke, a light-hearted glance at a sort of cross-cultural contact which was far from

---

[1]"Ot redaktsii," *Sovremennyi Zapad,* no. 1 (1922), p. 190.

[2]The poem was printed in a translation by the poet Elizaveta Polonskaia that is faithful to both the letter and spirit of the original (R. Kipling, "Ballada o Vostoke i Zapade," *Sovremennyi Zapad,* no. 1 [1922], pp. 3–5).

that undertaken by the journal. Kipling's primitive "East" and imperial "West" find common ground not in high culture but in battle. The two cultures drawn together by *Sovremennyi Zapad* — intellectual, avant-garde Europe and its Russian counterpart — were considerably closer to start with. In Kipling's usage the West would, no doubt, include Russia (with its own Eastern empire); the more narrowly defined West of the journal was distinct from Russia, though the distance was easily bridged. The cultural traffic, as reflected in the contents, was lively and diverse.

The different definitions of "the West" in the poem and journal are worth pondering for a moment, because they remind us of the breadth of Russian approaches to the West. Russia belonged to the West in some senses but not in others: that accounts for the ambiguity and ambivalence which color so much Russian thinking about their relationship.[3] If the West were wholly foreign, this book's subject would be much simpler than it is: the fine distinctions are always the hardest to make, and often the most consequential. As the twenties gave way to the thirties, the distinctions between Soviet Russia and the West were defined with increasing dogmatism by the state. Kipling's line about the divided worlds of East and West must have seemed less humorous in the mid-thirties than it had over a decade earlier. In the sphere of cultural interaction, for example, the gap widened: publication of foreign writers became more strictly controlled, and discussion of foreign developments more circumscribed. At the first congress of Soviet writers in 1934, which ended a literary era, Karl Radek pronounced the official word that Soviet writers had nothing to learn from the decadent likes of Joyce and Proust. And in Soviet literature itself, as these chapters show, the "invented" West in its varied forms lay beyond an increasingly distinct border.

That border had long figured in Russian fiction: it was not raised by the Revolution. But the events of 1917 initiated a remolding of Russia's identity, and this process prompted new ways of looking at the West. Pilniak had written in *The Naked Year* (1922) that "the Revolution has set Russia in contrast to Europe." The character who says this means that Russia is now shedding its westernized skin and reclaiming its native mentality. But the statement can also be read neutrally, as a general description of the Revolution's impact. The

---

[3]Marc Raeff comments interestingly on this problem in "Russia's Perception of Her Relationship with the West," *Slavic Review* 23, no. 1 (1964): 13–19.

radical reshaping of society gave a new context to questions that Russians had often addressed: what were their country's fundamental characteristics, and what was its relation to the West?

The state developed its answers to these questions; those policies belong to the history of Soviet foreign and domestic affairs. While ideologically the Western countries were antagonists, they were important to the pragmatic Soviet state — in part as tools for speeding economic progress. In literature the West was a creative tool, used to explore changes of a more varied and abstract sort.

There are books that analyze the image of a foreign place in a given country's literature. What has interested me is how a foreign culture (conceptions of it, ideas associated with it, real or fictional experience in it) is used by a writer to explore — sometimes to discover — his own country. What I find of post-revolutionary Russian literature, which may be true of other literatures in times of comparable upheaval, is that the foreign place most crucial to the country's self-definition was a fertile literary source. For Russia, this place was the West — and in the twenties and thirties the many-meaninged West figured in literary efforts to probe national and individual identity.

National identity is always called into question by revolution; the individual's relation to the nation, a perennially live issue anywhere, was spotlighted by the founding of a system that championed collectivism. The theory and reality of individual life are necessarily connected to the ideal and real nature of the society to which one belongs. Those works which interrelate the two most revealingly — Mandelstam's articles and travel essay, Bulgakov's novel, the plays of Olesha and Platonov — seem to me of particular significance. These are not the only works linking both aspects of identity. The West involves national and inner landscapes in Fedin's novel and Platonov's story, where it can be seen as a metaphor for an oppressive aspect of the state. Nearly all the writing discussed concerns the two to some extent, though one may predominate. Some works (ranging from "The Scythians" to *Time, Forward!*) focus on the nation's identity, using the West largely in political and historical terms; in others (*Flight* among them) individual identity is in the foreground. Mayakovsky's comic-book epic and his poems, lyric and programmatic; Ehrenburg's satirical mixture of autobiography and exposé; the West as fantasy ("Italian Sunshine"), as formalistic device (*Zoo*), as intellectual heritage (Mandelstam) — all these types, and others, are part of the story. As I have emphasized, each must be interpreted in its own context, and not projected directly onto an ideological screen. Taken together, these artistic inventions of the West span the literary stances of the era. Many of early Soviet literature's faces are in the mosaic I have tried to create.

The difficult matter of setting the figurative borders that delimit individual and country is a conspicuous feature of this mosaic. As should now be clear, I speak of border-drawing in two principal senses. One concerns the external border that distinguishes Soviet Russia from the West, or from the world as a whole; there are also internal divisions governing the relationships of populace or individual with the state, and of individual with self. People as well as institutions formulate these lines. Some writing of this era of upheaval reveals borders that are rigidly or falsely drawn — "falsely" in that they damagingly confine. Russia and the West are often set up as opposites, and may be rigidly polarized. This happens, for example, in works built around the venerable notion of Russia as the land of promise and the West of doom. Shaginian's game of proletariat and plutocrats and Mayakovsky's "150,000,000" are of this type; so is such diverse fiction of dissimilar periods as "The Third Capital" and *Time, Forward!* Lyrically and rhetorically, Pilniak develops a belief in Russia grounded in nostalgia and faith, and in a notion of Spenglerian phases that finds Russia rising and Europe moribund. Kataev declares optimism justified, thanks to industrial know-how, industriousness, and ideological zeal. His West is also perishing, falling at the rate of Russia's ascent. *The Hurdy-Gurdy* — one work which suggests that Russia is being falsely defined and pushed in damaging directions — questions such absolute dichotomies. Platonov shows that it is dangerous for natives and foreigners alike to regard Russia as "light" to the West's "dark." For Russia to assume the role of socialist paragon blinds it to reality: no amount of rhetoric will turn image into fact. In *A List of Assets,* Olesha asserts that Soviet rhetoric about the West is at one with reality — but so awkwardly that he implies the reverse. The playwright himself proposes faulty definitions: he identifies individualism with the West and then discredits the West, sweeping individual freedom and capitalist perfidy into the same category. Both things, in the play's shaky logic, belong outside the Soviet border.

Olesha's comments on his work indicate that this vision of polarity was not bound to be widely shared by his peers. Every intellectual, he had written, desires artistic and individual independence — a desire he calls "an idea of Europe." In the play he takes his metaphor literally, thus making these freedoms alien. Mandelstam, whose concern with the individual pervades his art, also links Europe to the idea of the individual's primacy — but Europe in his definition is within Russia, inseparable from it. Certainly a geographic border exists, and historical and cultural differences. But that border marks a distinction rather than a separation. The "native" city of which he writes in "Humanism and the Present" is a place of no definite nationality, but one where the individual can thrive. The "gold coinage of the European humanistic heritage" is common currency there; Mandelstam suggests that it can be removed from circulation only at Russia's peril. Some literary figures (like Olesha's heroine) accede to the sanctioned definitions of individual and country; in the "Arshak" section of Mandelstam's "Journey to Armenia," the individual succumbs, rather than accedes, to a loss of autonomy. The foreign conqueror who now rules has established power by divesting the native sovereign — the poet, and the individual — of his sovereignty. "Journey to Armenia" celebrates the satisfactions of exploring life's patterns through one's own eyes. It offers one glimpse of the state constraining independent vision, erecting borders that block the individual from himself.

With the formidable power of his imagination Bulgakov punctures boundaries, thus letting loose those problems of authority and art that had been barred. The limits of society in *The Master and Margarita* are shown to be too narrow, illegitimate because they exclude qualities that belong within. These internal boundaries necessitate the border crossings Bulgakov orchestrates. In his novel, more directly than in other works of the period, the reader is made to see the need for drawing borders anew. It is telling that the contemporary West is absent from *The Master and Margarita*: it is not to a more tolerant West, for instance, that the hero exits. That would have been meaningless, for both writer and creation need the native environment. The West as an actual place is irrelevant — and not just because it was difficult to get there. Russia was what concerned Bulgakov; commitment to Russia, too, explains Mandelstam's principled refusal to travel to Europe. In much fiction involving emigration (including Bulgakov's *Flight*), the West is no magnet either: Russia is the only place that matters. Nearly all the works presented express the author's deep attachment to Russia and preoccupation with its fate. That is a quality of Russian writing that survives to the present.

The literature of the Soviet period's first two decades is very much alive in the Soviet Union. In the intermittent cultural thaws since Stalin's death, long-unpublished works, long-ignored writers, and long-taboo issues have been openly discussed. Writers who came of age in the late fifties and after continue to be influenced by the techniques and concerns of the generation that experienced the Revolution. The questions raised in the twenties and thirties about the developing Societ system and the individual's relation to it are still being asked, in fictional and nonfictional forms. To understand current approaches one has to know their roots, which lie in pre-revolutionary culture and in the less widely known writing of the Revolution's early years. The barrier between the Western reader and the post-revolutionary writer — of the first years and of years since — is one I hope to have diminished.

Literary border crossings are being overshadowed these days by actual ones: the Third Wave of emigration is bringing an important segment of Soviet culture to the West. A leading journal of the new emigration is the Paris-published *Kontinent* (the title itself declares the natural connection between the West and Russia). Two recent issues contain a memoir by Viktor Nekrasov that focuses on what keeps the continent divided. Nekrasov (one of the editors, and a major literary figure since the forties) calls his piece "On Both Sides of the Wall"; he begins and ends at the Berlin Wall, and pauses frequently to ponder the absurdity and tragedy of the line separating the politically defined "East" and "West."[4] That political border marks art as well as life: of all the features of the "real West" (to recall Tynianov's distinction between "real" and "imagined"), it most affects how contemporary Russian writers, émigré and Soviet, use the West in literature. But present political terminology should not obscure the West's other associations, or the limitless meanings the artist can give it. Were the border to be opened by some new regime — whatever its stance toward the West and toward ideas linked with it — forms of the West would continue to figure in Russian literature, as they did for centuries before 1917. Defining what is Russian, in individual and national terms, and exploring what is human will never cease to occupy Russian writers. The West — in all its previous meanings, and in those yet to be invented — will be part of that process.

---

[4] Part 1 of "Po obe storony Steny" appears in *Kontinent*, no. 18 (1978), pp. 55–116; the second and final part is in no. 19 (1979), pp. 77–156.

INDEX

INDEX

Pilniak, Boris (Cont.)
— *Naked Year, The,* 38–39, 192
— "Old Cheese, The": thematic
    commentary, 87–90; and *A List of
    Assets* (Olesha), 115; mentioned, 77,
    80, 91
— *O.K.,* 47
— "Third Capital, The": thematic
    commentary, 38–47; contemporary
    criticism, 47, 48; and *The
    Hurdy-Gurdy* (Platonov), 69; and
    "The Old Cheese," 89; mentioned,
    14, 49, 60, 69, 194
— *Volga Flows into the Caspian Sea,
    The,* 39, 62
— in *Now in the West* (Nikitin), 140–41
— on his use of passages from other
    fiction, 42n
Platonov, Andrei
— *Chevengur,* 63–64
— *Dzhan,* 63
— "Epifan Locks, The": thematic
    commentary 175–79; and *The
    Master and Margarita* (Bulgakov),
    187, 190; and *Time, Forward!*
    (Kataev), 179–80, 182, 183;
    mentioned, 161, 162, 163, 171–72,
    193
— *Foundation Pit, The,* 62–63
— *Hurdy-Gurdy, The:* thematic
    commentary, 64–68; and "The
    Epifan Locks," 175; mentioned, 14,
    193, 194
— "Pushkin, Our Comrade," 178
— contemporary criticism, 62
— on Russia's borders, 8
Platonov, S. F.: on the historical role of the
    foreigner, 159–60
Polonsky, Viacheslav: on "The Third
    Capital" (Pilniak), 47
"Production novel." *See* Five-year-plan
    fiction
Prompartiia (Industrial Party) trial: and *A
    List of Assets* (Olesha), 111
Prussianism and Socialism (Spengler), 36
Puni, Ivan: in *Zoo, or Letters Not About
    Love: The Third Heloise*
    (Shklovsky), 96
Pushkin, A. S.: "Autumn (A Fragment),"
    26; on Chaadaev's view of Russian
    history, 18–19
"Pushkin, Our Comrade" (Platonov), 178

Radek, Karl: on Proust and Joyce, 192
Red Cavalry. See under Babel, Isaac
"Red pinkertons": defined, 55; success of,
    56
Remizov, Alexei: in *Zoo, or Letters Not
    About Love: The Third Heloise*
    (Shklovsky), 96
"Resurrection of the Word, The"
    (Shklovsky), 91
"Return." *See under* Tikhonov, Nikolai
Revolution of 1917: changes caused by, 2;
    divides transitional periods in
    Russian history, 11; and European
    supporters of the Third
    International in literature, 48–49;
    first anniversary of, *Mystery-Bouffe*
    (Mayakovsky) written to celebrate,
    51; relationship to other Western
    revolutions, 15–16
Rodchenko, Aleksandr, 119–20, 144n
Russian in the Shadows (Wells): and *Julio
    Jurenito* (Ehrenburg), 129n
"Russian identity," defined, 3

Saga of a Society Lady, The (Shaginian),
    76
Scythians, defined, 31
"Scythians" (literary philosophical
    group), 29n, 31
"Scythians, The." *See under* Blok,
    Aleksandr
Sentimental Journey, A (Shklovsky),
    91–92
Serapion Brothers (literary circle), 172
"Shadow of a Friend, The" (Batiushkov):
    and *The Shadow of a Friend*
    (Tikhonov), 146
Shaginian, Marietta
— *Hydrocentral,* 62
— *Mess-Mend, or a Yankee in
    Petrograd:* thematic commentary,
    52, 56–60; contemporary criticism,
    59, 59n; and *The Hurdy-Gurdy*
    (Platonov), 68; mentioned, 14, 16,
    194
— *Saga of a Society Lady, The,* 76
— on *Julio Jurenito* (Ehrenburg),
    125–26
— uses pseudonym "Jim Dollar," 56
Shishko, A., *Appetite of the Microbes,* 50

INDEX

Waiting for Godot (Beckett): and *The Hurdy-Gurdy* (Platonov), 65, 68
Way Out to the East, The, 74
We (Zamiatin): and "Engineer Schvarts" (Kaverin), 173
Wells, H. G.: *Russia in the Shadows,* and *Julio Jurenito* (Ehrenburg), 129n
West, the: as brought into Russia by the visitor, 159–90; a declining civilization in contrast to Russia's young culture, 36; defined, 4n, 4–8; as defined in "The Ballad of East and West" (Kipling), 191–92; as defined in *The Contemporary West, 1922–1924,* 191–92; future of, 28–70; and emigration, 73–116; as an idea or set of ideas, 17, 102–3; personified by Woodrow Wilson in "150,000,000" (Mayakovsky), 53–54; Russia's challenge to, 28–34; Russia's nature relative to, 11–70; Russia's proximity to, 11–13, 17–27, 34, 37; Russia's self-definition, a dimension of, 2–3, 137; travel to, Dostoevsky on, 131, 132; travel to, pre-revolutionary, 73–74, 139; travel to, post-revolutionary, 74–77, 101–2, 119–21, 138–47; Tynianov on the "imagined" and the "real," 6–7, 13, 133, 137, 196; used by a writer to explore his own country, 193; viewed by pre-revolutionary Russian writers, 1–2, 139; viewed by Russian writers, 1917–1934, 2–8, 191–96 (*see also* subheading "thematic commentary" with individual titles under authors' names); viewed by Russian popular fiction writers of the early twenties, 48–52, 55, 56–60; viewed by the Soviet traveler, 119–156; viewed by writers about emigration, 115
Western Europe. *See* the West
"Westerners" (Slonimsky), 139
White Guard (Bulgakov), 80; and *Flight,* 84
Wilson, Woodrow: personifies the West in "150,000,000" (Mayakovsky), 53–54; Trotsky caricatures as menace to Soviet success, 54–55

Zamiatin, Evgenii: "The Cave," 79; *The Contemporary West* (editor of), 191; "In Old Russia," 79–80; *We,* and "Engineer Schvarts" (Kaverin), 173; and emigration, 104; on *Julio Jurenito* (Ehrenburg), 125
Zhukovsky, Vasilii. *See* "Singer in a Camp of Russian Soldiers, A"
Zoo, or Letters Not About Love: The Third Heloise. See under Shklovsky, Viktor
Zoya's Apartment (Bulgakov), 81

Designer: Janet Wood
Compositor: Viking Typographers
Printer: McNaughton & Gunn
Binder: John H. Dekker & Sons
Text: 10/12 Sabon
Display: Sabon